WAR IS NOT JUST FOR HEROES

USMC
OKINAWA

War Is Not Just for Heroes

WORLD WAR II DISPATCHES AND LETTERS OF U.S. MARINE CORPS COMBAT CORRESPONDENT CLAUDE R. "RED" CANUP

Edited by Linda M. Canup Keaton-Lima

Foreword by Colonel Keith Oliver, USMC (Ret.)

Hardcover edition published by the University of South Carolina Press, 2012
Paperback and ebook editions published in Columbia, South Carolina,
by the University of South Carolina Press, 2024

uscpress.com

Printed in the United States of America

The Library of Congress originally cataloged the hardcover version of this book.
The Cataloging-in-Publication Data can be found at https://lccn.loc.gov/2011049009

ISBN 978-1-61117-067-2 (hardcover)
ISBN 978-1-64336-486-5 (paperback)
ISBN 978-1-64336-487-2 (ebook)

Frontispiece: Staff Sergeant Claude R. "Red" Canup, Okinawa 1945. Charcoal portrait by E. L. Wexler, USMC combat artist.

Facing: Red and Marie Canup, Anderson, S.C., 1932. Claude R. "Red" Canup Collection.

With love,
in memory of my parents
Claude Richard "Red" Canup
(March 3, 1911–February 20, 1999)
and Clara Marie Bolt Canup
(July 27, 1910–July 10, 1983)

This book is for . . . Lou,
Lisa, Mark, Anna, and Ellen,
Karen, Caroline, and Marianne . . .
the best family in the whole world.

CONTENTS

PART 4—JAPAN

ILLUSTRATIONS

FOREWORD

> . . . I am become a name;
> For always roaming with a hungry heart
> Much have I seen and known . . .
> And drunk delight of battle with my peers.
>
> *Lord Tennyson,* Ulysses

He looked a little like Mark Twain. Same bushy eyebrows, same wry smile. Certainly not easily dazzled—and absolutely prone to the occasional prank, in both word and deed. Claude R. "Red" Canup—Captain United States Marine Corps Reserve, WWII veteran, crackerjack sportswriter, public relations executive of renown (especially in his native South Carolina), newspaper publisher/editor, author—epitomized the marine combat correspondent.

He was thirty-three years old when the all-business United States Marine Corps made room in its prestigious ranks for yet another "character." And he was seventy-four when it was my privilege to latch-on to Red at a meeting of the Iron Mike Chapter of the U.S. Marine Corps Combat Correspondents Association at Parris Island—his (and my) alma mater.

The fact that he and WWII photo ace Neil Gillespie were willing to motor down from the Greenville, South Carolina, area (a 250-mile trek) was impressive to us all. But the friendship that sparked between Red and me, and which extended to both our families, went far beyond merely impressive.

For my part, I was a twenty-nine-year-old first lieutenant, brimming with ambition, and convinced that public affairs work could be, must be, fun, colorful, and outside-the-box. So began a Canup-Oliver partnership that meant, for our wives and us, a slew of Marine Corps birthday balls, Combat Correspondent Conferences, and overnight stays at each other's homes. Our friendship grew to include (from me) a card on Father's Day and, always (from Red), tons of spot-on career and life counsel.

Suffice to say, 'tis an honor of the highest magnitude to be asked to pen the foreword to this important book.

1st Lt. Keith Oliver, USMC, and Capt. Claude R. "Red" Canup, USMCR (Ret.), MCAS Beaufort, S.C., 1984. Claude R. "Red" Canup Collection.

War Is Not Just for Heroes offers readers, especially those who knew Red Canup, a heartfelt look at what made the gravel-voiced rascal tick. Simply put, it was never about him; it was always about *them.*

Red believed, and put into practice, the notion that individual marines—or athletes or farmers or teachers—were the backbone of any large, worthwhile undertaking. And he set out on a lifetime mission of ensuring that, one by one, these genuine heroes were recognized—especially in their hometowns—for the duty they so faithfully performed on behalf of others.

The tome you are about to read is, of course, geared toward a particular kind of duty, performed by a particular kind of person. This is a story of the United States Marines in war. But Red's legacy, even in this age when news technology is evolving at a popcorn-popping rate, is that people matter. Individuals matter. Their lives, their deaths, their service to country and community matter.

To call *War Is Not Just for Heroes* a "labor of love" would be understated in the extreme. The author is Cap'n Red's own daughter, Dr. Linda Keaton-Lima.

Linda's exhaustive research, multiple drafts, and meticulous attention to detail have combined to make her Dad's story ring clearly with the authenticity it deserves.

Pulling from her veteran educator's penchant for getting it right, Linda has given marines—particularly aviation marines—a historical valentine that will likely find itself on squadron bookshelves from Cherry Point to Kaneohe Bay, and everywhere in between.

Perhaps more significantly, *War Is Not Just for Heroes* will inspire Defense Information School students and their civilian counterparts at colleges of journalism throughout the country to always place the hometown-raised individual "front and center" when covering our nation's battles. Like Ernie Pyle and Joe Galloway—and Rudyard Kipling before them—Red Canup has shown us how it's done. And daughter Linda, God love her, got it all down.

To those readers who will appreciate and perhaps even have opportunity to employ this book's people-first, one-story-at-a-time approach to journalism and public affairs, please allow me to leave you with the sign-off that Red himself used so often: *"Semper Fi!"*

Keith Oliver
Colonel, U.S. Marine Corps (Ret.)

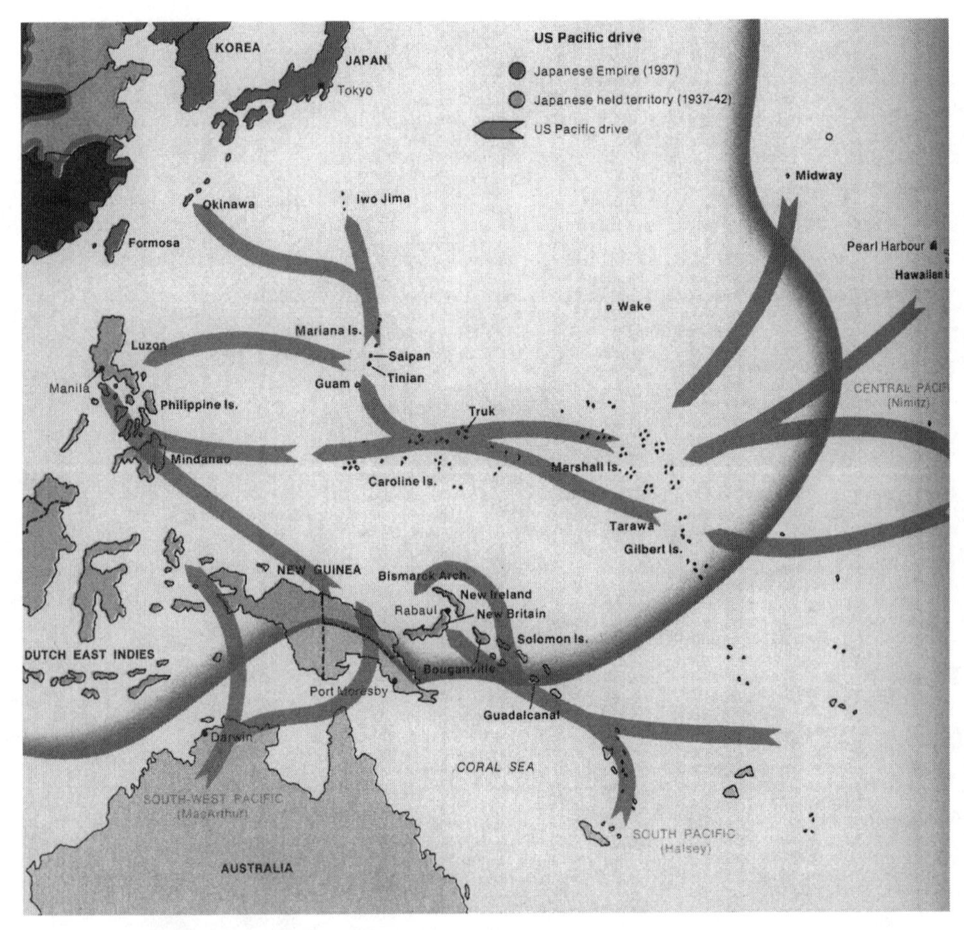

The U.S. Pacific Drive, by the Marine Corps Historical Division. Courtesy of the Library of the Marine Corps, Quantico, Va.

PREFACE

Lest We Forget Denig's Demons

On June 6, 1942, six months after the United States declared war on Japan, Lieutenant General Thomas A. Holcomb, commandant of the Marine Corps, advertized nationally for experienced civilian reporters to shore up his struggling combat correspondent group. Using the Associated Press wire service, he announced a change in combat correspondent recruitment guidelines, adding a five-year experience requirement. Unprecedented, the call for reinforcements opened the Marine Corps to "mature" reporters previously excluded from serving. All physical requirements for regular marines had to be met; six weeks of fighter training required. Reporters meeting the standards would receive sergeants stripes and sent overseas with combat units.

The same incentives offered earlier, without the five-year experience requirement, produced fewer CC candidates than expected; and, with the war escalating, more newspaper coverage of marine activities was needed immediately. Taking these factors into consideration, Holcomb made an administrative decision changing the concept of war correspondents forever: the Corps would field its own group of experienced correspondents. Skilled newsmen serving as CCs would ensure marines received deserved recognition in print. With expanded eligibility, the call issued by the Marines Corps attracted experienced reporters, those "recycled civilians" nicknamed "Denig's Demons."

Brigadier General Robert L. Denig, handpicked by Holcomb to head the newly formed Division of Public Relations and lead the adjunct CC group, personally selected the recruits from written applications and letters of recommendation. Each successful candidate received a letter from Denig with instructions to enlist and then proceed to boot camp—again stressing that the Marine Corps' physical requirements had to be met before the candidate could become a CC.

Dispatch, story, article, report—all terms used interchangeably for a combat correspondent's writings. During World War II, the main sources for war news were nightly radio broadcasts, weekly movie reels, and daily newspaper

S. Sgt. Claude R. "Red" Canup, Yontan Airfield, Okinawa, 1945. Claude R. "Red" Canup Collection.

stories. CCs were to write "print ready" material enabling newspapers to use articles without further editing.

Dispatches were seldom found on page one. Always marked "Delayed" because of censoring and location often "Somewhere in the Pacific" for security concerns, CC articles were feature stories. Not having the time-saving, uncensored wire service capabilities of civilian correspondents for reporting daily war news, marine combat correspondents wrote about individual leathernecks and marine life in the Pacific, and chronicled eye-witness accounts of other marines.

An unusual mix of news savvy civilians answered the call. My father, a small-town newspaper editor, was among those selected. Writing hundreds of stories about his fellow marines, Claude R. "Red" Canup introduced countless newspaper readers to members of Marine Aircraft Groups 45 and 31. Dispatches ranged from reports of MAG 45 living the jungle life and flying protection for anchored ships to accounts of MAG 31 emptying Okinawa's skies from day one of the invasion and occupying Japan, the first U.S. military to do so.

Red, always the meticulous record keeper, filed the last carbon copy of every dispatch in his seabag. Safeguarding these dispatches has been my mission turned passion for almost three years. More historically significant collected in this book than when first published individually, his dispatches report marine aviation activities from a new perspective—the Marine Corps' own.

Gathering background for my father's story, I searched out the most accurate combat correspondent history available. I interviewed two experts in the field, Captain Jack Paxton, USMC (Ret.) and Colonel Keith Oliver, USMC (Ret.). Both were friends of my father and former marine CCs themselves. They currently work with combat correspondents—past, present, and future. I am deeply indebted to them for their interest and support.

I first contacted Jack, since 2005 the executive director for the United States Marine Corps Combat Correspondents Association. Over five hundred members strong, USMCCCA is the only professional organization of its kind in U.S. military services. Recognizing the importance of civilian support to the Marine Corps, the association's prestigious Brigadier General Robert L. Denig, Sr., Distinguished Memorial Performance Award is presented, when warranted, to an accomplished civilian communicator for a special and significant contribution to the marines. Two-time Academy Award–winner Tom Hanks received the 2010 award for his HBO series *The Pacific;* the 2011 award went to Chip Jones, the author of *War Shots,* the story of Norm Hatch, a combat cameraman during World War II.

Jack shared his extensive knowledge of CC history during phone calls and through e-mails. According to Jack, the idea of marines writing about marines was on the drawing board before Holcomb recalled his good friend Denig from retirement on June 30, 1941.

A thirty-six year marine veteran, Brigadier General Denig returned committed to these goals: that individual marines would see their names in hometown newspapers, that enlistment would increase, and that nonmilitary reporters would receive any assistance needed to report leatherneck news. Wise to the importance of keeping the American public informed and perceptive in his belief that marines writing about marines would be a morale booster, Denig advanced the concept of combat correspondents. Reporters, he envisioned, would ensure marine families received information not otherwise available and the general public would stay abreast of leatherneck activities from wherever marines served.

Before Pearl Harbor, Jack noted, DPR began focusing on the need for reporters and photographers, training a limited number on its own. Only after the United States declared war on Japan December 8, 1941, and the Marine Corps' heroic Wake Island defense receiving little publicity did Denig receive permission from Holcomb to begin actively recruiting civilian reporters. If ten experienced newsmen could be recruited to jump-start the CC group, the agreement was another ten would be authorized.

Denig sent First Sergeant Walter J. "Joe" Shipman, DPR, to canvas the closest pool of potential CC enlistees, city rooms of local newspapers. Wearing dress blues, Shipman walked ramrod straight into Washington, D.C., newsrooms bearing an offer from the Marine Corps: sergeants stripes plus a Pacific combat zone news beat in exchange for enlistment and boot camp graduation. An opportunity to write eye-witness accounts of marines from combat zones proved quite a sales pitch. According to Jack, Cissy Patterson, publisher of the *Washington Times-Herald,* lost most of her reporters to the Corps. She complained directly to President Franklin D. Roosevelt, and word passed quickly down the line that Denig should expand his recruiting area.

As the war escalated the need for CCs grew faster than reporters could be recruited from newsrooms. Thus the June 6, 1942, nationwide announcement adding the five years experience requirement and opening the CCs to previously excluded reporters.

In a taped interview Red recalled, "After the word got out, reporters from around the country, definitely older than most recruits and not exactly 1A, immediately began gathering required paperwork. For most of us, a place in the group was our last chance to serve. Deals sealed only after boot camp. Stripes awarded after being schooled in 'the marine way' of reporting news—the five W's slightly revised. Just the facts: 'who'; 'what'; 'when' (DELAYED); 'where' (SOMEWHERE IN THE PACIFIC); and everybody knew 'why.' We couldn't write about ourselves and, as in all good reporting, no editorializing.

"Elite, unique, handpicked, working from combat zones—the group drew news professionals like a magnet," he noted. "Classified 'public relations personnel,' often referred to as 'reporters,' and even more often called 'combat correspondents,' the terms got a bit confusing—particularly with journalists, reporters, artists, illustrators, photographers, cinematographers, public relations specialists, radio broadcasters, and magazine personnel enlisting.

"I sucked in my gut and squared my shoulders," Red continued, "when I told folks I was joining the marines. After a long three months of training, we newly minted Denig's Demons were shuffled and dealt to marine groups shipping out or in combat zones. My new friend and fellow CC Phil Storch and I headed for Santa Barbara, assigned to Marine Aircraft Group 45, almost ready to pack up."*

Jack recalled a conversation with one of the first civilian reporters to come on board with the CCs, the late Samuel E. Stavisky. Sam related that in March 1942, he became the fourteenth reporter to enlist in the group. Assistant city editor of the *Washington Post,* Sam telephoned Denig to enlist. Denig immediately sent his sergeant major over to sign up Sam.

Already turned down by the army and navy because of poor eyesight, Sam's acceptance required a waiver. Brigadier General Denig issued the waiver, and it was denied. Lieutenant General Holcomb issued another waiver; it was denied. At this point the leader of the Marine Corps personally intervened with the Navy Department, which then as now administers the Marine Corps. Meeting face-to-face with Secretary of the Navy Frank Knox, Holcomb secured the waiver. Sam revealed that his greatest fear was not the enemy but that something would happen to his glasses. *Marine Combat Correspondent* (1999) a humorous, historical narrative of his combat correspondent days reporting from Guadalcanal and the Solomon Islands is a good read.†

On February 6, 1943, after recognizing an official military occupation specialty (MOS) was needed for the group, Holcomb issued Letter of Instruction #337 to all commanding officers. It read in part:

> The Division of Public Relations is charged with responsibility for all matters having to do with the administration of public relations and is charged with the coordination and administration of Maine Corps Public Relations personnel, equipment, and activities. It shall provide trained public relations personnel for the Marine Corps.
>
> . . . The assignment of all public relations personnel will be made by the Commandant.
>
> . . . Enlisted men of the first four pay grades assigned to public relations shall be designated "Public Relations personnel," and upon subject assignment the service record book of the individual concerned will be prominently marked "Public Relations personnel" on the outside cover.
>
> . . . The promotion of Public Relations enlisted personnel will be made upon recommendation of their commanding officer, such recommendations

* All tape recordings are part of the Claude R. "Red" Canup Collection.

† Samuel E. Stavisky, *Marine Combat Correspondent: World War II in the Pacific* (New York: Ballantine Publishing Group, 1999), 8.

> to be sent to the Commandant via the Director, Division of Public Relations.
>
> . . . Insofar as consistent with directives from other responsible commanders, the following instructions will govern the handling of press releases:
>
> The unit commander to which a Public Relations correspondent is attached is responsible for the accuracy of facts and general tenor of articles and news items written by combat correspondents under his command.
>
> . . . Combat Correspondents are specially trained to perform the duty which the name implies. Their status is similar to that of Quartermaster, Paymaster, Ordnance, Engineer or Communications Personnel. They are basically Marines. The purpose of Combat Correspondents may be delineated as follows:
>
> 1. General Marine duties.
> 2. Collect military information and facts of historical value to the Marine Corps.
> 3. Collect, prepare and forward for publication news items and articles of interest to the American public.*

Jack maintains contact with the most highly distinguished cinematographer of the war, Staff Sergeant Norm Hatch, who landed with the marines on Tarawa—one of the first, fiercest, and bloodiest battles of the Pacific. Norm waded in with his fellow marines, not carrying a rifle but a 35mm camera, filming the battle from a standing position.

In an e-mail to Jack, Norm recalled that before leaving San Diego, he and John F. Ercole, the only two professionally trained motion picture cameramen in the division, planned ahead. "We knew we were going somewhere in the Pacific far, far away from any resupply source, so we convinced our photo officer and the quartermaster that we should go to Hollywood and purchase as many as possible 16mm handheld cameras, developed for the amateur trade, and the color film magazines to go with them so we could train other members of the organization in the art of movies. Johnny and I knew we could not cover the activities of a 20,000 man division in battle, and if one of us or both were killed or wounded coverage would be made.

"All of the members of the photo section survived Tarawa and all except me shot color. Consequently, when the film *With the Marines at Tarawa* opened,

* Thomas Holcomb, Letters of Instruction No. 506, 2195-30, AO-278-nsh, 1943, General Alfred M. Gray Research Center and Archives, Library of the Marine Corps, Quantico, Virginia.

my black and white film was tinted to a rosy hue so there wouldn't be drastic cuts from BXW to color. They needed to use my film. I was the only movie man on the beach for the first day and a half. Our coverage of Tarawa in color was the first battle so filmed. Use of color was quickly taken up by the other services as well as the Corps. After Tarawa, all Pacific battles that the Marines fought were filmed in color."

More than one thousand marines died during the seventy-six-hour battle. Japanese losses numbered near four thousand. After reviewing the film, President Franklin D. Roosevelt granted special permission for parts to be shown in newsreels. The president felt the public needed to see Tarawa's casualties to prepare for future battles and to rev up financial support. Bond sales ballooned—and for a time marine enlistment numbers fell.

In 1944 Hatch's work won the Oscar for Most Outstanding Documentary Short for *With the Marines at Tarawa.* He later traveled for the Treasury Department on the fourth war loan drive. On March 26, 2010, Major Norm Hatch, USMC (Ret.) was honored by ABC's *World News* as the show's "Person of the Week."

Combat correspondents today are placed under the military occupation specialty public affairs. Continuing Denig's Demons tradition of reporting, public affairs personnel "tell it like it is" wherever marines see action. Keith chairs the Public Affairs Leadership Department of the Defense Information School at Ft. Meade, Maryland. New public affairs officers (PAOs) receive training there in methods of managing public and internal information and community relations.

PAOs are essential personnel for marine bases in today's world. Unlike WWII's censored, snail-mail news delivery system, news now travels at the speed of light, available twenty-four hours a day at the click of a button or touch of a finger. Working with the media, the public, and base personnel, PAOs closely coordinate release of information and procedures with the base commanding officer. Keith's *Command Attention* (2009) is a public relations textbook applicable to many organizations.

Between 1995 and early 1998, my father taped highlights of his CC days and penned many notes, preparing perhaps to write his marine story someday. Suffering a second heart attack in late 1998, my favorite marine died February 20, 1999. All the direct quotes from him found in this book are from these tapes and notes. Every story has been carefully retyped from his saved dispatch copies. Any and all mistakes are mine and not intended.

If he were here today, my father would smile and say, "Hot damn, golly gee, and that's swell," knowing his yarns, as he called the dispatches, are now seen as significant to Marine Corps aviation history. The dispatches report incidents that my father either observed firsthand or verified from participants or witnesses. Important not only for their content, the dispatches also represent the only intact collection of original writings—the actual output—known to exist of any WWII marine combat correspondent.

Dispatch copies and the resulting printed articles are extremely rare finds. My brother, Dr. Claude R. "Buzz" Canup, and I plan to donate our father's carefully saved collection to the General Alfred M. Gray Research Center and Archives in the Library of the Marine Corps, Quantico, Virginia. Claude R. "Red" Canup's will be the only combat correspondent's collection, the only dispatches, housed there.

A visit to the National Museum of the Marine Corps, Triangle, Virginia, near Quantico, finds only one reference to the unique WWII combat correspondent group. Sergeant Louis R. Lowery, combat photographer, is credited with taking the first picture of marines raising the first flag at the top of Mt. Suribachi on Iwo Jima. The museum has recently approved the addition of two tributes to the early combat correspondents: a memorial to General Denig, his "Demons," and all CCs; and the addition of a cinematographer to the existing Tarawa tableau. Each is privately funded. The Denig Memorial was dedicated in late 2012.

Only a few names from that first CC group are remembered today, and their important assignment to report leatherneck activities back to families and communities is all but forgotten. My hope is my father's writings found in this book will call attention to this duty so ably performed by Denig's Demons.

Brigadier General Denig's instructions to a group of the first CCs in early 1942 were simple: "Give most of your time and attention to the enlisted man—what he says, thinks, and does. If Pvt. Bill Jones of Cumberland Gap wins the boxing tournament, tell the people of Cumberland Gap about it."

My father followed Denig's instructions. The excerpt below is taken from a September 1, 1945, letter from my father to him:

> Since joining your Division 19 June 1944 I have had the pleasure of serving with newspaper men from every part of the country, all heralding Marine Corps victories. I shall always be proud of the honor of having been a Combat Correspondent for the Marines themselves, as well as publishers and the public, looked to your little army for news about the Corps, its generals and its privates.
>
> It was my privilege to be up front in the last 12 months of the war, moving forward with Marine aviation from the Western Carolines to Okinawa [and now to Japan].
>
> During this exciting period my squadron made headlines, including the first kill by Okinawa-based Marine pilots, and also the last kill of the war.

> Night fighters I covered re-wrote the record books, and I wrote the stories of the only eye-witness accounts of the airborne suicide attack on Yontan.
>
> But my deepest satisfaction was in helping see to it that there were no unknown Marines. The Joe Blow stories seemed to count most with the men and their families. To some, they probably were more important than any making headlines.*

Of great loss to us and to future generations are the dispatches, photographs, and films that disappeared through the years as well as the unrecorded personal stories of most of the original marine combat correspondents. In my father's honor and as a tribute to all WWII marine combat correspondents, I have assembled this collection of his writings and told his story. Lest we forget, Denig's Demons lived and reported eye-witness accounts of marine history from the Pacific for leathernecks, their families, and the American public.

* This letter is part of the Claude R. "Red" Canup Collection.

ACKNOWLEDGMENTS

There are many to whom I owe thanks, many who provided help or support during the writing of this manuscript. I would like to acknowledge the following people in particular.

My mother and all the military wives who waited, prayed, loved, and cared for us WWII kids.

My husband, marine veteran Louis Lima, who earned sainthood these last years for his support, encouragement, patience, and weekly bouquets of flowers. And a special thanks for prodding me at crucial times with reminders that Red's stories are part of a history that should not be lost—and that he is looking down and smiling.

My daughters, Lisa Marie Keaton (Mrs. Mark) Wilson and Karen Shirley Keaton (Mrs. Curtis) Maxon, whose love for Granddaddy Red inspired this book.

My granddaughters, Anna Elizabeth and Ellen Marie Wilson, Caroline Keaton and Marianne Marie Maxon, my sunbeams, who are daily reminders of how blessed I am.

My brother, Dr. Claude R. "Buzz" Canup, for his support and for preserving the dispatches, and his children, Scott Richard Canup and Catherine Elizabeth Canup (Mrs. Garrett) Scott, and his grandchildren, Parker Davis and Hammond Elizabeth Scott, the remaining Canup clan.

Colonel Keith Oliver, USMC (Ret.), my father's good friend and my cheerleader extraordinaire, for believing so strongly in my ability to organize this treasure trove of information, his prayers along the way, and writing the book's foreword.

Colonel Walt Ford, USMC (Ret.), editor/publisher of *Leatherneck Magazine,* for recognizing the historical value of my father's dispatches and bolstering my confidence at crucial points along this journey.

Captain Jack Paxton, USMC (Ret.), executive director of the United States Marine Corps Combat Correspondents Association, my father's colleague, and the number one supporter of the CCs, for sharing his extensive knowledge of combat correspondent history and for his continuous support throughout this project.

Connie Ann Canup (Mrs. Kenneth) Hall for her valuable recollections of WW II days and for saving her Uncle Red's letters to her father, Orville McCarty Canup, a southern gentleman with remarkable insight, a no-nonsense demeanor, and a heart of gold.

Barbara Jean Edmonds (Mrs. Edward) Welmaker (Aunt Georgia Lee Canup Edmonds's daughter), my lovely, gracious cousin, for her family history, support, and encouragement of this endeavor long before it became a book.

Linda Haines Fogle, assistant director for operations of the University of South Carolina Press, for rescuing this book and for her continued support.

Ly Vang, my good friend, for technical assistance above and beyond the demands of friendship.

Steve Hurt for his assistance preparing photographs and line art.

Red Canup, in his tent, reporting from the field, Yontan Airfield, Okinawa, 1945. Photograph by T. Sgt. Charles V. Corkran, DPR with MAG 31. Claude R. "Red" Canup Collection.

PROLOGUE

The Cardboard Box

War Is Not Just for Heroes is my father's story. The story of the cardboard box is mine. The pages that follow detail the transformation of the contents of a cardboard box to this book. Step by step—often not taken in order—the manuscript took shape. It was assembled in ever changing parts, and I never knew the best fit until the last revision, never sure until now which revision would be the last.

The significance of this book will never be measured by the number of years spent researching and piecing together information. The significance will be measured by those special heroes who say, "That's me," or by a relative or reader who spots a familiar name and says, "I remember," or when someone who just happens to love marines and reading about World War II says, "What a story!"

Summer 2008

Opening the box delivered to my front door was emotional. I knew it would be. Here were my father's treasures, packed after his death some nine years earlier. Someone else's treasures are hard to sort, especially your father's. In the box were copies of his combat correspondent dispatches, their planned donation to the Marine Corps long overdue.

Filed in three faded dispatch binders neatly labeled in my father's block-style printing, the dispatches were in excellent condition after being safely transported in his seabag from halfway round the world more than sixty-five years ago. A duty was owed before sending the stories on to the Corps, and I read all of them.

There were more treasures in the box. Stacked near the bottom were my father's personal files—some filled with his notes, some with articles other

Linda (at age three) and Red Canup, Anderson, S.C., June 1944. Claude R. "Red" Canup Collection.

reporters published about his combat correspondent career. Proud as he was to be a leatherneck and a combat correspondent, my father never wrote about his Marine Corps days—though he loved telling stories of them with his signature dry wit. Every dispatch, article, and page of notes was a revelation to me.

Neither the neatness nor organization of my father's files was a surprise: such traits essential early in his newspaper career. In addition to his coverage of seasonal high school and college sports and his feature stories, his column, "Here We Go Again" (originally "On the Sidelines"), ran for more than twenty-five years in the *Anderson Independent.* Published with his picture seven days a week in the upstate South Carolina newspaper, his name and face were recognized by more folks in the Carolinas and Georgia than "you could shake a stick at," as we southerners say. Friends and faithful readers opened morning newspapers to the sports page first for Red's humorous comments on everyday issues, encounters rambling around the countryside, and take on sports headlines.

Sitting amidst the box's contents, I made a decision—the consequences of which rippled through the next three years of my life. My daughters should have copies of Granddaddy Red's writings to pass on to their daughters before I passed his carefully saved dispatches, his legacy, on to the Marine Corps.

Starting the Project

I began photocopying the dispatches with great care. Each onionskin page was removed from the binder clasp, gently placed on the copier, and carefully replaced. My intent was to slide the copies into plastic sleeves and make notebooks. After a hundred or so sheets, I changed my mind. The notebooks were becoming too heavy to hold comfortably for reading. My new plan was to retype the dispatches into a continuous flow, separate by title and date, add copies of articles and pictures, and have copies bound.

A major decision was not to include every dispatch. Combat correspondents were to write something about every marine in every squadron to which they were assigned. My father accomplished this with two-line promotion stories and listings of leathernecks from every state. Every promotion and listing story included the marine's street address, hometown, state, parents' names and full addresses plus the same information for wives. Some even included social security numbers.

The listings were repetitious. State group information was often repeated in stories featuring individual marines. Promotion stories, identical wording for dozens of marines written for dozens of different hometown newspapers, proved not only to be tedious typing but even more tedious reading. Clustering promotion stories and state listings in separate chapters was information overload. Rethinking my goal, I deleted all state listings and most promotion stories.

My true "aha" moment came when I realized that I also needed to delete multiple accounts of the same event written for every participant's hometown newspaper. As each story contained all the names involved, I chose one per incident.

The Letters

Typing, deleting and organizing completed, I continued my search through the box's contents. Finding letters my father wrote to his older brother Orville, a WWI veteran, was quite a discovery. I positioned excerpts among the dispatches beginning with my father's arrival at Marine Corps headquarters in Washington, D.C., in June 1944.

The letters added a personal connection to his stories. Finding the intact set was a miracle. After my uncle's death on September 20, 1989, his daughter Connie sent the letters back to her Uncle Red. Originally mailed from "somewhere in the Pacific" to Anderson, South Carolina, they were returned to my father decades later in Greenville, South Carolina, via New Mexico and Colorado.

Thoughts and feelings expressed brother to brother, told of the toll war takes on the human spirit. In many letters my father asked his brother not to share information with other family members, to avoid adding to their worries. Other letters were clearly meant to be shared, the last months of the Okinawa campaign in particular too hectic to remember what had been written to whom.

The letters add opinions, humor, recollections, and reflections not allowed in the official dispatches.

More Treasures Revealed

The box contained many more treasures—official and personal letters; restricted handouts; a 103-page booklet with maps, "Guide to Japan," dated September 1, 1945 (a week before the first MAG 31 planes landed at Yokosuka naval base); photographs; newsletters; church service bulletins; articles other correspondents wrote; clippings of many of my father's published stories. Most will be donated to the Marine Corps.

The Ulithi Diary

Pages torn from my father's pocket-sized diary were found clipped together, tucked inside a folder. The entries, jotted down through most of his MAG 45 deployment, documented his daily activities and added to my understanding of life on the tiny, peaceful island and to the emotional highs and lows my father experienced—a stymied combat correspondent writing about pigs, lizards, and natives instead of missions flaming Japanese planes.

Jet Stream Article

Another treasure in the box was an article about my father published in *Jet Stream,* the official newspaper of the Marine Corps Air Station Beaufort, in the South Carolina lowcountry, dated January 13, 1984, and titled "Marine Aircraft Group 31 Historian." Written by Sgt. Hugh Hawthorne and carefully laminated by my father, the article noted that his saved dispatch copies were the only recorded history of the MAG from D-day Okinawa through five weeks of occupation duty at the naval base in Yokosuka, Japan.*

Read separately, the dispatches report accomplishments of individual leathernecks, enlisted men and officers, with human interest stories mixed throughout. Read together, the dispatches tell the story of the MAG's heroic role in achieving air superiority from Kyushu to the southern Ryukyu Islands, the only land-based air support early in the Okinawa campaign.

Presidential Unit Citation

I discovered a shorthand notation indicating the MAG was awarded the Presidential Unit Citation. Piquing my interest, I contacted the MCAS Beaufort for

* Hugh Hawthorne, "Marine Aircraft Group 31 Historian," *Jet Stream* (MCAS Beaufort), January 13, 1984, 1–2. Hawthorne revealed the *official* history of MAG 31, based at Beaufort, devotes barely two paragraphs to the important part the MAG played in the Pacific campaign. Red's dispatches, he noted, contain hundreds of pages of *unofficial* history detailing the MAG's historic role through his reporting of the day-to-day activities of its heroic men.

verification. The Second Marine Aircraft Wing, of which MAG 31 was a member group, received the Presidential Unit Citation for participation in the history-making Okinawa campaign. This award is similar to an individual marine being awarded the Navy Cross, the highest individual honor given. The Presidential Unit Citation was awarded to only four marine units (First Marine Division, Sixth Marine Division, Second MAW, and Marine Observation Squadron 3) for their contributions during "Operation Iceberg," the code name for the Battle for Okinawa. A copy of the citation, a comprehensive synopsis of MAG 31's heroic actions on Okinawa, is included in chapter 12. Assigned by DPR, my father was not eligible for the award.

Giretsu Attack on Yontan

In a letter he wrote to General Denig, I discovered my father wrote the only eye-witness accounts of the giretsu attack. This was my first clue that my father's post-attack reports were historically important.*

I found the dispatches and also found a newspaper clipping written by a civilian wire service reporter quoting Sergeant Canup. Combat correspondents could not write for news services; they could serve as conduits for information. The fastest way to get news published was to be quoted by a civilian reporter, bypassing the censors. I wrote an article for *Naval History* (June 2010) entitled "Giretsu Attack" using the dispatches.

Tactical Air Force, Ryukyu Islands

Found deep in the box was a tattered mimeographed handout, run from a typewriter-cut stencil attached to a hand-turned drum, printed front and back, one copy at a time—the paper, similar to construction paper, separating at the folds. The "restricted, source unknown" handout contained organizational details of Tactical Air Force Ryukyus and a three months' long day-by-day history of the most important happenings on Yontan Airfield, Okinawa, from April 7 to July 6, 1945. The organizational information appears in chapter 7; the history in chapter 11.

Along with other little known information about TAF, the handout listed every squadron of every participating Marine Aircraft Group—MAGs 14, 22, 31, and 33—with the officers, types of planes, squadron identification numbers, and nicknames. Three groups made up the TAF Ryukyus Fighter Command—Marine Air Warning Group 43, 2ndMAW, and 301st Army Fighter Wing. My father's dispatches from Okinawa contained 2ndMAW MAG 31 squadron nicknames, not identification numbers.

* See Robert Sherrod, *History of Marine Corps Aviation in World War II* (Baltimore: Nautical and Aviation Publishing Company of America, 1987), 404–5, for a brief overview of the giretsu attack.

From the handout, I also learned one aircraft squadron, VMF (N) 533, Black Mac's Killers, joined MAG 31 six weeks into the campaign. This explained my father's many dispatches about Black Mac's Killers. Operationally assigned to MAG 31, administratively they belonged to another group.*

I developed an e-mail friendship with Colonel Marion "Black Mac" Magruder's son Mark. He sent his father's squadron roster enabling me to identify pilots, and I returned the favor by providing copies of dispatches my father wrote about his father and Black Mac's Killers. Mark's book about his father is titled *Nightfighter: Radar Intercept Killer* (2012).

The 31-Magazette Newsletters

Another discovery, included in chapter 12, are two MAG 31 newsletters published from Chimu Airfield, Okinawa, on August 17 and 20, 1945. Probably the only copies in existence, these newsletters contain interesting history and little know facts—particularly about General Douglas MacArthur's instructions for the Japanese envoy traveling to Manila to receive the terms of surrender to ferry back to the emperor.

The MAG began packing for the initial occupation of Japan shortly after the August 20 newsletter. Only these two issues were found.

Personal Tapes

Tapes dictated in the later years of my father's life were in the box. They include a wealth of information and also humorous stories of the escapades of the marine correspondents in Japan. Transcribed excerpts have become an important part of this manuscript.

Photographs

Finding titles for the loose pictures in the box proved to be something of a scavenger hunt. Information gleaned from dispatches helped with a few—Tune Toppers band and Doughboy Chapel. More were identified sifting through pages of captions my father filed with his dispatches. By matching the activity pictured—cleaning aircraft guns, loading auxiliary gas tanks, sleeping after combat—to typed captions, I was able to identify additional marines.

The Project Becomes a Manuscript

As I organized materials, two story lines developed—one without combat and the other packed with details of the last great military campaign of World War

* "90 Days of Operation Tactical Air Force Ryukyus, April 7–July 6, 1945," Claude R. "Red" Canup Collection.

II—both parts filled with detailed information describing marines in the Pacific. My father's collective writings became his story.

The dispatches transport readers to a different era. In stories my father wrote from notes taken during debriefings, young pilots seem to come to life exuding determination to win the war. In many dispatches my father used direct quotes from the pilots to lead the reader through dogfights from first sighting to flaming finish. In other dispatches the marine aviators describe kamikazes taken out just before crashing into ships, both planes scrambling to get away from deadly ack-ack streaming from the gunners below.

When I discovered the Marine Corps archives held not one original dispatch and would gladly review my father's copies for acceptance, I decided that his stories and saved handouts should be submitted to this archive. Although my father's personal letters also contain interesting information on marine aviation, I decided they would remain with the family.

Archives are crucial for preserving valuable papers; but, by this time in my endeavor, I decided the dispatches and materials should be made readily available to others interested in marine aviation in the Pacific during World War II. The dispatches contained too many heretofore little known, or unknown, details; and, they were too well written to be read only by researchers and family members. Although publication had never been my intent, submitting a manuscript was the only means to accomplish this.

I willingly admit here I knew nothing about submitting a manuscript. Even though my father's dispatches constitute by far the majority of this book, the unknown variable that soon emerged was the amount of time needed to flesh out a presentation worthy of his writings and the history he preserved.

My husband, Lou, cautioned not to let publication become my new goal. He reminded me that I had succeeded in my original intent—to preserve my father's writings and the story of his life as a combat correspondent for my daughters, Lisa and Karen, and for their daughters—if the manuscript was never accepted.

Lou's warnings could not prepare me, however, for the most difficult part of submitting a manuscript for publication: the waiting. The manuscript was never rejected, but I pulled it from one well-known publisher because of time—more than a year—spent waiting to hear if it would be accepted.

There was a fringe benefit to this wait time: I used it to write several magazine articles. One I have mentioned. Another, "Combat Detour: Marine Night Fighter Squadron 542," was published in the May 2010 issue of *Leatherneck,* the magazine of the marines. Colonel Walt Ford, the editor/publisher, accepted the Squadron 542 article almost immediately—for publication a year later—but, it was accepted. This instantly boosted my confidence. After the article appeared, he told me the former VMF (N) 542 pilot whose photograph—

asleep, exhausted after a night of combat—was included in the article (p. 176) requested extra copies for his grandchildren. The marine was identified by matching my father's caption to the subject matter. That one request from the pilot, a marine my father knew personally, reinforced my dedication and determination.

Even though the article is now two years old, recently I have been contacted by relatives of marines pictured or named in "Combat Detour."

Final Thoughts

When I began this project, I was thinking of my children and grandchildren, but as it progressed, it became clear that children and grandchildren of other WWII marines could relate to my father's dispatches. I also hope that marines of all ages, military scholars and historians, WWII veterans and their families, and those who enjoy reading about the war will find my father's story interesting and the history he wrote both valuable and entertaining. Aviation enthusiasts in particular will find my father's dispatches about night fighters in the black Okinawa skies just like being in the cockpit.

Often referred to as "the greatest generation," my father and his peers experienced both the Great Depression and World War II. Growing up during hard financial times and accustomed to doing without, these men went to war and experienced some of the worst conditions imaginable. Those who returned stayed on point keeping America and our freedoms safe by their participation in continued military service, government, politics, and communities.*

Sharing my father's contribution to the preservation of Marine Corps aviation history has been very gratifying. I knew very little about marines' island hopping across the Pacific when I started this project. Now I feel as if I have been there.

Proud to be an enlisted Joe Blow, my father used the power of the press to ensure the contributions of these leathernecks were recognized. Each time a plane took off, the work of every nuts and bolts leatherneck in the squadron made the mission possible. Dispatches detail many essential duties and name enlisted marines checking them off.

The cardboard box is being readied for one last trip to the General Alfred M. Gray Research Center and Archives with my blessing. I now know appreciation of my father's CC writings will extend far beyond the box. His voice, along with the voices of other leathernecks met during his Pacific travels, will be heard loud and clear each time this book is read—and Denig's Demons will be remembered.

* Tom Brokaw, *The Greatest Generation* (New York: Random House, 1998), xvii–12.

PART 1

Answering the Commandant's Call

1. RED CANUP, COMBAT CORRESPONDENT

Private Claude R. "Red" Canup, thirty-three, newly graduated Parris Island "shitbird" was anxious to get on with the business of writing about marines. The Marine Corps' promise—boot camp graduation secured his acceptance into the combat correspondents, the unique adjunct fighter-writer group of the Marine Corps Division of Public Relations. Formed to inundate local newspapers with more marine news than any other branch of service, combat correspondents had fascinated Red for years. Now, at almost twice the age of most Parris Island graduates, the South Carolina native had successfully completed the marines' physical and fighter training requirements.

Nineteen forty-four was a monumental year for the new marine. Red applied for the CC group in January and received acceptance in March. Inducted in April and boot camp completed by June, Red was assigned to marine headquarters in Washington, D.C., for indoctrination. September found the marine in California assigned to marine aviation. And, from August 1944 through November 1945, the former small town editor wrote 398 aviation dispatches for the USMC Division of Public Relations.

He remembered his first assignment. "I joined MAG [Marine Aircraft Group] 45 as it was packing up at Santa Barbara," Red narrated on tape."With a brief liberty stop at Pearl Harbor, we embarked on what turned out to be a slow boat trip to peaceful Falalop Island, Ulithi Atoll, the western most Allied outpost in the Pacific at that time. We sailed September 1944. I wrote many stories after we landed and began living, if you could call it that, on Ulithi using the usual war-safety dateline SOMEWHERE IN THE WESTERN PACIFIC. Combat never reached Ulithi, but the mile by half-mile "fly speck" island was turned into a strategic base for shipping and staging. Man, was it crowded! My group's highly trained pilots ended up flying protection for the island and hundreds of ships gathering there for the Iwo Jima invasion. Combat correspondents were given quite a bit of freedom writing what they could dig up about their fellow marines. The stories were censored at the base wherever we were. Our intelligence officers got first crack at my stories, and then the Pearl Harbor censors. Nothing got by that would make the Nipponese happy."

Red's second assignment was with Marine Aircraft Group 31, 2nd Marine Aircraft Wing, for the invasion of Okinawa. The campaign began Easter Sunday, April 1, 1945. The MAG, commanded by Colonel John C. Munn, took possession of Yontan Airfield on April 3, two days after First Division Marines had cleared the airfield of Japanese soldiers.

The 2ndMAW Corsairs flew combat missions from the base on April 7, the first day the field was fully operational. Night fighter Hellcats took to the air a few nights later. Skilled pilots protected the airfield and ships, day and night. For this the marines had trained. Three weeks into the campaign the rains came, record setting monsoons. For this the marines had not trained. The mud, sinking planes and filling boots, had the leathernecks cursing but not beaten.

Red interviewed leathernecks flying and servicing Marine Corps fighter planes throughout this last great campaign of World War II—from Yontan and Chimu airfields on Okinawa to Yokosuka naval base, Japan.

From many Pacific war zones combat correspondent dispatches provided the only news, the only eye-witness accounts, the only written histories. This is true of Red's MAG 45 and MAG 31 dispatches, written while covering his Pacific news beat.

After the Japanese surrendered August 15, 1945 (V-J day), combat correspondents became correspondents. Three months later, on November 15, 1945, Red's discharge papers arrived from marine headquarters to Yokosuka naval base.

Discharged as a technical sergeant in San Francisco on December 15, 1945, Red returned to South Carolina to become the first full-time sports editor of the *Anderson Independent.* Known by friends and colleagues as "the Dean of South Carolina Sports Writers," he would smile broadly at the title and attribute this distinction to his longevity in the field, writing for the newspaper for more than a quarter of a century.

In 1960 Red accepted the position of sports information director for the University of South Carolina Athletic Department, working with his good friend Warren Giese. Remaining with the university until mid-1962, he resigned to return to Anderson as editor/publisher of the *Anderson Free Press,* a weekly tabloid whose subscriptions and advertising tripled under his supervision.

In 1963 Red was named the first public relations and advertising director for Greenville-based Daniel Construction Company (later Fluor-Daniel, Inc.), remaining there until his retirement in 1986. While working for the company, he coauthored *Charles E. Daniel: His Philosophy and Legacy* (1981) with W. D. "Bill" Workman, Jr., the former editor of Columbia's *State* newspaper.

With a communications career that spanned three distinctly different fields—newspaper, military, and construction—Red worked his craft for more than a half-century. According to him, "Every dollar I earned came from writing, and whatever the career, I always promoted somebody or something."

A member of the Marine Reserves since November 23, 1948, Red received a captain's rank in the Retired Marine Reserves, April 1, 1958. He was a life member and ardent supporter of the United States Marine Corps Combat Correspondents Association.

In 1997 Red wrote a colleague, "I'm 86 and I can still say I am a Marine, and that's something special." And so are his dispatches. Connecting his writings is the underlying theme *War Is Not Just for Heroes*—a title found penciled in the margin of his notes and a belief held high by all participants in every mission he covered.

On February 23, 1999, a bitterly cold snowy day in Anderson, rifle shots of the United States Marine Corps honor guard echoed through the pines. *Taps* sounded. Wind ruffled edges of the draped flag as Claude R. Canup was laid to rest. Today a bronze plaque marks the grave site and per his request displays the proudly worn, time-honored United States Marine Corps emblem—once a marine, always a marine.

The Role of Combat Correspondents

"General Denig knew what he was doing putting us combat correspondents up front. Being interviewed or having pictures taken really made marines happy. Officers and Joe Blows both grinned from ear to ear for the camera and came around to show me clippings sent from home. Nothing meant as much as getting mail from home, except getting mail from home including a personal clipping.

"Some correspondents were too gung-ho on the front lines, got too close, and got themselves killed. Of course you can't be a marine and not be gung-ho. I was just fine dodging bombs waiting on pilots to get back, but I would have loved being assigned to a big navy carrier. But, the navy didn't want combat correspondents on board till near the end of the war.

"Admitted or not, in the beginning when we first enlisted, not knowing anything about marine guidelines and censors, all of us had visions of being the enlisted version of Ernie Pyle pounding out dispatches on lap-balanced portables, runners carrying flimsies to beaches, boats waiting with motors running to relay the latest news to destroyer-protected ships for transmission. We soon found that was not even a remote possibility and got with the program.

"We never knew if the dispatches reached headquarters or if the dispatches were distributed and published unless we actually saw the dispatch in print. I kept in touch with several members of General Denig's staff, who often mailed me clippings. When a newspaper printed a dispatch, a clipping was supposed to be mailed back to headquarters. Half didn't do it. When a leatherneck got word from home that he 'made the papers,' we all celebrated.

"Some officers never got comfortable with the whole CC idea. I was supposed to be assigned to a night fighter squadron after MAG 45 on Ulithi, even had orders, but the CO didn't want me. Found out later I didn't have BO—he was having some kind of problems at the time and didn't have much use for anybody. Anyway, I had been waiting for combat assignment for months and joining MAG 31 was my ticket.

"Being enlisted with public relations stamped on us, some officers didn't like us around—but orders were orders, until they got changed. One squadron commander told me the only thing he had against me was not being G.I. enough. I don't know what the hell he expected. I was not career military and took leave of a civilian job for a year and a half to write about marines. Well, commands changed pretty often, and he soon was reassigned. We met up later got along fine.

"Some friends and relatives want me to tell about my marine experiences. I have consented to recount a few that might be of interest to somebody simply because they happened so long ago and maybe they are a bit uncommon. At any rate, they did happen and they are true."

RED
February 17, 1998, tape recording

2. FROM SIDELINES TO SHORELINES

Red showed an early affinity for both sports and reporting. He had a successful career as an editor at an Anderson newspaper and a young family when the war broke out. Nevertheless Red answered the call of Commandant Holcomb.

Nicknamed "Red," Claude R. Canup, the youngest of nine children, was born in Pendleton, South Carolina, March 3, 1911, the wedding day of his oldest sister Jane (Mrs. Ernest P.) Werner. Other siblings were James J., Orville M., Icy (Mrs. John L.) Palmer, Georgia Lee (Mrs. Robert F.) Edmonds, and Oda (Mrs. Richard) Byars. Two other siblings, Dalton and Myrtle, died at young ages. His parents, George "Pap" Alexander and Hulda Marietta Wood Canup, relocated to Pendleton from the mountains of Habersham County, Georgia.

According to Red's notes, Pap was appointed police chief in Pendleton after Stark Whitlock got killed. While serving as chief, Pap also managed Riley's Store on the town square. Bootleg whiskey, covered with cabbages and transported by wagon from nearby mountains, was sold from an adjacent alley. Red's first job, for which he was paid with candy, was distributing grocery orders from a wagon pulled by Orville.

While Pap served as police chief, so the family story goes, a short-term prisoner in the jail learned Pap could not read. A deal was struck. During the time remaining on the inmate's sentence, he would teach Pap to read in exchange for his bootleg whiskey recipe. Pap learned to read a few words, and the former inmate, whose name today appears on a popular brand, left town with the recipe for the best whiskey he ever tasted. Or so the story goes.

As happens, customers would not, or could not, pay their bills. In 1919 the grocery store closed, and the family moved to Anderson. Orville and eight-year-old Red rode on the wagon loaded with household furnishings, the family milk cow tied to the rear. Red's second job was making sure the cow kept pace.

Both Pap and Orville secured jobs with Duke Energy, Pap as a streetcar motorman and Orville with the hydroelectric plant on the Seneca River at Portman Shoals. Attending first grade in Pendleton, Red enrolled in Anderson's East Whitner Street School for the second and third grades, West Market Street School for the fourth through the seventh, and Boys High School for grades eight through eleven.

According to Red, "I attended Boys High School and wanted to play on the football team coached by Carroll 'Frog' Reams, who later became a life-long friend and principal of Boys High. I was so skinny that I had to wait a year to put on enough weight and played one season in 1928."

Red's first military experience also came in 1928, when he volunteered for summer camp with the Citizens Military Training Corps (CMTC) for young men at Fort Bragg. Training with the army for a month, he drilled and got a chance to fire the historic Springfield '03 rifle.

In autumn 1929 Red's football days ended and his newspaper career started, both as a result of a hopelessly low math grade. Ruled academically ineligible to participate in sports but attending every football practice, Red wrote stories for the afternoon newspaper, the *Daily Mail,* from the practice field. The following year, partly to escape full-time work in one of the many textile mills and partly to earn a diploma, Red repeated the math class, first period every day, and—as he used to laugh—added the twelfth grade to the high school curriculum. The remainder of the day he spent covering area high school sports, graduating in 1931.

Red's tapes detail another story of the origins of his sports writer career. "Coach Reames took the team over to Furman in Greenville to see a day game," he said, "and it was sleeting and snowing and raining. It was just a miserable day to be watching a football game. I looked across the field and saw all those guys sitting up in the press box out of the weather. I decided then and there that I wanted to be a sports writer."

In those days Anderson County had nineteen textile plants, eight cottonseed oil mills, and thousands of farms, mostly growing cotton. The boll weevil struck hard as early as 1920, and that, combined with the 1929 stock market crash, meant much suffering for the mill and farm workers of Anderson County. In 1932, if an unskilled mill worker was lucky enough to find work, the pay was ten cents an hour. Farm laborers were happy to work for food and a place to sleep.*

Red and Clara Marie Bolt married in 1932. Marie, nicknamed "Tiny," was the only girl of seven children born to Eudora Broadwell and William Frank Bolt. Her siblings—J. C., Sam, Grady, O. B., Cecil, and Albert—all lived in Anderson, and most were brick masons. Married nine years before the birth of their first child, Linda Marie, they lived around the corner from the newspaper.

On December 8, 1941, the United States declared war on Japan. Red, then thirty, registered with the draft board. When Commandant Holcomb issued his call for experienced journalists, Red summarized his newspaper work experience in his January 13, 1944, application letter for consideration as a combat correspondent:

> I, Claude Richard Canup, 32, entered newspaper work in the autumn of 1930 on the Anderson, S.C., *Daily Mail,* contributing by-line stories on football games.
>
> I was made sports editor of *The Daily Mail* in 1931. For the next seven years I was supervisor of the sports departments of both *The Daily Mail* and *The Independent-Tribune,* and have written a daily column on sports for one or the other since 1932.
>
> I became telegraph editor of *The Daily Mail* and *The Independent* in 1938 and have served in that capacity ever since, meanwhile continuing to supervise sports and cover major games.
>
> From 1931 to 1938 I did general reporting in addition to my sports work, such as covering strikes, killings, and court.
>
> I have been managing editor of *The Daily Mail* for the past several years.
>
> In addition to my newspaper experience I have had five years with the Anderson, S.C. radio station WAIM, as both a sports and news reporter, but have not been on the air regularly since 1940.
>
> In my newspaper work I have enjoyed the fullest co-operation of my fellow employees and all with whom I have come in contact. What success I have had in this field is measured by the friends I made in this climb.
>
> Finally, as a newspaper man, I am at my best writing about the other fellow, and not myself.†

* Hurley E. Badders, *Anderson County: A Pictorial History* (Norfolk, Va.: Donning Company, 1983), 113–14.

† Red Canup's letter of application is part of the Claude R. "Red" Canup Collection.

"I received my acceptance letter from General Denig March 16, 1944, the day my son Buzz was born," Red reminisced on tape. "The letter stated, 'This division has requested the Procurement Branch, this Headquarters, to authorize your induction into the Marine Corps for Combat Correspondent duty, provided you meet the physical requirements for general service.' In 1944 times were hard financially and giving up my newspaper job to go to war at my age had some folks thinking I was several bricks shy of a full load. Adding in Marie, Linda, and my new son Buzz—plus joining the marines—folks were sure I was just plain nuts."

Red learned that he was classified as "essential personnel" only after being accepted for the combat correspondents group. "I went to the draft board," he continued, "and told the chairman I was not essential to the war effort sitting on my tail in the newspaper office. I was joining the Marine Corps. I was sworn in at Columbia, South Carolina, April 1, 1944, and reported for boot camp at Parris Island."

Every Parris Island boot leaves with stories. Red was no exception, his swimming test fiasco a favorite. Never a swimmer, he splashed around in the water—flailing his arms and legs, sometimes combining dog paddling with toe bouncing across the pool bottom—and in four or five foot water, he clowned around eliciting lots of laughs. And, as on many other occasions, his antics combined with dry humor paid off.

"That boot camp was something," Red recounted, "I was thirty-three and most of the guys there were barely eighteen. I had a pretty rough time with the swimming test. I passed all right, not with flying colors but a lot of laughs, and made friends with the lifeguards in the process. Swell guys."

There was also his famous lawn mower story. While policing the grounds, he was commanded to cut the grass. Red looked everywhere for a lawn mower. None could be found. After hearing this report, the officer issuing the order was not amused and answered, "Well, Private Canup, I guess you'll just have to shit one." Red found a lawn mower.

"When I left boot camp," he continued "I was a marine private—not a P.F.C. but a buck private. I remained a buck private until I had orders to report for duty in Santa Barbara later that summer after interning at Marine Headquarters in Washington.

"In the marines at that time a combat correspondent was automatically made a buck sergeant before being assigned because he needed a little weight as he perused his duty through various ranks of the corps. A sergeant in the Marine Corps got quite a bit of attention."

3. LETTERS BEFORE ULITHI

June–September 1944

*A short furlough in Anderson was followed by a long bus trip to Washington, then a military hub in full war mode, and Red was as far away from home as he had ever been. Writing to his brother Orville, Red shared experiences from his first day in the big city. New jobs and an influx of government workers, mostly women, saturated the Washington economy and strained housing. The National Mall filled with new buildings, and the law of supply and demand in many instances overrode price controls.**

Most of Red's military salary went to Marie in the form of an allotment check, standard practice for military wives. With little money left over, the weeks spent in the big city presented an unexpectedly expensive indoctrination period for the former small-town editor.

WASHINGTON, D.C.
JUNE 19, 1944 (MONDAY PM)

I finally reached the city after a long bus trip. Luckily had a seat—back one—all the way and slept four or five hours. Felt like hell when I got here, but shaved and polished up a bit feeling somewhat better before going to Marine Barracks at Navy Yard.

Finding my way around here is as much of a problem as I may find once I get into the jungles. Place is spread out and barracks are in Washington and the Navy Annex, location of my office, stands out like a sore thumb on the other side of the river in Arlington, next to the big War Department Pentagon

* Focus group research conducted by the editor, October 10, 2010.

building about which you have read so much. My bus goes through—that's right—the Pentagon. It's a big place and no wonder people get lost in it.

I'm having a bit of tough luck from the start. Orders haven't gone through, and I must buy my own dinner and supper for three or four days and also purchase a GI raincoat which costs about eight bucks (it seems to rain here often). Don't issue them here. Other than being lost and forking out more cash than I'm making, I'm okay. Still haven't gotten over having to leave the family. Makes me want to be a civilian again.

The work here is interesting and right down my alley, and I am sure I will enjoy it. Don't know how long I will be here but certain it will be a month or more. At least that is what I have been told off the record. Fellows here are nice to work with and hours are fine—9 AM to 4:30 PM—and I don't have to be back at barracks until the next morning. Such liberty! And no money!

I understand promotion to buck sergeant will be coming a few weeks before I ship out. Maybe then I can come out ahead of Corps financially. Once my orders are received at the barracks, I will be paid car fare and for dinner and supper—eat breakfast at barracks. The men here tell me you've got to live close to break even on the subsistence pay. I don't doubt it.

This is so different from Parris Island that I am bewildered by it all. I can't get used to being treated like a Marine and first sergeants and master sergeants insist that I quit saying "sir." That is a bit strange to a former "shitbird." When I get used to the whole place I think I will like it very much. While in the office, I can go down to cafeteria in the building most anytime and grab a bite or a drink.

I believe I will be home at least once before being assigned to a regiment or division. I got that pretty straight from a staff sergeant here in the office, who was a combat correspondent in the Guadalcanal invasion, now assisting the many bosses. I never saw so many men with authority in one place!

Haven't been able to get my seabag from city. Must go to a little trouble for it and likely will get it brought in by Navy tomorrow. Met an AP man from Charlotte today. He came in two days ago on the same assignment as mine. Also met a guy from Hartwell on bus. Don't remember his name. He is a dog-face and hadn't been home in a long time. Seems he is messed up currently with a pregnant member of the service. He is more concerned about things here than in Ga.

It is about quitting time so I can stop appearing busy for the rest of the day.*

* All letters from Red Canup to his brother Orville are part of the Claude R. "Red" Canup Collection.

WASHINGTON, D.C.
JUNE 23, 1944 (FRIDAY MORNING)

Thanks a lot for the money order, but I fear you need it more to pay taxes to support this outfit than I do. I am holding it for a while though and will send it back if I get paid soon. Everything has changed financially since that hurried letter to you which was not intended as an SOS. I did have to dig heavily into my reserves for a few days but meanwhile I got a semi-monthly check for ten bucks and this morning I drew subsistence pay of $4.80 for the last four days of this week. I have found that by eating a big breakfast (four eggs yesterday AM) at the barracks I can get by on the $1.20 daily they allow for two meals.

I am eating at the Stage Door Canteen most every night. They have a new shift nightly so nobody knows you're coming so regularly. Swell place and exceptional hostesses. The other night the wife of Major General L. D. Gasser of the Army sat with two other correspondents and me and told us many interesting stories. This one she gave me permission to use. It seems she sent a telegram to Eisenhower's boy who received his commission as second looey at West Point the same day Ike started the invasion. Since Eisenhower means Iron Hammer and you can't send straight congratulatory telegrams now, Mrs. Gasser—good friend of the family—sent this clever wire: "Iron Hammer preferred selling above par. Iron Hammer common expected to rise."

Thought this was very clever and she gave me permission to use it. I thought Readers' Digest might pay ten bucks for it. When I checked here in the office about sending it in, I unhappily learned that Marine writers can't accept pay for published stories. So I wrote the darn thing up and turned it in here for any use they see fit.

Doubt if I'll have much, if anything, fit for our paper before I sail. Nothing here of interest to folks at home except things men in office feel have either been over-done or not worth doing. They laugh about a boot camp story because so many have been written, so I didn't mention mine.

I'm on fire watch tonight from 2 AM till 6 AM. I simply patrol the three-deck barracks and look for anybody smoking in bed—suppose to remove cigarette from mouth of any man going to sleep with a lit one.

I'm still a bit bewildered by things here but am gradually falling into step. Going from the strictly GI extremes at the Island to this set-up snowed me for a while. I leave the Navy Yard about 8:30 AM and don't have to check back until 7 AM next day. I can't get accustomed to not saluting officers everywhere but have found they apparently don't want much of it.

The barrack's life is also very unusual. Must be a couple or three hundred men here and all are veterans of some Pacific campaign, or about to go over. Many are back here recuperating and are a good lot, but many are also strange.

Most are infantrymen, pfcs or corporals with a few sergeants. They don't talk much and sleep a lot. Seem to live in a world by themselves and are not very lively. Occasionally they go out at night.

I understand four correspondents are about ready to check out. Two are veterans and two are rookies who will receive their sergeant's rating this week. Seems you get three hash marks not long before traveling orders are handed out. These new men have been here six weeks or so. Seems the average is a couple of months.

Nothing much to do here except walk and I am getting out of shape fast. I am drinking some beer and a little liquor. Liquor costs too much. Beer prices okay. I have visited a number of recognized lounges and, to use a South Carolina or Georgia expression, have been shitting in high cotton at times.

I have been around to the White House but haven't seen Frank (FDR) but did see his car and a hundred secret service men yesterday AM. I haven't seen General Vandegrift, Commandant of Marine Corps, either but he beats me here every morning and usually is around when I leave. He rides in a three-star Packard. General Denig is out of town but I may meet him before I leave.

By the way, I'm not buying a raincoat for a while because am likely to be issued poncho or something on coast. Meanwhile, field jacket and khakis are uniform of the day.

*Red's salary was $114 per month when he was discharged on December 15, 1945, at the rank of technical sergeant.**

WASHINGTON, D.C.
JUNE 30, 1944

I'm afraid you're going to have to wait on those ten bucks because I am about ready to start on them. Liquor is too high in the night spots—or the day spots for that matter. You can't turn around for less than a buck—never seen anything like it!

We had an informal talk from a correspondent just back from many months in the jungles. He didn't pull any punches and said it was plain hell. It seems the life of a combat correspondent is not what it should be because so much extra stuff is expected of him or may be forced upon him, such as guard duty, etc. It depends on what outfit a fellow joins and how he gets along with the noncoms and officers. He said the jungle is hell on clothes and typewriter and

* Claude R. Canup, DD 214, military discharge form, Claude R. "Red" Canup Collection.

nothing stays dry. It seems being under Jap fire or bombing is only a tenth of the worry. He said most men crack up at night while in foxholes.

Another correspondent just back told us to have a big time while we could because we would have plenty of time to think of the nights we went to the barracks instead of staying in town and enjoying life. But, the way I got this damn thing figured now is that I may as well shoot the works as far as I can in this city because from here out there won't be much if any enjoyment. These correspondents tell some mighty unpleasant stories and suggest that we enjoy life while we can. That's the spirit I'm taking. Even walking around helps ease the tension, but drinking beer also helps. Liquor takes care of itself at these damn prices. If I don't start getting more sleep I believe I'll be safe from cracking up because I probably will be catching up on sleep over there!

The first correspondent told us of many things we should buy to take over such as three fountain pens, a water-proof watch, and woolen socks (cotton socks last only four hours wading through swamps or cutting through jungle) and some more non-issue stuff. If I am carrying that over, the Marines will have to supply it. Oh, yes. The correspondent says all of us can expect to have malaria at least once. He's had it four times and looks as if he may break down any minute. Hell of a case, he is. I'm hoping they send me somewhere in China—anywhere except the jungles.

I still don't know when I will check out but it seems no time soon. Still you can't tell. I probably will get my sergeant's rating in another two or three weeks. I will make more, and over there I will get the 20 per cent extra for foreign duty. But, shortly after the promotion goes through, I will head for the coast—so I am in no big hurry. It seems certain that I will get another furlough (five-day delay in route) when I head west. Policy here is to give it to men shipping out. Fellow won't need a furlough where we are going. The best I can learn is that it is possible I might become attached to headquarters or service command with either fourth or second division. Those are the veterans of Tarawa and other engagements of importance.

I have seen a few interesting spots here but haven't scratched the surface yet. From where I sit, I can look across the street on Arlington Cemetery. Most everyday somebody is buried, and the soldiers fire a volley of shots. It is a regular occurrence. I have picked out my spot, one that is shaded most of the time.

I went on a Potomac cruise last night just to get a feel for the water—didn't feel any ill effects and drank beer a good bit of the voyage. Get a good skyline view of Washington, or part of it, from the water. The airfields look great at night. Think I'll go maybe once a week because I can get a pass—service men get passes to most everything except bars.

I went to Griffith Stadium Wednesday night and saw Washington and Detroit. It was a pretty lousy game and I almost went to sleep—probably would have had a crazy gal Marine not been sitting near. She was pulling for the winning team, had plenty to cheer about—and, boy, did she raise hell.

That afternoon I had to deliver Saipan copy to 12 newspapers, radios, and news agencies in town. I didn't have a great deal of trouble finding them but walked most I have since leaving PI. Didn't get to see anybody of any note because it was time of day all were out. Studios here are just so-so and newspaper offices not so hot—disappointing. I don't think I would be interested in working at any of them.

Most watering holes here are air conditioned, and after the heat of the day it is a pleasure to go to one of these places for a few beers. Ten cents a glass or two-bits a bottle. Some of it is fair. Most liquor is about fifty or sixty cents a drink.

I went to a place Saturday with two of the men. When orders were taken, they said beer. I asked the price of a shot of bourbon, and the waiter said fifty cents. I said make that three beers. Some gizmo sitting at the next table must have thought it was funny and had the waiter bring me a couple of drinks of bourbon. I didn't know who that Santa Claus was, but I liked the idea so well I bought a couple. That made me feel pretty good—best I've felt since being here. Of course, I thanked the gentleman with all my southern appreciation, and he seemed to enjoy paying for the damn stuff as much as I enjoyed drinking it. He turned out to be a hell of a nice fellow.

I got letters from my platoon leader and from one of my drill instructors at Parris Island this week. The drill instructor wrote he and two other Marines went to Port Royal the other night, got fairly well soused, and started walking back to the Island. They got a lift and tried to pay the driver thinking they were in a cab. After arguing a little when the guy would not accept the dough, they discovered that General Vogel, commanding officer of the Island, was in the backseat. He is still trying to figure out how they escaped the brig.

If I can get along as a boot that well and win the friendship of those men, I've got a hunch I can make friends over yonder pretty well. I know it will be rugged living just about all the time and plain hell much of the time, but that seems to be why I got into this outfit four months ago—and there ain't no way to get out!

WASHINGTON, D.C.
JULY 5, 1944

I spent a little of my dough last Saturday afternoon for presents for Linda and Marie. By the way, if there is anything you want here let me know and I will try to find it. I sent Linda one of those little tricks that snow when you pick it up and shake it. I have always liked those but never could find one in Anderson.

I had a most relaxing time Monday. After finishing work at 4:30 PM, I decided not to follow the gang down town and guzzle a few glasses of beer. Instead, I walked across the street to Arlington National Cemetery. For about an hour and a half I just strolled through the place, reading the names on grave markers and thinking—a guy can do a hell of a lot of thinking in a cemetery. His imagination can run away with him about such things as the battles those fellows were in and those he might be in himself.

Object of the trip was to see the Tomb of the Unknown Soldier and, if these words are the proper description, the tomb and surrounding marble structure are beautiful in a simple yet architectural sort of way. Seeing beautiful memorials such as that touches places inside a person that ordinary events won't ever reach. I was impressed, too, with the guard that walked the tomb post. He was spick and span and his rifle and bayonet—shoes and belt—flashed in the bright sunlight. I just heard three more volleys in the cemetery. It seems as if they bury someone every hour.

An MP told me General Marshall ordered the night patrol doubled throughout the cemetery. While visiting grave of his first wife he found evidence of sexual activities going on over there. It seems it is—or was—a favorite place for that with so many women living nearby. It's a hell of a thing, but that's the way I heard it.

One of the correspondents awaiting assignment lives near New York and he and another writer and I plan a trip to the big city. Trip will take only a little while and ticket will be around five bucks. We can get a weekend pass without any trouble. This is the best chance I ever had and probably will ever have to see the town and maybe take it in just a little bit.

You have probably taken enough company time reading this so I'll knock off—remember, keep your muzzle pointed toward the targets at all times!

SANTA BARBARA, CALIFORNIA
SEPTEMBER 2, 1944

My company has secured for the day, and what a day! It is just like being back in boot camp. I am writing this at 4:15 PM while I wait for chow and am I hungry!

While we are marking time here, before shipping out, for some reason or another the group has been formed into companies, and we are being put through a combat conditioning course which is just like I got down at PI, except in some instances worse—hiking with full packs, splashing ashore in mock invasions, firing weapons, hitting the deck, guard duty. If we stay here much longer, I will be fit for the infantry and will probably wish I was in an outfit that is going to storm a beach-head. I am now a rugged individual again with only a few days of conditioning.

Results of drinking nights in Washington showed up with combat training starting back here, but now I am feeling much better and moving around helps pass the time away. I could be getting out of all this if I wanted because I have run into some stories—already have sent seven back to headquarters—but I realize the need for being in top shape and am getting as much of it as I can.

We mustered at 7:30 AM and drilled a while and then saw a movie before chow. The movie was about what we might have to face some day. This afternoon we mustered again at 12:30 PM, did a couple of hours of maneuvers, and then had an hour of combat swimming.

Swimming here is not like Parris Island—a new style under less favorable conditions. The only way I can navigate is to take a deep breath and set sail, kicking and stroking. When I come up for air I have to stand. That works swell in water up to my shoulders, but today for the benefit of a colonel all non-swimmers were put in 12 foot water and told to shove off. Well, I shoved, as did lots of others. Some made it and some—well, they rescued everybody without any casualties! But I didn't mind that so much except that we had already been released and dressed before the colonel arrived and had to strip and hit the water again. And, it is not hot out here. California prides itself on its cool summers and this is one of them.

Also, today for the first time we had to jump off a 15 foot tower into 12 feet of water, and I jumped. Can't believe it, can you? I wouldn't do that unless I was in the Marine Corps. You somehow get the courage to do things you would not do as a civilian.

They have a 30 foot tower here, too. Will I jump? That, my friend, is something again. I'm not saying, but if it comes to a showdown I probably will. Non-swimmers may get out of it. Some guys stay up for hours before they jump, and two refused to leap today. I speak of a 15 foot tower now as nothing! Was I scared to jump? Well, in a sense I was—but I didn't hesitate. That is one thing in my favor; and the life guard, a new friend of mine, says I did right well considering the fact it was the first time and I can't swim. I will have to do it every day—and every day will be just as hard. Here swimming is a two-week course—I hope we will be out of here before I have time to finish it. I have been ready to sail since we got here.

I don't know why I can't swim. I try hard enough and I am not afraid to get my head wet. Maybe I try too hard, but I try because I sincerely want to become a fair swimmer. The 15 foot jump is to build confidence. I guess it is okay, but I feel I could do just as well down there in four or five foot water kicking around and coming up for air when I need it. The life guards are swell and maybe they can do something with me before it is over.

I lost my five-year-old Kaywoodie pipe while hitting the deck—what a day! If you can find a pipe, please send it when you get my new address.

I don't go for this territory at all. It is beautiful and probably swell if a guy could dress as he pleased, go out when he pleased, spend all the money he pleased, do everything more or less when he pleased. It would be a great place to vacation. It is different from home. They go in for color out here in a big way, especially the resort cities. I haven't seen much of Santa Barbara, but the guys say Frisco and L.A. are the best towns. Nothing much here except lousy beer, high priced liquor and a fair number of women. But the gals out here are not as good looking as back home. May be they've got the beauties cornered in Hollywood. I would like to make it to Hollywood while we are here, but we are packed up and you know what that means. We can still go to Santa Barbara.

The afternoon paper tells of a heavy attack on one of the Bonin Islands. I predicted weeks ago we might go there, and I still haven't changed my mind. If the place is invaded soon I believe we will head for it. I understand we will be stationed in a hot spot and all the heat won't come from the sun. There is much scuttlebutt where we are going. All of it is just guessing. The Bonins still look like the best bet with the coast of China No. 2 on my list. But, wherever it is, I hope we will shove off right away.

I wrote a friend at Stockton the other day about getting together. The only problem is my dress shoes were shipped away in my seabag last Sunday. They let my outfit go on liberty in field shoes but can't go over 50 miles in them. Stockton is up the coast on the other side of Frisco and way more than my field shoes can go.

I got into a great outfit, but since things have turned out as they have, it would have suited me better to have flown on across and joined an outfit in the field. Waiting is hell, and the way things are going I could drown before leaving the States!

PACIFIC OCEAN POLLUTED; CANUP'S PIPE OVERBOARD

Here's ominous news from the South Pacific. Red Canup, the Independent sports editor, who is a Marine Corps combat correspondent for the duration, has lost his Kaywoodie pipe.

"This may affect the course of the war if something isn't done in a hurry," writes Red, as he can't concentrate on licking the Japs without a suitable pipe. The missing pipe is five years old, fully flavored, black and a little battered from banging on a desk, but still quite serviceable.

There's no percentage in anybody around here looking for the pipe, however, as it isn't near. Red dropped it overboard into the Pacific Ocean.

"Without my favorite pipe," writes Red, "I'm going to be terribly handicapped. The Navy Department, however, doesn't seem unduly alarmed over the situation."

Anderson Independent
Undated clipping, circa September 1944
(reprinted with permission granted from the *Independent-Mail*)

SANTA BARBARA, CALIFORNIA
SEPTEMBER 7, 1944

It looks like this is it after the days of waiting. I believe we will shove off Saturday or Sunday. I could be wrong again, but don't think so.

Tonight I am having a last fling in town—another one. There is plenty of liquor in this town, and we got our share early in the evening—Phil and Sam and I are here at the USO to write a couple of letters—and I am feeling no pain.

I wrote 11 more stories today, all of them about promotions. That makes 18 written out here, a good start.

I don't believe now it will be the Bonins. I have no idea. Keep writing, but it will be censored. Please look out for the family, and I will let you know as soon as I can if this really is it. I hope so.

SANTA BARBARA, CALIFORNIA
SEPTEMBER 8, 1944

This is it! We got word this afternoon, and by the time you get this letter I will be sailing the Pacific. Destination is somewhere between Saipan and China or Japan. Many are guessing the Philippines, but not me. I believe that will be purely an Army show. I've paid close attention to lectures lately and have tried to reason a few remarks out. That is why I don't think we will hit the Philippines. Don't believe now it will be the Bonins. Some of the officers know and say it is close, though.

The scuttlebutt is that the island on which we will pitch camp has not been taken. So just for the hell of it you might watch closely for invasion news over that way during the next seven days to three weeks. It really doesn't matter since any place from here on out will be a hot spot.

From all I've been told this particular outfit is going to see things that no other aircraft group has seen lately. Something new, it seems, has been added,

Sergeants Red Canup and Phil Storch, USMC combat correspondents, 1944. Claude R. "Red" Canup Collection.

and we are it. I expect that the worst part of the whole deal will be the bombing attacks and that will depend on how many planes the Japs want to sacrifice to keep us on our bellies for a few hours each day. I have no illusions about an easy time, but I firmly believe I will get back and be home to greet Santa Claus in 1945.

There is no last word. I know you will keep an eye on the family and whenever you can, please do some things for Linda that you know I would do—and for Buzz, too, when he gets old enough to know. I will be forever grateful for any help you can be to Marie. I hope I am not expecting too much of you.

SOMEWHERE ON THE PACIFIC
SEPTEMBER 22, 1944

Received your letter yesterday, and it was better than anything else I could have gotten for it was the first word from home since several days before I sailed.

When you were riding the waves of the Atlantic—along with your horse—going to that war to end all wars, I doubt if you thought your baby brother would be in a similar position some day. Well, here I am—probably a hell of a lot better off than you were in 1917—but you might say in the same boat. We are probably living pretty much like you and the gang did when you went over to call on Wilhelm. To me there appears little difference between transports in the two wars from what I have seen and heard. Either way, it is hard on the posterior.

The water is so calm it is like riding a Pullman. I am on deck, and as I glance out to the horizon, the sea is as smooth as glass. Weather is perfect, and I haven't been sick—eating like a pig and feel great. The sea has been kind to us but a few of the men got sick. Anyway, the two meals daily are too good to miss.

I'm happy to learn that Buzzy apparently has not forgotten that stubby hair of mine, and am glad he delights in "feeling for hair" while you are playing with him. Be a good "father" to him whenever you get a chance—I don't want him to forget what a man looks like!

It has been my pleasure to meet some of the officers on board with whom I will come in contact and from whom I can get news items. I hope to start sending back stories sometimes this month.

We have heard the good news being made by the Marines out here in this lake, and I guess the papers have been full of it. I can't say anything more—the censors!

PART 2

Ulithi

4. TOJO'S FRONT YARD

September 9–October 15, 1944

*On October 9, 1944, Red and Marine Aircraft Group 45 arrived at Falalop Island, Ulithi Atoll, for the invasion. The island was deserted. Scuttlebutt had the MAG moving on. But the "fly speck" of an island—with enough land for an airstrip and a lagoon large enough for an anchorage—was strategically located for staging and shipping. The MAG landed, pitched tents, and within the month tested their newly constructed airstrip. Highly trained pilots began flying defense for the base, and ships gathering in the lagoon for the Iwo Jima invasion, the airstrip transforming Ulithi into the U.S. base closest to Japan.**

Red chronicled everyday life on the crowded, humid island—teeming with mosquitoes, overrun with lizards, peppered with wild pigs—with gusto worthy of a battle zone. His dispatches originated from "Fly Speck Hotel," the Ulithi press tent.

Shoving Off

"Sea travel meant new adventures," Red reminisced. "Shoving off from Port Hueneme September 9, 1944, for 'somewhere in the Pacific' our MAG squadrons, including night fighters, were aboard merchant marine craft *Dashing Wave.*† That was quite a feeling sailing under the Golden Gate from San Francisco and steaming out into the open sea. It was the first time aboard a ship for most of us, hanging over or sitting on the rail waving good-bye to the fading skyline.

* Claude R. "Red" Canup Collection.

† Robert Sherrod, *History of Marine Corps Aviation in World War II* (Baltimore: Nautical and Aviation Publishing Company of America, 1987), 474.

"'NOW HEAR THIS!' boomed the PA system. It was a new alert for us but heard many times before we returned to the West Coast. The captain's startling announcement told us to back away from the rail because falling overboard was not reason to stop the ship. We got the message.

"But after a few more miles, the ship slowed to practically a stop, a Coast Guard cutter pulling alongside. To our amazement one of the crew brought a dog to the rail and lowered it to the cutter for a return trip to the shore. We got that message, too!"

*From Red's 1944–45 diary**

September 9 Left Santa Barbara in trucks 0900. Sailed from Port Hueneme.
September 10 Uneventful day. Sky overcast. Received Red Cross kits.
September 11 Men heard the first news broadcast over the PA. Cheered to get word. Told letters would be mailed at first port helped morale. Many began writing.
September 12 Practiced firing anti-aircraft guns, good shots. Perfect weather.
September 13 Usual routine.
September 14 Wrote letters.
September 15 Docked Pearl Harbor 6 PM. Spotted land about noon. Got haircut ship's barber in afternoon, 50 cents. First impression of harbor 'How could Japs have sneaked into a place like this?'
September 16 Interesting day watching ships come and go.
September 17 Attended communion service aboard ship conducted by Chaplain Bell of Texas. Simple but impressive. More men came aboard. First day of round of liberty.
September 18–23 Usual routine. Getting hotter and hotter.
September 24 Father Norton preached Protestant service. Good.
September 25 Read detective stories.
September 26 Interviewed officers about night fighters.
September 29 Ship crossed date line. Retiring on Thursday and rising on Saturday.
September 30 Usual routine.
October 1 Attended church services.
October 2 Wrote letters.
October 3 Arrive Eniwetok 0700 and left at 1900. One isle showed signs of heavy shelling. Took on boat crews. Mailed letters.
October 4 First day in waters of Jap-held islands. No concern.

* Red's Ulithi diary is part of the Claude R."Red" Canup Collection.

October 5 Told first time officially our destination is Ulithi group of islands in Carolines. It is 85 miles from Yap.
October 6 Usual routine. No new dope.
October 7 Air raid alert tonight. No planes came over. Shore partners named.
October 8 Reached Ulithi. Dismal day. Much rain. Troops held aboard. Rumor we may not stay here. Attended church service.
October 9 Some went ashore today. Bright and hot. Still scuttlebutt we may leave. Many ships here. No Japs.
October 10 More men ashore. I'm on mess detail at midnight. Met Sgt. Wm. Couch of 542. Old Anderson friend had been aboard all the time. Big ship. Talked of Anderson. Mail call—12 letters. Very hot. Little excitement likely.
October 11 Arranged to send grass skirts home when our ship returns to Hawaii. $8.

SOMEWHERE IN THE PACIFIC
OCTOBER 11, 1944

If this is it, then I suppose I will be around long enough for someone to invent rocket ships that will leap the ocean. In other words, your brother now has the feeling that he will live to see the day his head will resemble a bowling ball. And, hair won't have fallen out from being afraid of the fast moving Japs. They can really scram, I suppose, and stay scrammed.

I haven't been to our island reached Sunday, but it looks quite inviting after so much time on this trusty ship.

What do you mean do they have gardens on these beautiful Pacific islands? Haven't you heard that the leaves and vines and bugs are edible? Why bother working a garden? These natives could teach you and me a thing or two, I believe.

Nothing much to tell about Pearl Harbor—place looked mighty secure—and defiant. No blackout there. Nobody sleeping now.

Here it is either raining or hot as hell. Reminds me a little of Parris Island and California. The rain doesn't seem as wet as the S.C. rain—does that make sense? You can readily see how the heat is affecting my head already.

I am glad the trip is over. I do not want to be a seaman. You may not learn where I am but don't let that concern you. I don't know myself except that the papers use to refer to this area as Tojo's front yard. Now it is mine.

October 12 Went ashore in afternoon and pitched tent at edge of clearing deep in island. Rain & much mud. Now on K-rations. (Falalop Island.)
October 13 Living next to Couch and having lots of fun camping despite rain.
October 14 Touring island for stories.

October 15 Attended church services in Army Chapel. 1st Lt Clarence B. Finsaas.

Ulithi

"Ulithi, an atoll of several islands and referred to as a 'fly speck,' was the westernmost post for Allied Forces in the Pacific," Red recounted. "Flying defense, Marine Aircraft Group 45, fighter planes and torpedo bombers, was sent to protect the fleets rendezvoused there for the invasion of Iwo Jima. At one time most of the Fifth and Seventh U.S. fleets, a smaller part of the Pacific fleet, and British fleet representatives were at Ulithi. There were hundreds of ships from huge aircraft carriers on down to destroyer escorts.

"For a while, MAG 45 was as far along the road to Tokyo as any American troops had traveled. Overnight the Philippine invasion relegated us from the grandstand to the centerfield bleachers."

ULITHI—OUR PRESENT STOP
BY USMC COMBAT CORRESPONDENT CLAUDE R. CANUP

Ulithi is one of the 48 island clusters which make up the Caroline group. It is in the Western Carolines, roughly about halfway between Guam and Palau, the latter only 530 miles from Davao in the southern Philippines. Yap, one of the Jap fortresses in the Carolines and still held by the enemy, is just a few minutes by air from Ulithi to the southwest. Turk, strongest of the Caroline Islands and in the center of the group, is several hundred miles to the east of Ulithi. Like Yap, Turk is bombed frequently and has been neutralized.

Ulithi was taken without a fight. The Japs, whose entire fleet was said to be docked in the Ulithi harbor about three years before the start of the war, never bothered to defend the island, pulling out ahead of American troops.

Ulithi was occupied by army troops in late September following on the heels of the invasion of Peleliu and Anguar in the Papau group by Marines and soldiers. In early October, Marine Aircraft Group 45's land echelon and a battalion of Seabees went ashore quickly building an airstrip and cleared coconut groves for tents, Quonset huts, workshops, mess halls, and a base sick bay. Wide roads were cut through the thick jungle growth from one end of the island to the other. Within a few weeks the island's face had been changed from a primitive jungle to a busy Marine air base.

Mog-Mog is the most popular island at Ulithi for the greatest number of visitors who stream into the lagoon on ships of the fleet, cargo vessels, and troop ships. Mog-Mog is the liberty island.

The Carolines were discovered by Spaniards. The actual land area of the 48 clusters of 600 islands and islets which make up the group is only 525 square miles, but the ocean they occupy amounts to 820,000 square miles—or an area roughly ¼ the size of the US. It is 1,700 nautical miles from the eastern to the western islands of the group and 550 miles from north to south. (October 1944)

5. MARINE AIRCRAFT GROUP 45

October–December 1944

Red spent the peaceful months on Ulithi primarily writing human interest stories about life on the tiny coral island. The airstrip constructed by Seabees in record-breaking time became the "Times Square of the Pacific." The population increased so quickly, the tents were so closely packed, that finding space for clotheslines and trash proved difficult. Drinking water, full of chlorine, came from hanging bags, and the first building built, the mess hall, ended almost a month of K-rations.

MAG 45 pilots flew defense, never spotting a bogey. Meanwhile marines played basketball, softball, and chased pigs for recreation—and waited for new orders.

An example of Red's original dispatch form follows. All others in this book are edited.

SAMPLE DISPATCH

Clark C. Campbell
8 February 1945 — #158-Canup
With Pix MAG-45-46 — EPD

By Sergeant Claude R. Canup, of 711 South Manning Street, Anderson, S.C., a Marine Corps Combat Correspondent, formerly of the Anderson Independent-Daily Mail.

Somewhere in the Western Pacific (Delayed)—.Keeping the sting in a night fighter squadron of Hellcats is the job of Marine First Lieutenant Clark C. Campbell, Elizabeth, Pa., whose squadron is in Major General Louis E. Woods' Fourth Marine Aircraft Wing.

Doughboy Chapel, Falalop Island, Ulithi Atoll, November 1944. The chapel was constructed entirely of coconut logs by thirty army volunteers in seventeen days. Claude R. "Red" Canup Collection.

Lieutenant Campbell, 24-year-old native of Elizabeth, is ordnance officer of a squadron that left Cherry Point, N.C., last summer for this Western Caroline island. He enlisted in the Marine Corps December 13, 1942, and was commissioned May 19, 1943. He recently was promoted to his present rank.

Son of Mr. and Mrs. W. C. Campbell, 245 Center Avenue, Elizabeth, the leatherneck officer was employed in a steel mill and taught school before entering the service. He is a graduate of State Teachers College at California, Pa.

This night fighter squadron has been flying protection for this atoll and shipping in these waters.

-USMC-

HAPPY BIRTHDAY, STAFF SERGEANT KOON

If prizes are offered Marines with the most birthdays observed in this theater of war, then Staff Sergeant Benjamin W. Koon, Dixon, Ill., will have a better than fair chance of being a winner. Today "Somewhere in the Pacific" he is observing his third in this theater. He is 23.

Koon, who was married three months ago, spent his birthday on Ondonga in the Georgia group a year ago and spent the one before at New Caledonia. He enlisted January 1942, and this is his second trip out. An electrician with a Marine aircraft unit here, he lived with his grandmother in Dixon before joining the Corps. (12Oct44)

MARINES SET UP

Marines who recently landed on this island have added the other "ten per cent" to the expression among American troops in this war that "ninety per cent of the fight out here is beating the island's jungle and insects." This Marine aircraft defense group has been here several days, and although Japanese forces are located within 100 miles, there has been no trouble from the enemy—just the lizards, making up the other ten per cent.

The place is crawling with the smaller variety but, as working parties slash their way deeper into the wilder parts of this island, they often find lizards over five feet long. All are harmless, regardless of size, and some are said to be edible. Even so, nobody has substituted one yet for K-rations.

This area had been included among Japan's inner defense. Today it is one of the most advanced Pacific bases of hard-striking, swift moving Marines sharing this island with army and Seabee units.

The only food on the island is coconuts. After the first fill of them, however, the men regard them as just something else to be cleared away from the bivouac area. (14Oct44)

DOUGHBOY CHAPEL

MAG 45 and the Seabees coming ashore with them to build an airstrip found a new 200-seat chapel on the island. The structure, erected in the center of the 'flyspeck' island by an army infantry outfit, is appropriately named Doughboy Chapel.

Built in 17 days, the 30 men contributing their labor knew they would not be on the island long enough for more than half-dozen religious services in their new chapel made entirely of coconut trees. Asked if the volunteers built the chapel for other men who would fight the war from here or for the natives, one of the soldiers Private Ray S. Rosales, 20, Minneapolis, Minn., spoke for all of them when he said, "We built it for no particular persons, combat troops, or natives. We built it to glorify God."

First services were conducted by First Lieutenant Clarence B. Finsaas, Superior, Wis., army chaplain. He revealed the men planned the chapel in route here. It is copied from Memorial Chapel on Guadalcanal, built in honor of the Marines who died there. (15Oct44)

COMMANDER CONGDON

Lieutenant Colonel George E. Congdon, 46, Santa Barbara, Calif., brings a multiplicity of experience to his role as air base commander here—now the closest American post to Japan. The Colonel's first assignment was as a World War I gunners mate, overseas for 19 months. More recently commanding officer of a Marine aviation unit in Santa Barbara, the Colonel organized this frontline base so quickly the bivouac area was almost completed with tents, mess hall, and offices before the last man came ashore.

He has a systematic method of accomplishing goals with a minimum of delay. This approach almost overnight changed the island's jungle terrain from coconut trees and underbrush to fresh cut roads, crisscrossing this "fly speck" island.

Retreating Japanese troops left nothing of value behind; but, within a few days of the Marines coming ashore—thanks to the Colonel's expertise—the island turned into one of the most functional advanced bases in the Pacific.

Before entering the service, Lieutenant Colonel Congdon was a division manager for Westinghouse Electric and Manufacturing Company of Detroit, Mich. The Cornell University graduate, commissioned in 1932, won letters in football, baseball, and swimming. (16Oct44)

October 16 Sun out for change. Moved from shelter half to pyramid tent with seven others. Mailed story No. 21.

October 17 Had movie tonight. Got pictures of CO of island for story.

October 18 Discussed possible transfer to 542(N). No changes soon. Inspected strip with Com. Smith.

October 19 First fresh water bath since US. Bathed in helmet. Clear for a change.

October 20 Showered from oil drum. Sent in couple of stories.

October 21 Spent day working on tent area. Place much improved. Japs left nothing.

October 22 Opened seabag & discovered everything wet. Bag had been dropped in sea while unloading. Had to wash all. Attended church service. Heard Seabee chaplain.

October 23 Had 6-hour movie tonight. Too much of good thing. 3 features.

October 24 Spent much time with Lt. Engelmeier picking movie site. Island crowded with arrival of 2 more flight squadrons & naval unit.
October 25 Working on Christmas story & other yarns. Another brother team.
October 26 Finishing touches on strip.
October 27 Strip opened. 4 transports came in today. Met Marine Maj. Gen. James T. Moore, C.G. of 2nd Wing. Got story & pix of strip.
October 28 More planes coming in.
October 29 Turned in revised story on strip. VMF (N) 542 planes came in.
October 30 Pix of 542 mail call. First since Aug. 20 at (Cherry) Point.
November 1 Starting third calendar month overseas. Time going fast.
November 2 Turned in movie yarn.
November 3 Got off couple more war stories. Interviewed Maj. Wm. Kellum. Informed I'm going to Native Island next Wednesday for story.
November 4 Tied up today with rush stuff for Capt. Ridder to take on visit to Capt. Wilson at Peleliu. Finally finished night fighter yarn.

MARINE AND ARMY BROTHERS MEET

Not long after Marine Master Technical Sergeant Montie E. Kaiser, 27, landed on this base, he found his brother Army Captain Alfred E. Kaiser, Jr., 33, sitting in a jeep on a jungle road. Neither man knew the other was on the island.

Both are from Seattle, Wash., and were partners in a mining business before Montie joined the Marines in January 1942. This is his second time across, first spending six months on Guadalcanal. Alfred joined the army in August 1942, attended officers' candidate school, and is commander of a combat engineering company.

Another brother Arthur E. Kaiser, gunners mate second class, is also serving overseas. (4Nov44)

MARINES CHANGE TUNE

A Marine night fighter squadron here wore some notes off "No Letter Today," juke box favorite where there are juke boxes. The more they sang, the sadder became their voices. Now the tune has changed to "Happy Days Are Here Again." The reason is first mail call in almost three months and their first overseas! The squadron averaged between 20 and 30 letters per man.

Fifty nine letters from the same girl were received by Private First Class Bert Hathaway, 30, Birmingham, Ala. "Happy" Hathaway, as the boys call him now, received a total of 63 letters. Sergeant Raymond H. Broerman, 21, Cincinnati,

O., gathered 65, and Sergeant Walter L. Padbury, 27, Richlands, Va., collected 63. Corporal William A. Couch, 19, Anderson, S.C., received 51 letters.

Squadron mail clerk Corporal Robert J. Scary, 20, Waterford, N.Y., estimated between six and seven thousand pieces of mail were received in one day. The squadron moved so fast since leaving Cherry Point, N.C., the mail had a tough time catching it.

But, what has made the Marines so happy has the censors adjusting their glasses and filling their stamp pads. They have to read all the answers. (4Nov44)

MOVIES MAKE IT "REEL"

"When you leave here stay to the right of the screen. A bomb drop is to your left." The warning from Second Lieutenant Ralph W. Engelmeier, 24, Pittsburgh, Pa., recreation officer of the Marine aircraft group stationed on this island, reminded the men where on this little island they were watching the movies this night.

The location of the outdoor movie theater has been changed so many times to accommodate the growing numbers of movie goers, it is often hard to remember where on this "fly speck" the theater is located a particular night. Watching three movies one after the other can disorient even a night pilot.

Marines here find the nightly entertainment location and the title of the featured film don't matter. It's the only show in town. The movies have several reels, and the middle one seems to always end during an exciting scene. The men scream bloody murder.

That's what happened the other night to Sergeant Matthew J. Wozniak, 22, Brooklyn, N.Y., trying to change the reels as quickly as possible. "Home in Indiana" was showing and just as the beauty went up on the balls of her feet, poised for a dive, the reel had to be changed. Sergeant Wozniak almost had to call for protection.

The films arrive on board a movie ship which anchors in the harbor. All the recreation officers from the different branches exchange features on board. Taking into account all the ships anchored here and all the squadrons stationed here, just executing an exchange can be quite an accomplishment.

When a permanent site for the open air theater is found, the airplane cloth screen will be placed in the center so the picture can be watched from both sides. Seeing the scenes reversed won't matter to Marines standing or sitting on the ground with scraps of boards and logs for the seats. During a recent three features program, some stood half the night watching—sometimes in rain. (4Nov44)

MARINE BROTHERS MEET IN PACIFIC

It is a long way from Brooklyn to this island, but a couple of brothers met here recently for the first time in almost a year. Albert, 19, joined the Corps January 1943 and Leonard, also 19, enlisted October 1943. Both are corporals.

Leonard Meadows, whose outfit was on the island early in the occupation, heard his brother was coming ashore. When Albert disembarked, he was stunned to find Leonard waiting for him on the beach—another "what are the chances" coincidence. (4Nov44)

MARINES REMEMBER FOLKS BACK HOME

There were no newspaper ads to remind them, but Marines on this island did not forget the folks back home. With Christmas coming, Marine ingenuity rose to the occasion.

MAG 45 began Christmas shopping months ago while still in the States—long before civilians gave the day much thought. All the way out here from the West Coast, these Marines kept their eyes open for more than Jap planes and subs. They were on the alert for Christmas gifts. The stop at Pearl Harbor helped.

After they landed here and squared away, the men discovered the island offered little in the way of Christmas presents. But, traditional with the Corps, the leathernecks improvised.

Many selected coconuts from nearby trees, polished the husk, carved out season's greetings, added addresses, and mailed them—in the raw, so to speak. (4Nov44)

MARINE NIGHT FIGHTERS FLY PROTECTION

Major William C. Kellum's night fighter squadron is flying protection over this island. Since the planes went up, the Japs have not tried to send anything down.

The Major's Hellcats followed the squadron's ground echelon by a few weeks. Within five and a half hours after the first plane landed, regular patrols had been started to guard this vital base and its harbor. The first night the Hellcats took over the sky, a Marine remarked to his buddy, "Now that those babies are up there, I feel much better down here."

The pilots of this principally defensive unit may never be aces in respect to the number of Japanese planes shot down, but the men who fly these especially radar-equipped Hellcats were ace pilots before they left the States. They had to be the best day fighters to meet the requirements to be trained as night fighters. They are expert instrument fliers. Major Kellum remarked many times, "I would stack them up against anybody."

Major Kellum, who realizes that his men are eager for an opportunity to tangle with the enemy, would like nothing better himself, but he points out that his squadron can accomplish its mission so far as defense of this base and its shipping is concerned without bagging a single plane, without firing one round, as long as their presence keeps the Nips out of this area.

Exactly what these Hellcats are protecting is classified. The pilots, however, are eager to mesh with the enemy that their presence has discouraged. But, while the comforting drone of night-fighters' engines takes the place of the wail of the siren, their mission is being accomplished without firing one round. (5Nov44)

November 5 Missed religious service. Busy on story at strip.
November 6 Storm flag up. Raining & strong wind. No storm. Ate with Couch. Read clippings.
November 7 Still blowing showers, but storm went to south of us. Put in whole day at typewriter.
November 8 Too rough for trip to Native Island.
November 9 Went to Native Island with Col. June, others. Friendly people. Cute kids. Few men. Men and women only dress to waist. Rough trip back in LST. Lost dinner. All got wet.
November 10 Felt like hell today. Began aching all over as did two weeks ago. Same kind of fever.
November 11 Armistice Day here. What a joke! No celebration. No call for it.
November 12 Went to church. Good sermon.

NATIVE LAUGHS AT LIGHTER

When Seabee Commander G. Wood Smith, Kirkwood, Mo., failed to produce fire from his expensive cigarette lighter, a native triumphantly applied flint to wood and provided a light for the commander and himself. The dark-skinned man laughed loudly about the lighter that would not light.

First Lieutenant Sam R. Smith, Greensboro, N.C., thought the incident so amusing that he asked the principals to go through it again so that he could get a picture. Next day Lieutenant Smith learned that his camera was not focused properly. Now he is hoping word does not get back to the native of another failure of the Smiths—and the white man's fancy tricks. (10Nov44)

MARINES MISS NATIVES

Marines at this base are anxious to see the natives, but none are to be found on this island. All innocent by-standers have been removed for their protection, which means all the natives are on a nearby island, only with the commander's permission can anyone visit.

When our forces occupied this atoll, under the command of Commodore Oliver Kessing, Chapel Hill, N.C., the natives on this island were moved to a nearby island where others of their tribe live. So quickly were they whisked away—for their own safety as well as the convenience of the new occupants—very few troops saw them. In the event the Japs decide to come back, the natives will be comparatively safe on their own island. It has no military value.

A visit to Native Island is made each week by Navy Lieutenant (jg) James E. Norton, Washington, D.C., chaplain for the Marine base defense aircraft group here. A trip with the "padre" fills in the missing blanks about the natives. First impression is the natives are very religious, Catholic, and they are friendly. All of them wave and smile at visitors.

The natives are fond of American cigarettes, many of them becoming chain smokers overnight. K-rations have been a big hit. Photographers would be disappointed. They are not like popular Hollywood variety natives and have little to offer in the way of souvenirs.

The natives are short, slender and lithe, except for the women who lose their girlish figures almost as soon as they attain them. They have light brown skin and wavy black hair.

The natives on the atoll wear as little as possible, but the women appear modest enough in their attire, a piece of cloth about the size of a bath towel drawn tightly around their hips. The Army provided the women with skivvy shirts. The shirts were accepted by all the women, and all wore them, but cut two holes in front for the sake of comfort. The Army didn't bother with clothing after that, and now the women don't wear shirts, with or without holes. The men wear breechcloths around the waist and drawn between the legs, just enough to keep their modesty. The temperature averages 80 degrees the year round, with humidity 84–86 per cent. They rely on rain for their drinking water, and that is sufficient averaging 105 to 141 inches annually.

The lure of the islands would be shattered for Marines visiting Native Island if they made the trip with travel poster images in mind. The girls don't swish around in grass skirts and dance on the beach. They marry when they are 12 to 14 years old as a rule and either carry or are trailed by children malnourished, covered with sores and flies. One of the most unusual sights on the island, a baby sucking coconut milk out of an American beer bottle through an improvised cloth nipple.

Natives eat bread, fruit, coconuts, yams, tropical chestnuts, and sugar cane. A few chickens run wild on the islands. Marines found several pigs tied to trees. Pork, chicken, and fish make up their meat diet except for occasional K-rations.

Tools are scarce, but the men seem to do a good job with what they have. A few seaworthy crudely made boats are used for fishing. The male natives hunt fruit bats, known as flying foxes, for fur and meat. Ropes are made of fiber from hibiscus and used for fishing nets and securing rafters of huts.

The natives need a few lessons in personal hygiene and camp sanitation even with their custom of bathing two or three times daily. As a rule, venereal disease is found throughout the Caroline tribes. Yaws, skin disease, boils, and ringworms are widespread. Tuberculosis takes a heavy toll. Their teeth decay fast because of lack of minerals in their diet and oral hygiene.

Medical assistance is now being provided by Navy Lieutenant Commander Victor S. Falk, Wauwatosa, Wis.; Navy Lieutenant Daniel V. Jones, Norwood, O.; and Navy Lieutenant Kenneth G. Ruedy, Encino, Calif. They are in the medical corps of MAG 45. Colonel Frank M. June, Santa Ana, Calif., is commanding officer.

The natives will come out of this the heavy winners. Their stakes are small, their casualties few. Yet, they are reaping a golden harvest of care and attention from their visitors who when they sail will leave them much better off than when they came. (12Nov44)

MARINE FALLS FOR NATIVE GIRL

Don't feel sorry for Marines fighting in jungles when you see pictures of American troops kissed by beautiful French girls. Remember those travel posters of pretty native girls dancing on moon-lit beaches, the lure of the islands.

I recently visited an island near this base on which only natives live, and one cute, bronze-colored girl in particular won my fancy. I could not take my eyes off her as she stood in the doorway of a hut. She reminded me of the girl I left behind in South Carolina.

I wanted to hold her and talk baby talk, but we had orders not to touch the natives. It was easy to see my girl in the doorway where this one stood, because the native must have been about the same age as my girl. At least the native looked almost four years old, the same as my little daughter. (12Nov44)

WAR IS NOT ALWAYS LIKE SHERMAN SAID

Nobody out here will question General Sherman's statement that "war is hell," but on rare occasions his statement could stand an amendment. Such as the evening this conversation was overheard at the Marine air base here.

Devil Dog, "How did you like the ice cream we had for supper?"

Leatherneck, "I didn't go to chow . . . too busy drinking cold beer." (12Nov44)

BASKETBALL "FREEZE" REVISED

Marines have added something new to basketball, but fans in the States will never see this combat revision of the controversial "freeze" play.

Out here men snatch a few minutes of basketball on improvised courts with only one basket nailed to a coconut tree. The play is hot and furious—hot because of the temperature, furious because these leathernecks love to shoot. Nobody wants to freeze the ball.

Several men were playing recently when the freeze play revision was first observed. All were scrambling for the ball wanting to shoot. Suddenly each player froze in his tracks, every one looking up. Competition could be hot and furious, but stop on a dime when planes roared back from a mission.

Nobody moved until after they peeled off for the landing. The cue to resume the game and end the freeze play—when a Marine counted silently and then shouted, "They all got back!" The Marines had scored again. (14Nov44)

November 13 Couch and I gathered shells in afternoon after I turned out few stories in morning.

November 14 Feeling worse than hell. Not sleeping good. Bones ache. Talked with Capt. Wm. Shand, Jr. My new CO. He played for Carolina. We know many of same people.

November 15 Most of fever gone today but my eyeballs ache.

November 16 Feeling about normal again and going after stories.

MARINE OFFICERS NEW DUTIES

Major Nelson A. Kenworthy has been appointed executive officer and air base planning and developing officer of the Marine air base command here. He formerly was commanding officer of the service squadron of the aircraft group which is on this island.

Major Kenworthy, native of Plainfield, N.J., is former operating manager and operating superintendent of Rockefeller Center, Inc., New York City.

Captain William M. Shand, Jr., who has been with the MAG as supply and evacuation officer since last September, is the new commanding officer of the service squadron. He is a former attorney. He and Major Kenworthy entered the service in the summer of 1942.

Captain Shand is assisted by Second Lieutenant Brent E. Bradley, personnel officer, Fort Bragg and Danville, Calif.; Commissioned Warrant Officer Arthur E. Johnson, Gettysburg, Penn., adjutant; and Master Technical Sergeant Carl J. Raitano, Pittsburgh, Penn., squadron sergeant major. (15Nov44)

MARINES KEEP SPORTS ALIVE

Sports are so popular at this air base that some leathernecks have been known to pass up evening chow simply to finish a game of basketball which is the most popular sport. The business at hand has been too urgent to clear off enough of the jungle to construct a baseball or softball diamond.

Everything in the way of sports is improvised except the athletic equipment—the best that could be secured before sailing from California. Sports gear includes boxing gloves, punching bags, baseballs, softballs, gloves, mitts, basketballs, footballs, fishing equipment, swimming goggles, picture puzzles, and parlor games such as monopoly and checkers.

The Japs come first but Marines nevertheless find time for recreation usually at chow time or just before dark. Of course, dark comes early to the islands—no twilight leagues here.

Girls and food are the chief subjects of conversation for Marines on this island, but sports run third. (15Nov44)

FITTING PUNISHMENT FOR AXIS LEADER

One of the favorite pastimes of members of MAG 45 stationed here is to lie in their bunks in the evening and offer suggestions for the worst punishment for Hitler and other Axis warlords.

Going all of his buddies one better, Corporal Vernon E. Jones, 20, Nashville, Tenn., came up with a double-barrel proposal. All present agreed it would settle more than one post-war problem.

The southerner, attached to a night fighter squadron, proposed that certain Pacific islands be set aside on which the Jap warlords could be exiled.

The voices faded into sleepy silence after other Marines added to that thought. One leatherneck declared that he would be content for the rest of his life if he knew Axis warlords were out here slowly and painfully dying of fever—further tormented by flies, rats, and lizards. (17Nov44)

A MARINE AND THE JUNGLE MYSTERY

Long after this island was secured, a leatherneck walked through a section one night. When darkness falls over the jungle, it is pitch black. On this night the leatherneck could not see his hand before him as he walked toward camp. He felt he was being followed—he heard movement behind him. He stopped—only silence—and darkness.

He moved slowly forward again—cautiously—drew his fighting knife. He stopped again. This time the movement behind him neared. No question. He was being tailed.

The Marine quickly, silently stepped off the trail, behind a coconut tree and waited. The sounds of a slow, creeping-like movement neared. A five-foot lizard, slowly crawling along the edge of the path, came into view.

The leatherneck kicked dirt at it and watched the "granddaddy" reptile disappear. (17Nov44)

November 17 Wrote story on Capt. Shand.
November 18 Smith & Davis got pix of 542 pilots.
November 19 Went to church.
November 20 Checked pix. Half no good.

MONK SHAND OF SOUTH CAROLINA

One of the biggest thrills out here is to meet somebody from your hometown, or someone who knows someone from the part of the country you call home.

When Captain William M. Shand, Jr., turned out to be "Monk" Shand, the former University of South Carolina football player, I hurried around to his tent. For more than an hour we talked of practically all the important games in the state during the time he played before we both became Marines.

Captain Shand is now commanding officer of the service squadron of MAG 45 stationed here. Previously he had been logistic officer of this aircraft group in charge of landing operations. He credits having the physical stamina to do his job to playing football during the days of the 60-minute men with no substitution rule allowing a player to be taken out and put right back into the game.

The former Gamecock tackle and co-captain finished law school at the University of South Carolina and plans to return to Columbia to resume practicing law. (19Nov44)

LOVE AND THE CENSORS

Absence makes the heart grow fonder. So does the censor.

Notices placed on bulletin boards here show the censors have a sense of humor. But more than that, they encourage letters full of sweet nothings for wives or sweethearts. Here, for instance, are things they want your Marines and other fighting men to put in letters—things that will pass the censors:

"Love.

"Friends, shipmates and relatives, including your mother-in-law, if you have one.

"Entertainment, religion, art, music, books, and hobbies.

"Matters of business, personal finances, your plans after the war is won (unless those plans include revenge upon the censors).

"Your personal needs or wants for soap, fruit cake, razor blades or whatnot.

"Love.

"The latest (clean) jokes.

"Love."

Such things as ship movements, weapons, casualties, and location should not be mentioned for two reasons—security and the censor. (20Nov44)

MARINE "DISCOVERS" PACIFIC

Since shortly after this Pacific atoll was occupied, a Marine night fighter squadron has been on nightly patrol duty. Recently, however, the war's tempo was stepped up, and now the night fighters are supplementing day patrols, flying both day and night.

"You know," remarked one of these highly trained instrument fliers, "I sort of welcome this chance to double up. I had never had a good look at all the surrounding water in broad daylight."

He added as an afterthought, "There's a lot of it, isn't there?" (22Nov44)

A MARINE'S MARINE

"Bo" Bodanski has been a Marine for 20 years. This story is about an unsung hero who was a leatherneck before some of this war's Marines were born.

"The way I look at a fellow becoming a Marine," says this 48-year-old master technical sergeant, "is this way. This is a select outfit. Marines are known and respected the world over as fighting men. They fight rough and hard, and sometimes they have been known to live the same way. Just as it is a select outfit, it is a tough outfit. When a boy joins the Marine Corps, he is no longer a boy. He's a man. I'm not one to go out and beat the bushes for recruits. They should come to us. A man should be honored to call himself a United States Marine. I'm proud of the Corps. Nobody can touch its record. I've been in so long I feel like a member of a big family.

"You'll never hear a Marine gripe about something big—about fighting against heavy odds, about working sometimes all day and night to get a job done. It's the little things—like somebody using your bathing water or leaving the cap off your tube of shaving cream. Sure, you'll hear a Marine kick about a lot of things—maybe everything under the sun—except his outfit."

Like all older Marines, Bodanski says the Corps is not as tough as it used to be. Maybe not, but the Japs think so. This is Bodanski's second tour of duty out this way, and he has spent his entire time in aviation. Now he is in charge of a carpenter shop for the aircraft group stationed here.

Asked how long he planned to stay in the service, Bodanski said, "I don't know. Never gave it much thought. I was 22 when I joined, and I've never known anything except being a Marine." (22Nov44)

MARINES COPIED BY DRAGON FLIES

When the Marines' influence started showing among the natives, everybody took it in stride—wearing shoes, smoking American cigarettes, eating Marine chow. People everywhere pick up habits and customs from visitors.

When insects begin copying the island's newest inhabitants, Staff Sergeant Robert C. Peverly, 24, Decatur, Ill., wanted to share the quirk of nature. He described how dragon flies were imitating combat patrol pilots' tactics—diving and buzzing off other insects—a fighter plane after a bomber. As can be surmised, the sergeant's audience wasn't impressed.

"What should a dragon fly do to interest you guys?" Sergeant Peverly joked. "Carry a tail gunner?" (22Nov44)

November 21 Wrote four stories.
November 22 Turned in 43rd story.
November 23–24 All is quiet.
November 25 Sgt. Lincoln of WASP came ashore. Met him. Got stories.

ONE PLANE FAILED TO RETURN

They packed the kid's things the other day and sent them home.

He was a young fellow, not yet 20, but he was a good gunner. He proved that a number of times, but something went wrong the other day. Some thought the kid's number came up. Others spoke softly of the bomber flying too low. All offered a silent prayer when the plane failed to return.

The kid's name doesn't matter. He was just another Marine. He was just another boy from down the street. You may not have known this particular kid, but that doesn't matter either. All of them look pretty much alike once they are in the planes with all their gear on. He might have been that kid down the street you knew when he went to school or delivered your paper.

He isn't with our outfit anymore. He's in a better place. As war goes another kid is already on the job in his place. Another plane is already in the air flying in the spot left by the one that is somewhere on the bottom of the sea. "Missing in action," that's all the kid's mother and father know about the mission their son flew the other day—a mission from which he did not return.

Just a line or two appeared in the paper—a mere mention of "one of our planes failed to return." You read on to see how the war is progressing in other theaters. You put down the paper. We are still losing planes, men and ships but we are moving in the right direction. You told your friend that you felt good this morning after reading the war news. You told him that we have the Nips on the run and that it shouldn't take too long now to win. You felt pretty good. The enemy had suffered a stiff blow from those Marine bombers. You thought we did a swell job and were glad to see we lost only one plane—one plane. The plane the kid was in. The kid who told you about earning money to buy a bicycle. The kid your wife said was "courting the girls" just before he went off to boot camp. The kid you thought looked mighty sharp in his Marine greens when he came home on furlough last winter.

The same kid whose seabag was packed the other day.

You say you'll buy another war bond in his memory?

That's swell, mister.

But don't forget, there are a lot of kids out here. (23Nov44)

SOMEWHERE IN THE PACIFIC
NOVEMBER 24, 1944

Your letter and clipping came today. I was sorry to see that Georgia Tech didn't do so well against Miami, but they simply got out of their league. So the Clemson Tigers have a ball club for the homecoming fans. That is swell. Don't see how they continue to play that kind of ball with the sort of material available, or is somebody kidding. Got two letters yesterday from Jess Neely. Rice is doing pretty good, still had a chance to win the conference title when he wrote. He sent along some clippings showing standings of all the teams in the country and most of the results of the big games for the season to that date. I shared the clippings with Captain Shand who likes the sport as much as I do.

Marie wrote the kids had been sick with colds. With her having no help now, it would be a hell of a fix for her to get run down for lack of sleep and rest. Can't have that with the old man almost on the other side of the world. I wouldn't have been too much help the way I've felt over here. Must have picked up something on an island I visited. For a few days I felt worse than hell—aching all over with some kind of fever—bones and eyeballs hurt—but I'm fine now after another bout of the same thing.

Armistice Day was a joke here—no celebration with no call for it—but Couch and I visited the beach and collected a few shells and then went to church. I'm attending every service I can.

There isn't much to report from this side of the map. The novelty of setting up camp wore off fast, and now we are down to the business at hand. The island is getting crowded. No matter how long I stay here or anywhere out this way, I don't think I will ever get used to the heat. I thought we had some hot days in South Carolina, but not every day as the case is here. Now and then a breeze will get misplaced and blow through the tent. No extra charge for that.

Well, the chow line is getting short—I'm near the mess hall—so I speck I should grab my mess gear and wait it out. That is, after I put on some clothes. I'm so accustomed to lazing around these rocks, basking like a snake, that it will be hard gathering steam to go to chow. But, from the weather reports out your way, steam is what people need the most. Remember, keep your coal bins full and don't kick the covers off.

MARINES 1, PORKERS 0

When a shrieking squeal pierces through the jungle, it means only one thing—more pork for the natives' tables.

After the American occupation of this island, the original inhabitants were transferred to another. The natives carried their bundled possessions but were unable to grab their wild pigs roaming Ulithi. Catching pigs is a new challenge for the Marines stationed here and a fun sport. The captured pigs are given to the natives after the pigs, some weighing over 200 pounds, give the Marines a lot of laughs.

It is not unusual to see a mud-covered leatherneck smiling triumphantly leading a roped pig along a path. After all, it's no easier to catch a pig on this jungle island than it is in Missouri. (24Nov44)

SEABEES FILLING THE OCEAN

Seabees, who have done just about everything else in this war, are now filling in the ocean. Commander G. Wood Smith, Kirkwood, Mo., commanding officer of the unit of Seabees known as "Bat Out of Hell," has revealed that his outfit, working here more than a month, has added half an acre to the size of the island.

This was done by dumping coconut stumps, logs, and roots on the beach and into the water. They have been secured and are withstanding the pounding of the waves.

MAG 45 did not need the extra "land." The Seabees are dumping hundreds of truckloads of logs, stumps, and roots into the Pacific to clean up the island and remove breeding places for flies and mosquitoes. (24Nov44)

ALARMING

The most alarming situation on this island was the official raising of the United States flag.

Marine, army, and navy officials were on hand for the ceremony. The flagpole was made of old pipe. A band played and there was a guard of honor.

At exactly eight bells, Old Glory was unfurled into the breeze blowing off the Pacific. The eight bells were sounded on the gas alarm. (25Nov44)

THINGS THAT SELDOM HAPPEN

The heat is blamed for this one.

Technical Sergeant Ralph M. Wersonick, 22, Albuquerque, N.M., had been payroll clerk almost two years in the Marine Corps in the States. When his outfit came out here recently, he took another assignment.

Then came pay day. Wersonick, who was to receive $105, signed the SMR wrong—and every Marine on the island was paid on schedule except the former payroll clerk. (25Nov44)

November 26 Finishing touches on strip. Went to church.
November 27 Went aboard WASP. Interviewed M C Capt. Rosacker. Ate quart of ice cream. Saw white woman. Nurse aboard hospital ship SOLACE. Saw battleships ALABAMA, MASSACHUSETTS and others. Wonderful experience.
November 28 Wrote most of day.
November 29 Turned in 50th story.
November 30 All is quiet.

ANOTHER GEM OF THE OCEAN

Stepping down from one of the first planes to land on this island's new airstrip, the pilot of an army transport asked, "When did they build this island's new airstrip? I was over the island about two weeks ago and didn't see a sign of construction!"

That just about tells the story of the speed with which army combat engineers and Seabees slashed through swamps and coconut groves, hauling hundreds of truckloads of coral rock and sand to build this runway. When Army First Lieutenant Robert H. James, Marigold, Miss., landed the first plane here, one of the wheels burned rubber five feet and not a pebble moved.

Unlike many airstrips that have been made of coral rock, this one used a new technique. Stabilized coral required extra work leaving an element of doubt until the strip was tested, and tested it has been with most every type plane landing and taking off this strategically located airstrip.

Working around the clock, often to the tune of air raid sirens, the Seabees kept the heavy construction equipment rolling. Thanks to our pilots, not a single enemy plane came close enough to cause any delays in turning swamp areas into airstrip footage. Finishing the strip early is a testament to the teamwork of the Army, Marine, and Seabee units. Once considered a link to Japan's inner defense, this island is now one of our most vital forward bases.

The first night the strip's lights were turned on, the runway stood out like a main street—another Allied gem of the ocean. (26Nov44)

MARINE SERGEANT LINCOLN RECOMMENDED

Aboard WASP, Central Pacific—Marine Sergeant Thomas Lincoln, Jr., 21-year-old resident of Memphis, Tenn., has been recommended for the Bronze Star for his firing aboard this carrier. A gunner, the southerner fired the first shot off his ship in the recent sea battle off the Philippines.

This is the second carrier on which he has served. He was on the old HORNET when sunk in the battle of Santa Cruz two years ago.

Lincoln, who has been in more than a dozen air-sea battles off Formosa, the Bonins, Philippines, Okinawa and other islands, joined the Corps June 1941. He plans to remain in the service until he is retired. (30Nov44)

GUNNERS PRAISED, INJURED CAPTAIN TAKES OUT FIVE

Aboard WASP, Central Pacific—Almost a dozen Japanese bombers were spotted off the starboard side of the carrier WASP. Marine and Navy gunners laid down a wall of fire between the Nips and their ship. One of the Japanese bombers got through. In flames and full of holes, the bomber continued its suicide dive straight towards the flight deck and a gun tub of Marines.

Platoon Sergeant Dewey F. Murphy, Jr., Brownsville, Tex., screamed for the Marines to keep firing even though the plane was only 75 feet away. The bomber crashed into the sea only a few feet from the target, flames licking up around the gun tub, and hot oil sprinkling the flight deck.

WASP, a large ESSEX class carrier commissioned a year ago, carries a Marine gunner detachment commanded by Captain Ralph C. Rosacker, 25, Stafford, Kan., injured in the attack, who reported, "Planes were overhead trying to plant bombs on our flight deck." The Captain explained, "Our guns were pouring deadly fire at them. Suddenly I was hit and knocked to my knees. I was stunned and surprised, and when I realized I was down on my hands and knees on the deck I recalled that I had felt the same way once before. It was during a football game when I was blocked from the blind side. I felt no pain, just stunned and surprised. I didn't realize I was wounded until I stood up and tried to point with my left arm. I could not raise it. Then the pain really hit."

Captain Rosacker was given morphine and treated on the flight deck—remaining there for 45 minutes directing fire until the planes were shot down or driven away. He has been officially credited with contributing to the destruction of five planes during the attack.

Awarded the Bronze Star and Purple Heart for his actions directing fire against the enemy attacking one of our largest flat-tops, the Captain was in action October 13, 1944, off Formosa. (30Nov44)

MARINES "CONVERT" JAP

Aboard WASP, Central Pacific—Marines aboard this floating combat airport taught an unlikely candidate—a Japanese gunner fished out of the sea off the Philippines—to whistle the Marine Hymn and sing "God Bless America." Whenever a leatherneck came into view, the Nip would sound off with the Marine Hymn. The Jap knew a few words of English and also easily learned to enthusiastically sing Kate Smith's signature song "God Bless America" for an encore.

Abe, the prisoner, was transferred recently to another ship. He was assured before leaving that the Marines are looking forward to "visiting" Tokyo at the earliest possible date. (30Nov44)

MASONS IN THE PACIFIC

Masons aboard a Navy transport bringing MAG 45 to Ulithi last summer discussed plans for organizing a club after the occupation of this atoll had been completed.

So busy were all hands after the landing that nothing more was thought about a Masonic Club until recently. By then the Marines had discovered that a Seabee unit here had more than a score of Masons. Several Marines and Seabees swung into action, and within a week the Marcoba Masonic Club was organized.

Named Marcoba by Marine Captain Harry K. Trend, Bethlehem, Pa., the club is open to any Mason stationed on this island. First three letters in the club name represent the Marine Corps, the next three a Navy construction unit, and the last letter is reserved for the Army.

Twenty-eight men attended the first meeting, adopted the club's name and elected officers. Each man has been asked to look around for more Masons, hoping the membership will grow to at least 40. The average age of Seabees on the island is over that of the Marines; therefore, the majority of the club's members come from the Navy construction unit here whose nickname is "Bat Out of Hell."

The club meets every Monday night whenever conditions permit, and membership cards have been issued. Meetings are held in a mess hall, and beer and cheese sandwiches are served. (30Nov44)

MARINE PET PIG

A razorback pig is the biggest pet on this island. The two-month-old, 15 pound pork chop on the hoof is called "Butch." He is the pride and joy of his master, Commissioned Warrant Officer Arthur F. Johnson, Gettysburg, Penn., adjutant of the service squadron of MAG 45 here.

He has the run of the "officers' country" in a coconut grove just off the beach. He also has the officers on the run. Only this morning the Colonel threatened to throw Butch into the brig. It seems the porker has a fondness for shoes—a fondness for taking them from one tent to another. It is not unusual for an officer to find a pair of 10's under his bunk instead of his 8's, or maybe a 10 and an 8. As a matter of fact, Butch doesn't deal in pairs. He likes to mix them up—shoes and officers.

Not always does porky leave the right shoe in the wrong tent—sometimes, he a takes a shoe out into the jungle, that is where the Colonel found one of his.

Another thing about Butch is that he will not go near the water unless his master is with him. He won't even go to the beach alone. If a bath is timely, porky hops into his master's steel helmet of drinking water and tries to wallow. He is clean as a pup and acts like one, even to chasing cats.

To make sure Warrant Officer Johnson is not late for work, Butch grunts and "noses" him out of bed every morning at sunrise. If nudging with his nose doesn't do the trick, porky gently nibbles on his master's hand, and all his nibbling is not gentle. If another officer, no matter his rank, picks up the pig, porky bites—hard.

Butch wags his tail when he sees food—that is when he is not about to eat a lizard. Butch loves lizards. They may be able to move fast enough to catch flies, but they can't dodge the pig's front hoof.

For all his faults, the officers respect his ability to predict the weather. If Butch sleeps on folded canvas in the tent instead of under his master's bunk, rain before morning. For all his smartness and devilishness, Butch will not be adopted as a mascot. He really belongs to the natives. When he grows too fat to be a pet, he will be sent to them.

Then for the first time, he will live the life of a pig—for the short time he lives. (1Dec44)

December 1–2 All is quiet.
December 3 Went to church.
December 4–5 Sgt. Murphy came off WASP. Went to airstrip.
December 7 Caught boat to another island (identical). Went to CORNETTA, a film exchange ship. From there to YORKTOWN, big carrier for dinner. Then to WASP. Saw basketball game on hanger deck. Spent night on board. More ice cream. Saw Southern Cross first time.

"TUNE TOPPERS," MUSIC WHEREVER THEY GO

The closer Marines and other American fighting units get to the Japs, the higher goes morale, according to Commander Eddie Peabody, McHenry, Ill., who can speak on the subject of morale in the Pacific with as much authority as any man.

Commander Peabody, who is in charge of a strictly G.I. musical show, has traveled more than 70,000 miles by air all over this war theater. His "Tune Toppers" have been on every American occupied island and practically all US warships in the Pacific.

The seven-man show is now on its third tour; and, as usual, it is blazing the entertainment trail on the road to Tokyo. The former radio star, popularly known as the "Banjo King," led his musical seamen in a 60-minute funfest here recently. At the end of the show he revealed, "Our next stop is Leyte. We move right along with the troops, no matter where they go. We don't know what to expect at Leyte, but we will be there for our next show."

The Tune Toppers travel by air all the time. Their billing is so heavy they have no time to waste traveling by sea. They get to a new battle zone as quickly

Tune Toppers, a G.I. musical group, Falalop Island, Ulithi Atoll, December 1944. From the left: Musicians Second Class George Ramsby, Nicholas Drago, Joe DiLalla, and William Manzo; seated: Cdr. Eddie Peabody. Claude R. "Red" Canup Collection.

as their schedule permits. Men who have heard the Tune Toppers at rear bases and who have moved up look forward to the G.I. musicians' appearance at the new forward base—and they don't have long to wait. Commander Peabody and his boys are always close to the men behind the guns.

They were in Saipan less than six weeks from the day the bloody battle for that island was launched and were given a great reception by troops. Their largest audience was at Saipan, where one performance was seen by 19,000 men.

The Tune Toppers do not just visit the larger camps. They reach all of them sooner or later—mostly sooner. The size of the audience makes no difference. They are out here to make life a little merrier for the men away from home—for the men away from everything except the jungles.

The smallest audience the Tune Toppers have played for was one man. One wounded man in a ward by himself. Commander Peabody said the full 60-minute show was put on for the one man audience. "That's our job," he explained.

Hospital ships, carriers, battleships, cruisers, troopships, destroyers, and even the crews of submarines have been visited by this troupe. Wherever American fighting men come in the Pacific, they will at some time hear the Tune Toppers in person. That is more of a guarantee than a promise.

They have been to Peleliu twice, and each time the Japs were less than a mile away—but the show went on. Commander Peabody recalled that at Saipan the show was put on within 100 yards of the enemy. He said troops were relieved on one occasion to come off the front lines to hear the Tune Toppers. They had been up there 18 days he was told.

That is why Commander Peabody knows that morale among the armed forces is higher at the front than at rear bases because the men there are restless and want to be on the move. He has been on many fronts many times.

Other Tune Toppers in addition to the Banjo King are Musician Second Class William Manzo, Cleveland, O., guitarist; Musician Second Class Joe DiLalla, Cleveland, accordion player; Musician Second Class George Ramsby, Ligonier, Ind., base violin; and Musician Second Class Nicholas Drago, Cleveland, trumpet player and comedian.

A magician and an impersonator keep audiences entertained while the Tune Toppers catch their breath between numbers. Musician Second Class William Baird, St. Louis, Mo., is the magician, and Musician Second Class Larry Storch, New York City, keeps the crowd laughing with his impersonations. (1Dec44)

"H'YA, JOE!"

Private First Class Anthony Simonelli, 35, Cleveland, O., was in an audience with several hundred service men on this island to hear the "Tune Toppers," a G.I. musical unit playing all over the Pacific.

The five musicians on the improvised stage stepped under the spot light. There, third man from the left, with his accordion, stood Musician Second Class Joe DiLalla, Cleveland.

Simonelli and DiLalla, who had lived across the street from each other since they were kids, had last met in the spring of 1942. That was back in Cleveland.

Throughout the hour long show, the leatherneck couldn't keep still, so high was his excitement at the sight of an old friend. Finally the show was over and the two had about five minutes together. In those 300 seconds they relived years, going back thousands of miles to Murray Hill Road and other familiar places in Cleveland. Simonelli recalled how DiLalla never went in much for sports but stuck to his accordion entertaining the kids just as he is doing now. (1Dec44)

JOKE ON MARINES

The movie reached the scene where a man said to one of the beautiful, dumb blondes:

"You are so dumb you haven't enough sense to get out of the rain."

The Marines roared with laughter.

They were in an outdoor theater . . . and it was raining. (3Dec44)

ULITHI
DECEMBER 4, 1944

So some of the "won't go" boys are getting close to D Day? I can't believe it. Too bad they waited so long. They'll get in just in time to complete their training and get over here in time to do a year or more on guard duty or get stuck somewhere with a defense battalion. Or maybe, they'll be the chosen ones to mop up in China or the numerous little islands on which the Japs plan to go to heaven. They'll probably miss the big show—the biggest on earth.

The strategy you read in the papers is as good or better than the scuttlebutt we pick up here. Every day the report gets out that we are going somewhere—each day a different place. Scuttlebutt has us moving into Berlin, Tokyo, Manila, Bonins, Formosa, Hong Kong and points north, south, east and west. Nobody knows, of course, what the true dope is, but chances are it won't be too long before all hell breaks loose out here. And you can bet that I'll have a ringside pass. I only hope I don't have to rely too much on the pistol. I'm afraid I'm about as good a shot with it as you are with the shotgun. The Japs would be safe as the birds.

Everything here is about the same. The approach of Christmas has increased the mail around these parts. The men are receiving boxes full of goodies. I got another one today from Marie—a box of chocolate candy. You know how I go for that, and the fellows in my tent went for it too. It must have been five pounds of homemade candy! Please remember to tell the family not to send spam or canned peaches. I appreciate the thought, but we have enough here to be causing the shortages at home! I can always use stamped envelopes.

I could also use a package like Buzz, Linda or Marie. My morale has been going up and down lately, but it is on a high keel now, and I think it will stay there. Our wedding anniversary is the 7th of February. Thirteen years and I still prefer marriage to the Marine Corps.

MARINES VS. ARMY

Marines and soldiers, who work together and fight together, also play together.

An island softball league has been organized here and the eight-team circuit includes representatives of the army, although leathernecks dominate.

The league, first organized sports program on this atoll, operates in a parking lot just off the airstrip. In addition to men who have played little or no ball, some of the participants are former professional baseball players in the minor leagues.

All necessary gear is furnished by the aircraft group stationed on the island.

Organizer of the league is Marine Private Floyd J. Mercer, 18, Louisville, Ken. He is presently in charge of the Marine athletic department. (6Dec44)

KILLS JAP ON FURLOUGH

Miguel C. Castro, Oakland, Calif., has a personal reason for hating Japs. That is why he went Jap hunting on his furlough at Guam recently.

The 33-year-old native of Guam, who came to America in 1929, got a job in Oakland, married a Virginia girl in 1934, and came here in September this year with a Seabee unit as a metalsmith first class. After being here awhile, he was given a special leave of absence to visit relatives on Guam.

When he found his two brothers there, he was told how the Japs had overrun the Castro ranch and tortured his people before the Marines came. One brother still was inactive as result of mistreatment. His 62-year-old mother was dead. His brothers told him she died of exhaustion. All the Guamanians were worked hard by the Nips, his people told him. An uncle of the Castro brothers was tortured and put to death after being forced to dig his own grave.

He went back to the ranch with a brother and a cousin, and they killed one Jap straggler—the only one he was able to find before he had to return here. (6Dec44)

ULITHI
DECEMBER 6, 1944

A lot of people must have read that soldier letter in the newspaper. I got four copies of the one "dedicated" to me.

I don't think folks at the newspaper realize that we don't give a damn if the women's aide committee meets nor if the teachers stand an exam. We want to know if it has snowed, if the cotton crop was good, if anybody we know has died, if people are still being drafted, if the hooch shows at the fair were very hoochey, etc.

You should have heard some of the men, particularly me, cuss about the story mentioning how men had to stand in line two blocks long to buy shotgun shells. "After all, we aren't accustomed to having to stand in line" got a very negative response here—at least that is tame enough to pass the censor. As you know, in the service you stand in line for everything—and it didn't take long to get used to it.

The storm flag was up recently, and we had rain and strong winds. The real storm went south but showers blew for two days. Had to reschedule a few trips I had planned, but it was a good chance to catch up. Spent several days at the typewriter. Too rough to find any stories around the strip.

NAMES—ALL KINDS

Pilots sometimes have as much trouble settling on a name for their planes as do the happy couple expecting the blessed event. Many of the combat fliers name planes in honor of their wives. That makes the job simple, but others stay awake nights wrestling with the problem.

Here are some of the names of planes which operate off the strip on this island: "Song of Bernadette," "Round Trip," "One O'Clock Jump," "Melancholy Baby," "Millie Lou," "Midnight Train to Memphis," "Loaded Lady," "Addis," "My Devotion," "Chief Wahoo," "Hell'z-a-Poppin," and many others along the same line.

But the most unusual name which requires an explanation is the name of a night fighter captain's Hellcat. The big lettering shows his ship is known at the base as "BeBas." The story behind that name is that he wanted to give the plane a name similar to that of his wife. His nickname for her is "Be Boss." (12Dec44)

December 8 Still on WASP. Third anniversary of Pearl Harbor out here. No notice given date. Went ashore in boat with pilots. Rough sea. All got wet. Turned in 65th story.

December 9 Got more pilot pix (542N).

December 10 Went to church.

December 11 Rode out in harbor to watch blasting of coral.

December 12 Making plans for trip to Peleliu Wednesday. Got orders for trip today.

December 13 Raining hard, constantly this AM. First fresh fruit for breakfast. At 9:30 trip doubtful. No trip.

December 14 Went to Peleliu on R4D. Passed Yap. Ate K-rations aboard plane. Left 1130 landed 1400. Met S/Sgt. John Kirby, Capt. Earl Wilson. Public Relations Officer gone to Leyte. Saw Bloody Nose Ridge. Few Japs still there.

December 15 Left Peleliu at 0700 by R4D for Ulithi. Refueled at Anguar. Nice trip back. MAG-45 today joined 4th Wing from 2nd.

December 16 Took pix pilots.
December 17 Went to church.
December 18–20 Writing. Met Rear Admiral Reeves & got story.
December 21 Went on TBM strike to Yap in PBY. Cloudy, missed show. Went in for pix. No ack-ack. Piloted PBY part of way back. Nice ride.
December 22–23 Not much doing. Nurses off 2 hospital ships came ashore for officers' party. No see.

NAVY BROTHERS MEET

The Holley brothers of the Navy had a reunion on this island recently—their first in more than three years.

Chief Carpenter's Mate Fay A. Holley, USNR, member of a Seabee unit here, quickly arranged to get together with his brother Lieutenant Roy D. Holley, USNR, when he learned his ship was in this harbor. Last time they had seen each other was over three years ago in Bremerton, Wash.

Fay Holley lives in Medford, Ore., and brother Roy lives in Bremerton. They are the sons of Mr. and Mrs. G. G. Holley of Portland, Ore.

Prior to their coming into the service, Lieutenant Holley was employed at the Puget Sound Navy Yard, and Chief Carpenter's Mate Holley was a member of the Oregon State Police. (17Dec44)

In reference to the dispatch above, the Navy Department Public Relations Office in San Francisco forwarded a copy of the following letter to USMC Combat Correspondent Claude R. Canup.

Dear Sirs:
On January 24, received your information stating the meeting of our two sons somewhere in the Pacific. We appreciate deeply the courtesy of Sergeant Claude R. Canup, of Anderson, S.C., writing about this.
Sincerely yours, and the best of luck.
Mr. and Mrs. G. G. Holley
Portland, 16, Oregon

NO REPEAT PERFORMANCE

Some people may make the same mistake twice, but not Second Lieutenant Gordon L. Coles, Pendleton, Ore., a pilot with a night fighter squadron. Lieutenant Coles' most embarrassing mistake was made shortly after he began to fly when he came in one day for a landing and forgot to let down the landing gear.

Since then he has been given the nickname "wheels," and that is about the only name he gets out here from fellow pilots. He now has over two years of flying experience.

A member of the National Guard two years before he began training for his wings, Lieutenant Coles did a brief stretch in the army when his guard company was called out under the National Emergency Act. He received a discharge and became an aviation cadet in June 1942.

Twenty-three-years-old last June 28, the pilot received training in California, Texas, and Florida. He was commissioned October 1943 at Corpus Christi. Before entering the service, he was a student at Eastern Oregon College of Education where he played freshman football. (18Dec44)

IDENTIFICATION

A Marine intelligence officer received his Christmas present from his wife, thanks to the Post-Tribune of Jefferson City, Mo.

Second Lieutenant William N. Burks, Jr., Jefferson City, claimed an unidentified package as his own when one of the inner wrappings was revealed to be a copy of the Post-Tribune. He immediately recognized it as being his home town newspaper and closer inspection of the package revealed his name on another wrapping.

The outside address plainly read that it was to go to a particular squadron of the 4thMAW, but the name had worn off because of so much handling.

The newspaper was three months old, but Lieutenant Burkes said, "It's just like a letter from home." (20Dec44)

ADMIRAL INSPECTS BASE

Rear Admiral J. W. Reeves, USN, put his stamp of approval on this base during a recent tour of inspection in the Central Pacific.

He expressed particular satisfaction with air base facilities for MAG 45 which is operating here under the 4thMAW.

Following conferences with Naval and Marine commanders in the atoll, Admiral Reeves was said to have been pleased with the general operational progress on this base and the speed with which landing and construction missions had been completed.

He declared the base had already proved of vital importance to the Navy, which is now driving our striking power closer to the heart of Japan.

The Navy chieftain, who had inspected the base last summer a few days after the landing of Marines and Seabees, paid particular attention to the airstrip, which was completed ahead of schedule, and other facilities on the base that sprang up almost overnight between his visits. He also inspected offices and bivouac areas of the Navy, Marine and Army on the atoll.

Conferences were held with Commodore Oliver O. Kessing, commander of the atoll; Colonel Frank M. June, commanding officer of MAG 45; and Lieutenant Colonel George E. Congdon, air base commander.

Admiral Reeves, who slashes the Pacific's days into hours by air travel, came to this atoll in his private transport plane. While here, he continued to use the quickest mode of travel to the cluster of islands, hopping from one to another in a Piper Cub.

This base has been added to the network of sky lanes which link all Central Pacific forward areas and rear bases with scheduled flights by giant transport planes that carry service personnel, mail and freight.

And, from this base roar Marine bombers with their bellies full of destruction that is rained on enemy warships and by-passed Jap-held islands in the Carolines. (20Dec44)

December 24 Lots of beer for first time in weeks. Some cheer with Couch. Went to church. Saw boxing show. Wrote.

December 25 Went to Christmas service. Christmas dinner best yet. Ice cream. Turned in 3 stories & pix.

December 26 Wrote 4 stories.

SHORTEST AIR LINE

The Pacific may claim the world's shortest airline route—one mile. A Piper Cub operates between two islands of the atoll, making approximately 20 round trips daily hauling passengers and mail. The plane expedites the transaction of official business between the islands.

The Cub can make a round trip in six minutes. Dodging a coral reef requires about an hour for a boat to make that same trip. The inter-island air taxi, once used as an ambulance, was formerly based at the Naval Air Station at Pensacola, Fla. It is flown by pilots of a torpedo bomber squadron stationed here. Its flights are supervised by Major Braxton Rhodes, Jr., Pensacola, Fla., base operations officer.

The plane has a specially built 500 foot runway on one island and uses regular air strips on the others. (26Dec44)

ISLAND HOPPER

Corporal Everett E. George, Jr., Paris, Ken., knows plenty about island hopping in the Pacific. He leapfrogged from Pearl Harbor to Ulithi over a period of several months to rejoin his squadron.

Left at Pearl Harbor with a broken foot received while playing football last summer, George, 19, rejoined his squadron here on Christmas Day and sighed like a man who had just been relieved of a heavy burden. He said, "This is the next best thing to getting back home."

Before catching his squadron, the leatherneck was transferred to several outfits, landed on seven islands, and traveled thousands of miles by sea and air. From Pearl Harbor he went to Majuro, Kwajalein, Eniwetok, Saipan, Tinian and Guam. He flew from Guam to this island the day Santa Claus was making his rounds. (26Dec44)

MARINE SKY PILOT

Lieutenant (jg) G. Jay Umberger, Lebanon, Penn., recently assumed duties here as protestant chaplain of the Marine air base. Lieutenant Umberger, 38, is chaplain for navy and army personnel on the island as well as leathernecks of MAG 45.

He was welcomed to this atoll by Colonel Frank M. June, commanding officer of MAG 45, and Colonel George E. Congdon, commanding officer of the air base. Lieutenant Umberger, entered the service in 1943 and has visited 944 ships and performed 22 weddings.

Lieutenant (jg) James E. Norton, of Indianapolis, Ind., is the Catholic chaplain here. (26Dec44)

An Invitation for Red

You are cordially invited to attend dinner tonight
At the 542 Pilots Mess. Dinner is served at 1800
In the galley. Don't fail to be there.

MENU

Beef Pot Roast — Mother's Gravy
Fresh Mashed Potatoes — Buttered Corn
Raw Carrots
Butterscotch Pie
Bread — Butter — Jam
Cocoa
You've Gone Asiatic If You Are Not There

UNEXPECTED VISIT TO ULITHI

To more than 25 carrier-based fighter pilots, Ulithi was recently heaven on earth. Their ship's flight deck disabled while they were on patrol, the Hellcats could not land. They were 700 miles at sea, their fuel running low. Other flat-tops were crowded with their own planes. Flight officers went into a huddle quickly reaching a decision to save the men and planes.

The circling planes were ordered to land on a nearby carrier, refuel, and go to Ulithi. The young navy fliers did just that and hours later they spotted land. Spirits rose, then dropped, for fear it was Jap-held Yap Island. They finally heard the Marine air base radio which led them in circling jubilantly and peeling off.

These pilots may have to be reminded how beautiful Ulithi was with its palm trees lining the beach—but they will never forget how the landing strip looked. (26Dec44)

SPONSORS' PLUG

Now that Marines on this island have their own radio station and can tune in on the best American programs, the sponsors, who are not identified on shows to the armed forces, might be interested in a new game out here.

As men listen to the program in mess halls, libraries or their tents, they quickly add a plug for the sponsor at the end. Also, the businesses sponsoring shows and musicals are so popular for their programs and products that not a spot is played but that someone doesn't mention the sponsor's name.

The station is only five watts. It cannot be identified by call letters nor can the announcer say from where the broadcast is coming. Some of the leathernecks and other service men who occupy the island don't know the station is operated by MAG 45, and they don't know the programs cover only this island. But, that is the least of their concerns as long as they hear the day's top tunes by their favorite orchestras, singers, and laugh with comedians.

The station is so popular that "Tokyo Rose" is running a poor second. She is the dame whose futile efforts to demoralize American troops are beamed directly from Tokyo—her lies classify her program as a comedy. (27Dec44)

ULITHI, WESTERN CAROLINES
DECEMBER 27, 1944

This will be censored Thursday and within another week or so you should have it. This is damn swell mail service if you ask me. I don't know how long it will keep up. As you know, a reporter never lets the grass grow under his feet, and I keep up with answers to your letters because you can't tell what the situation will be after a while—and I want you to write back soon with another newsy epistle.

From all I have read in clippings and magazines that come directly from the States, the consensus is that something pretty big is in the making for next year. Maybe we'll get this one over with in time to shove across to Europe and help wind up the German deal!

You asked me how the Pacific looks from the air. After the flight to Peleliu a few weeks ago, I took a hop in a Catalina Flying Boat, a PBY. You've read much about them. They are great for ocean flying, and I felt pretty safe up there in the big navy ship as I looked down a few thousand feet between cloud banks at the blue Pacific. (Maybe I can get this through.) We were on a rather important mission and were on the lookout for anything that might be thrown our way—nothing came. We got close enough to a strongly fortified Jap-held island to get pictures.

I was invited to ride in the co-pilot's seat on the return trip, and the pilot asked me if I wanted to take the controls. I jumped at the chance, and the plane jumped at my touch. These big ships aren't as spry as the lighter ones, and I managed to keep to a fairly straight course and keep the nose level. It was lots of fun maneuvering it over thick cloud banks and through small openings between the clouds. We were cruising about 120 miles an hour at about 7,000 feet.

I'm planning to visit every island I can and go on the PBY missions whenever I can get a seat. They seem to like for me to go along, so it should be no trouble. I feel much more at ease in the PBY—which has landing gear as well as pontoons—than I did in the huge transport plane which can land only on the good earth.

The islands look good from the air. I have landed on three out here—this one, Peleliu and Anguar. I flew on an R4D to Peleliu which looked rugged. I visited Bloody Nose Ridge and there are still a few Japs on the island. The Marines had a hard time and lost about 1,200 men, as you know—but, you also read that the Japs buried over ten times that many. Our loss is too big a price to pay for all the Japs in the world.

Time is beginning to drag here, and being so close to the ocean doesn't offer much of a diversion. The beaches are full of sharp, jagged rocks—nobody wades into the surf barefooted, swims, or goes fishing much. I spend most of my time hanging around the airstrip looking for stories.

I was introduced to "torpedo juice" the other night. It is straight alcohol mixed with grapefruit juice and has the kick of a mule. I did not realize that I was drinking dynamite until I got up to leave . . . glad it was not far to my tent. Now I know why torpedoes really travel!

December 27 Lt. Bob Crosby ashore. Met him.
December 28–Dec 31 Usual routine.

MARINES GIVE UP SACK TIME

Usually only the enemy can keep a Marine from putting in his sack time. This morning the "Boondock Blackouts" accomplished that on a moment's notice.

The BB's are a Fifth Marine Division band of musicians and funsters led by Second Lieutenant Bob Crosby, "The Crosby without Hope." They landed here on a flight from Peleliu where they had played and clowned for men of the Pacific Fleet. Not scheduled to unpack their tunes and laughs on this island, Bob and his party of 31 leathernecks learned several squadrons of the 4thMAW were here. Plans were modified.

The short-notice event was publicized quickly. Within a few minutes sleepy-eyed Marines just off night duty were joined in the outdoor theater by others who could be spared from day duty. Leathernecks, soldiers and sailors came from all parts of the island by the hundreds swarming like our famous lizards.

The Pacific island touch was added—a ten minute shower drenched the crowd before the band struck the first note. (29Dec44)

FATHER MEETS SON

A midnight message signaled from a navy ship to the marine air base reunited a father and son after two and a half years. Metalsmith First Class Fred I. Carrigan, 44, is stationed on a ship recently anchored here. Discovering his son's unit was on the island, a meeting was set up with aviation Radioman Third Class James M. Carrigan, 21. Another son, Radioman Third Class Joe W. Carrigan, 18, is with the Navy in Panama.

"Pappa" Carrigan enlisted a week after Pearl Harbor. In 1931, the veteran of World War I, who served in France with the 34th Army Division, had been told he was "too old." War changed that. He is now on his second tour of duty in the Pacific. (29Dec44)

ULITHI, WESTERN CAROLINES
DECEMBER 29, 1944

I got a 12-page letter from my government friend in Washington. He wrote he heard by the grapevine that the Seventh Marine Division is being formed. The Fifth was completed only late in the spring, the Sixth sometime recently.

Looks like they are getting enough Marines to win the war. A couple of more divisions should do it!

Marie wrote Linda wanted to go to Greenville the other day and meet me at the train station. That's bad. I wish she could—but soon. However, I expect the time to roll by in a hurry before long. After all, I didn't come out here to write fairy tales, and from the way things are shaping up, it should not be long before I start making page one.

Come again, real soon.

FLYING COMMANDING OFFICER

Major William C. Kellum, commanding officer of a night squadron, is one of the most active pilots on this Marine base. He takes his regular turn on combat patrol and flies special missions in addition to his other duties.

The 29-year-old Major began his military training at the age of 16 when he joined the Reserve Officers Training Corps while a high school student. He continued the course during his student years at the University of California at Los Angeles and received a second lieutenant's commission in the United States Army Infantry Reserve in 1936.

The former Californian now lives in Varina, N.C., and was with 32nd infantry two years until September 1938 when he joined the Navy Reserve as a seaman second class. A month later he was appointed an aviation cadet and received his wings and commission in the Marine Corps in December 1939. His duties carried him to several stations, including the navy aviation factory where he was a test pilot, and Pensacola, Fla., where he was an instructor. He is a graduate of UCLA where he won letters in boxing and baseball.

The Major's old infantry outfit is now on Leyte. (29Dec44)

6. NEW YEAR, SAME ROCK

January–February 1945

Red's dispatches were well received and widely published. In fact they were so well received that his commanding officer arranged a transfer. Red's original orders would have assigned him to VMF (N) 542, a night fighter squadron; however, the squadron's commanding officer did not want a combat correspondent. Orders were changed, and Red was reassigned to MAG 31 for the Okinawa invasion. Ironically VMF (N) 542 was also assigned to the same MAG and headed to Okinawa on different orders by a different route.

January 1 Another good meal & beer.
January 2 Working on war diary.
January 3 More stories on pilots.
January 4–12 Usual routine.

HILL IS VERSATILE MARINE

Second Lieutenant Clyde H. Hill, night fighter in the Fourth Marine Air Wing, served as an enlisted leatherneck aboard WEST VIRGINIA and MARYLAND before receiving his wings and commission. Having attended the University of New Mexico, Lieutenant Hill was on WEST VIRGINIA's football team and MARYLAND's boxing team.

The 26-year-old New Mexican is recreation and welfare officer and assistant ordnance officer of his squadron in addition to being a flier. (2Jan45)

*Lieutenant Hill was killed in action on Okinawa. When his squadron moved to Chimu Airfield from Yontan Airfield, both on Okinawa, the softball field at Chimu was named Hill Field in his honor.**

PICTURE OF THE YEAR

How do you judge "picture of the year?" Why, of course, by how much and how loudly Marines laugh—and how many days they talk about it. Such was the case for "Hail Our Conquering Hero."

The leathernecks of the 4thMAW related well to the movie based on the story of six Marines just returned from Guadalcanal. For the information of those who poll theater goers, the sailors and soldiers here got just as big a laugh as did the Marines.

Men stationed on Pacific islands can't be choosy about their movies. They usually go to the outdoor theater without knowing the title of the feature. There is no doubt, however, about why they go—it's the only game in town and they love to laugh. The picture with the most laughs gets the most votes for "picture of the year." (4Jan45)

BIG JOB FOR TEXAN

One of the most important jobs with a Marine aircraft group is keeping parachutes in shape to save pilots and gunners in the event they are forced to bail out while on a combat mission.

Much of that responsibility in the air group stationed on this island is in the hands of Master Technical Sergeant Luther Leal, Jr., 26, Laredo, Tex., who is non-commissioned officer in charge of the parachute loft.

Leal, who joined the Marine Corps in 1942, sailed for overseas duty last summer. His group is attached to the 4thMAW. He was recently promoted to master technical sergeant, highest enlisted rank in the Corps. (9Jan45)

TYPICAL MARINE PILOT

Second Lieutenant Rodger "Ollie" Olson, 21, a Marine fighter pilot from Chicago, Ill., symbolizes the typical night combat flyer. Distinguishing himself

* *542nd Marine Night Fighter Squadron* (Baton Rouge, La.: Army and Navy Publishing Company, 1946), 54.

first as an exceptional pilot, he earned the opportunity to attend advanced night fighter courses at Vero Beach, Fla., and Cherry Point, N.C. He is presently flying night patrol defending the harbor and shipping routes of this atoll.

"Ollie" Olson is typical in another respect. Many of the night fighters attached to the 4thMAW were outstanding athletes before they became outstanding pilots.

The Hellcat pilot was previously stationed at Cherry Point before the 10,000 mile air and sea trip to Ulithi. (9Jan45)

The following story resulted from the one above. For continuity's sake, it is placed out of chronological order.

BLONDE AT ST. MARY'S

This story is a thank you for reading about local Marines in hometown papers. It is a ripple effect story that began on Ulithi, an atoll in the Western Carolines, when a mid-western Marine pilot was interviewed by a combat correspondent.

In January 1945, a story about a night fighter pilot—21-year-old Second Lieutenant Rodger Olson of Chicago—was flown via Pearl Harbor to the Public Information Section of Marine Corps Headquarters in Washington. A picture of the young pilot in the cockpit of his Hellcat accompanied the story.

One of the Chicago papers printed the dispatch. Miss Fredie Pignott of Chicago, a student at St. Mary of the Woods College near Terre Haute, Ind., saw the picture with the story describing "Ollie" as a typical Marine fighter pilot. She clipped the picture and carried it back to college.

The 125 girls of St. Mary's Guerin Hall were conducting a pin-up contest in search of their ideal man. Fredie showed them Olson's picture and shared with them his night fighter combat assignment in the Pacific. Validated by the typical "ah's" and "oh's," the picture was posted on the bulletin board with other contestants.

The pilot, now on Okinawa, was entered in the competition with fighting men from other branches of the service. As Fredie wrote, "It wouldn't be a contest without a Marine."

Representing the Marines from the Halls of Montezuma to the shores of Okinawa, Second Lieutenant Olson won the St. Mary's contest in a Pacific breeze—after all, 125 girls can't be wrong.

Acknowledging the results, the typical Marine aviator in typical Marine fashion said, "I am deeply grateful and honored by the vote of the girls of

Guerin Hall." He also said something about wishing he could get to Terre Haute for 125 days of liberty. (23May45)

ULITHI
JANUARY 12, 1945

Your first letter of the New Year arrived this morning and soon will be quartered in my seabag with scores of other messages of good cheer. I'm saving them to use after the war when all my friends and relatives have forgotten what a "great guy" and "swell fellow" I am. You see, right now I am one of the smartest, wittiest and most courageous men the world has known—simply because I'm rotting out here on a rock. So when I get back I will be just another guy named Joe to my friends and acquaintances—just as in the Marine Corps I'm a guy named Joe—one of nearly 600,000.

I hope you know I'm only kidding, just needed something to get off to a start with this answer to your kind letter. But really, you don't have to flatter me to stay on my mailing list. The letters mean more to me than anything else from the States. Boxes are appreciated, but a letter is only six cents and a box usually is five bucks or more. I had rather anybody thinking of sending a box write that many more letters.

Take for instance the cake and candy the folks mailed around the middle of October for my Christmas present. I haven't received it yet and probably won't this late. They had good intentions and I could use something unusual to supplement the Marine chow, which could stand plenty of supplementing at times, but the cake and candy are wasted now. I'm still mercenary enough to think of it in dollars and cents. They could have bought 100 air mail stamps for the price of that stuff, and I would have had 100 pleasant mail calls whereas now I have only the hopes that somebody got hold of the cake and candy before the maggots got it. You see, there's so little we need out here that can be put into a box. That is, a five-pound box.

My commanding officer of the wing was here yesterday. He likes my stuff and has arranged for me to be transferred in the near future. It is quite likely that not all the fireworks out here will escape me, and I should yet make the front page—or should I say, make it again. I like the play they gave the Christmas story. I will welcome a change. It is very tiresome trying to create stories with nothing of importance happening here—I have given out of rocks on this rock to turn over.

Now that you know where I am and the Navy has let out the news that this is a fleet anchorage, I can tell you of the trip I made to the harbor one day while the fleet was in. You've never seen so many damn ships. I often have stood on the beach and watched them come and go. It is an impressive sight. On my trip into the harbor on a Higgins boat and then a captain's dinghy, I visited a movie exchange ship that furnishes pictures to the fleet and bases here and caught rides to some carriers. I ate dinner on one carrier and spent the night on another and saw a basketball game on the hanger deck. I will not name them as it may not get through. I toured the ships—they are immense!

The flight decks are air strips, and the carrier-based aviators hitting islands from these ships are tops. Those are the boys to watch. Since my job is to sell Marine aviation, I would like to peddle the feats of those guys to the press. I'm sure that from here out people will know about Marine aviation. Some of the carriers have taken on squadrons of Marine fliers, and I am told I might have a chance later of serving on one—if the Navy breaks down and lets correspondents aboard.

Thanks for the letter you wrote about Buzz and the Christmas wagon you found and fixed. It really did a number on me. When he gets big enough to understand or starts talking a little, see if you can sell him on the idea that you are just pinch-hitting for his Daddy away on a little unfinished business but will be home about next Christmas. I'll even go so far as to shave off the mustache before I get home. On nights when I am really missing home, I like to sit on the beach and watch the multi-colored sky fade into dark blue. At nightfall the stars come out fast and thick. It is comforting to know that at least we are all under the same star studded sky.

While I was aboard one of the carriers, a Marine gunner who knows all about the stars showed me quite a bit. He showed me how to find the North Star and also pointed out the Southern Cross, which is not visible too far above the equator. First time I had seen it to recognize it—not a perfect cross because there is a fifth star. More perfect crosses are to be found, but they don't last many years. It seems the Southern Cross is to navigators below the equator what the North Star is to them above the equator. It makes sense. You know the First Marine Division shoulder patch shows the Southern Cross with Guadalcanal written down the center. The island itself is one of the beauty spots of the Pacific according to men who have been on dozens of them from the Canal to Saipan. Most of the lizards were killed when they remade the island—seldom see a five footer.

In answer to your question, I won't get to wear wings because I'm not in an aircraft wing, but I will be privileged to wear a shoulder patch of the wing to which I am attached when I am ordered back to the States.

I am writing this letter at night in my tent by electric light. That's how modern we've become. Just a few tents have lights—the sergeant major sleeps in mine!

January 13 First Lt. Louis Olszyk came to island. Completed plans for me to join new group for big operation. Place and date kept secret.
January 14 Pay day—$55.
January 15 Went to church. Washed. Wrote Linda and folks. Rested. Caught up on diary. Was three weeks behind, but nothing eventful happened.

This is the last entry in Red's diary.

NON-COMS FORM CLUB

Non-Commissioned officers of MAG 45 have organized a club and recreation center. Membership is limited to master technical sergeants.

The 30-odd charter members elected Master Technical Sergeant Robert L. Gumz, St. Louis, Mo., president. He is sergeant major of MAG 45.

Master Technical Sergeant Albert E. Pointer, 30-year-old veteran of the Solomon Islands campaign, is vice president. He has been a leatherneck since March 1933, serving the first five years as a line company Marine.

Master Technical Sergeant Carl J. Raitano, 24, Pittsburgh, Penn., is the club secretary. The 24-year-old enlisted in March 1942 and is sergeant major of the group's service squadron.

Master Technical Sergeant Willis C. Tapley, 22-year-old non-commissioned officer in charge of the quartermaster department, is the club treasurer. This is his second overseas tour. The resident of Byers, Kan., saw action at Samoa on his first tour. (15Jan45)

JAP PIN-UPS

American pin-up girls, their beauty gracing any place wherever there are fighting sons of Uncle Sam, won their first major engagement in the Western Carolines with plenty of charm and curves to spare.

It really was no contest and was not even intended as such—but, when the situation presented itself the Marines' favorite pin-ups walked away with more decorations than could be pinned to their pin-up costumes.

Jap pin-ups surfaced recently when leathernecks came back from a newly conquered island—their pockets and packs bulging with photographs and newspaper clippings of the Japs' prized pin-ups confiscated from enemy barracks as souvenirs.

After comparing them to our American beauties prominently displayed on every available surface in leatherneck accommodations, the Marines folded the

Jap pin-ups and crammed them into seabags to keep for souvenirs, not viewing. The American beauties winning the battle of the pin-ups—it was really no contest. (16Jan45)

INFLATION

Inflation here is reversed. Shortly after American troops landed and secured Fais Island in the Western Carolines, a recovery party of aviation Marines was sent ashore to Native Island to determine what Japanese material was worth saving.

One of the natives was very much attracted to a necklace worn by a Marine and wanted to buy it. Japanese money earned working in the mines had been exchanged for US currency, and the natives had done very well selling merchandise to the souvenir-hunting Americans. This native was prepared financially to close the deal.

Holding his cash so the denominations showed, the native wanted the Marine to point to the bill he would take in exchange for the necklace. The Marine pointed to a dollar bill. The native laughed, snatched the necklace, thrust a ten dollar bill into the astonished Marine's hand, and dashed away.

An island economics lesson is hidden somewhere in this exchange. (16Jan45)

ULITHI
JANUARY 21, 1945

I heard from my friend at Headquarters on the desk in D.C. He had not written in quite a while, and I was real happy to hear from him—for good reason. I'll quote you a paragraph from his letter: "Before I do anything else, I want to shake your hand on the story about the razorback pig that is the biggest pet and pest. It's a lulu of a story, of course, on the face of it. My congratulations are for the way you handled it. It's going to appear in our next clipsheet and should get good wide play." He handles much of the copy from correspondents—that is why I was so glad to hear from him. Word that my dispatches are being published keeps me digging for stories such as can be found on this rock. By the time you start digging in your garden, I don't think I will have to be digging for stories. There should be some big ready-made ones.

I've heard from headquarters about other stories. They are getting good play in places such as Flint, St. Louis, and Chattanooga, as well as around our neck of the woods. Three yarns were in last week's Marine clip sheet going out to every newspaper coast-to-coast. Also a Masonic yarn was sent to every Mason magazine in the country—29 of them. So my stuff seems to be going over okay even if the blood and guts are not included for the time being. Interest in this war's Joe Blows is alive and well.

The CO of our night fighter squadron really chewed me out the other day after he received a news clipping from his wife that was datelined Ulithi. It was her first knowledge of where he was and he did not know that I had received word from headquarters to finally identify our location rather than use the usual "Somewhere in the Western Pacific." He was so angry he forgot that our intelligence officers get first crack at my stories and then fleet headquarters, FMFPAC and finally USMC Headquarters. Will he apologize? I'm not holding my breath.

Marie sent pictures of her and the children. They were swell, and I had no idea that Linda had grown so much. Frankly, she doesn't look anything like the girl I left behind. She was just a little gal in shorts with a suntan last summer. Now she has her hair cut and in the picture is dressed in a new outfit Marie made for her. I suppose the suit and coat and cap make her look bigger and older. Anyway, she has changed. And, Buzz. Well, he's about the cutest trick I have ever seen. The little rascal is smiling in most of the pictures. I'm afraid I will have to become reacquainted with all of them when I get back. Marie looks just as pretty as ever. I may have mentioned to you before that I had a picture made out here and it seemed to me I looked every bit of 40. You see, I have a mustache now (wow!).

Oh, yes, about the pipe. If you get one, please airmail it. If you can't find a Kaywoodie, any good brand will do. Just don't send it regular mail. It takes too long and it may never catch me—didn't know they were so scarce.

VISITS BROTHER'S GRAVE

The McNeel brothers of Corsicana, Tex., joined the Marine Corps in 1942, and went through San Diego boot camp together. After basic training, 31-year-old Sergeant David C. McNeel was assigned to the First Marine Division and the 20-year-old Technical Sergeant Walton W. McNeel joined MAG 45. The brothers last saw each other in January 1943.

Sergeant McNeel's outfit quickly shoved off for Guadalcanal. He took part in some of the First Marine's fiercest engagements and David C. McNeel lost his life on "Bloody Nose Ridge" on Peleliu Island. One of the hundreds of white crosses there bears his name.

Technical Sergeant McNeel's aviation unit was at Pearl Harbor when the news of the Palau Islands attack was broadcast. It was months later before young McNeel learned that his older brother had been killed and was buried at Peleliu. Obtaining a pass to fly to the Palau Islands to visit the grave, Walton made pictures and sent them to his parents.

The younger McNeel's squadron is attached to the 4thMAW. (22Jan45)

SLINGSHOT BEDS

Marines never pass up a chance to add to their comfort here on our rock. The Japs didn't leave furniture so the leathernecks here improvise. An empty wooden K-rations box becomes a camp stool, writing table or trunk. Marines on this coral rock have learned to use anything and everything.

Old rubber inner tubes are the latest material on the most wanted list. Out here there is not much demand for slingshots, but "slingshot beds" are all the rage. The beds are made from frames of 4 x 4s, the "springs" are the woven four inch strips of inner tubes.

Those lucky enough to have these beds say there is nothing in these parts to match their sleeping comfort. Those who don't have them are gathering 4 x 4s and inner tubes.

Slingshot beds on this island were made by Technical Sergeant Gordon W. Bisdorf, 35, Norwood, O. He was assisted by Technical Sergeant Fredrick Gerke, 22, Grand Rapids, Mich. They have been together in the Corps since September 1942 and learned about slingshot beds from Major Kenneth Black on Ondonga Island in 1943. (22Jan45)

STAFF SERGEANT BUDGE ON SECOND TOUR

Marines back out here for the second time during this war find conditions as a whole much improved. Such is the experience of Staff Sergeant James E. Budge, 27, Grand Forks, N.D.

Budge, who was recently promoted to his present rank, has discovered on this tour of duty food served to his aviation unit is much better than the chow on Guadalcanal and Munda in 1943. The big difference, he says, is fresh vegetables, meat and eggs, which were a rarity in the early stages of the war. Also, now that Marines have fought their way thousands of miles north, living conditions are improved in that the most recent activity has been on coral atolls, where there is little mud no matter how much it rains.

Staff Sergeant Budge, who enlisted in the Marine Corps in 1942, is authorized to wear the Presidential Unit Citation with one star for the Guadalcanal campaign and the Asiatic-Pacific campaign ribbon with three stars. (25Jan45)

CHANGE OF COMMAND

A Marine officer who was in the thick of the fighting at Pearl Harbor is the new commander of the Marine air base on this island. He is Lieutenant Colonel Stanley W. Trachta, Alhambra, Calif.

He succeeds Lieutenant Colonel George E. Congdon, who has reported to headquarters of the 4thMAW for assignment by Major General Louis E. Woods.

Colonel Trachta, 33, is a native of Meeken, Co. He is a graduate of the University of Montana, and attended service schools at Camp Perry, Va., and a small arms firing school. He was commissioned July 1935.

Previous to taking over duties at this base Colonel Trachta was in the embassy guard at Peiping, China; with the fleet Marine force at San Diego, Calif.; naval air station at Pensacola, Fla.; served aboard WEST VIRGINIA, and was stationed at Edenton, N.C. He was in China three years and was with the fleet one year, being on WEST VIRGINIA at Pearl Harbor when the Japs struck.

Major Nelson A. Kenworthy, Rahway, N.J., continues as executive officer of the base. (29Jan45)

THREE JAPS FOUND AFTER THREE MONTHS OF OCCUPATION

Three Japs who escaped during the mopping up operations on this small island have been found in a cave on Native Island, a suicide bullet hole in each head. One rifle had been used, and the positions of their bodies indicated the three sat down, placed the rifle between their legs, clamped their teeth over the muzzle, and "died for the emperor."

The trio had water, food, and ammunition and were in no immediate danger of capture. Two searching parties had been successfully eluded. The officers here have determined the two Japanese imperial marines and the Jap civilian found their situation hopeless after the Marines built the air base here and became permanent residents. (29Jan45)

MARINES USE JAP CHEMICALS

Just as salvaged Japanese equipment is being put to good use throughout the Pacific, a Tokyo chemical firm's product is making work easier for Marine aerial photographers on this island.

First Lieutenant Sam Ray Smith, Greensboro, N.C., in charge of MAG 45's photographic laboratory, had tried for nine months to get a supply of ammonium chloride, both on the West Coast and out here. There was none to be had.

Things changed on a recent trip to Fais Island, occupied this year by Marines and other troops. Sergeant Edward E. DeFranco, New York City, returned with five jars of ammonium chloride taken from the Japs.

Ammonium chloride is used in standard and rapid fixing baths in the development of films. It saves time in turning out finished reconnaissance aerial photography.

Not to be overlooked either is the fact that "super-hypo" saves time in the darkroom—as hot as it is dark out here. (29Jan45)

THE FLEET AND SHORE LEAVE

Ulithi's harbor is full of ships, and the island has been secured. Sailors anxious to break the monotony of months on the water are coming ashore. What they are finding is a scene much like a stateside park in California or Florida, a beach with coconut groves. What the seamen are looking for are souvenirs and natives, both in short supply on this island.

The air strip is a virtual beehive of activity with planes of all shapes and sizes coming and going day and night. All this activity is a bit unusual for our visiting sailors, but our lizards ranging in size from a little more than an inch to six feet really capture their attention. Nuisances much like roaches, they get into everything but unlike roaches they grow large and bite hard if bothered.

Cold beer is another reason the sailors want to come ashore. Often the beer is special for them only and after months at sea they deserve the treat. Those of us stationed on the island find life can become as monotonous on land as on sea. After a while the most exciting thing happening is mail call for the fleet gets its mail here also. (6Feb45)

PACIFIC TIMES SQUARE

With the war moving nearer Japan, this island might as well be called the "Times Square" of the Pacific. All branches of the service have men regularly passing through here, and permanent personnel include Marines, Seabees, Coast Guard, and several units of navy and army aviation.

When the fleet steams in, almost everyone on the island runs across a friend or relative or someone who knows someone. It is said if you don't find someone you know on this island, you don't know enough people. (8Feb45)

RIGGERS RATE HIGH PRAISE

A Virginian and his crew are experts at repairing and inspecting life-saving and safety devices used by Ulithi's pilots and gunners. Unless a job and a life

Sgt. Claude R. "Red" Canup, "Fly Speck Hotel" Press Tent, Ulithi Atoll, 1945. Claude R. "Red" Canup Collection.

depends on parachutes not much thought is given to the important work done in the parachute loft of the aircraft group here.

Marine Warrant Officer George Hayes, 44, Fredericksburg, is the parachute officer in charge of the vital parachute loft. The riggers are also known as jump masters. Specially trained for their jobs, riggers handle a sewing machine with the skill of a seamstress. They do more than sewing, repairing and packing "chutes." They drop supply cargo "chutes" in emergencies to stranded pilots and crews on land or sea. They inspect and repair life rafts and safety belts. Approximately 450 parachutes are inspected monthly.

One of the latest safety innovations introduced out here is the combination parachute and para-raft used by gunners and passengers who constantly fly over water day or night. It is attached to the parachute harness. On a forced jump, each man has his own raft and is not faced with the problem of remaining afloat in the sea with only a "Mae West" inflatable vest to keep from drowning. The raft, tightly packed, is automatically inflated when released just before the jumper drops into the water. The jumper rises to the surface, inflates his life jacket and crawls into his raft. (8Feb45)

ULITHI
FEBRUARY 8, 1944

Here I am, at five minutes until 11 o'clock, pecking on a typewriter that long ago should have been covered up. As a matter of perfect frankness, it was until one letter back. You see, I'm just getting back from a very bad effort at a movie, and a few with the pilots, and I felt I should sit at my desk and write Marie and you, also.

You should see my desk—I really shouldn't be writing about my desk because out here the small fry aren't supposed to have a desk—and here I am writing on probably the best desk on the whole island, outside of some of those behind which sit the guys with the chickens or scrambled eggs on their caps, or the little silver stars!

But there is a story to this desk, and I don't think I have ever said anything about it to anybody in a letter. I'm sitting here one day and I'm thinking how much better a real desk would be than the crate on which I am writing. There is a desk nearby, a desk much too fancy for this part of the world.

A carpenter comes in, and I ask him if he can duplicate the desk for two cans of beer. The carpenter stands there with almost a jeer on his face thinking I am trying to snow him and expecting me to promise him a couple of cans of brew. I calmly get up—that is the only way I get up these days unless there is more important business in a safer place—and reach under my sack and pull out a couple of cans of Blue Ribbon. His tongue hangs out like a tired mule—the Seabees, who can perform miracles, are given credit for my stash.

Well, he takes the beer and leaves. I didn't see him again; but, I walked in the tent a few days later, and there was my new desk.

The Plexiglas cover is another story. Plexiglas is hard to come by out here—unless you have a photographer with you and can promise to get someone's picture in their hometown newspaper.

MARINES NEEDLED

A needle indicates the progress of Marines in their advance toward Japan. It is the inoculation needle. Helping troops ward off diseases prevalent in war zones, the aviation leathernecks of the 4thMAW are among the first to take "the works." Alerted by the needles to a probable move, the Marines have been immunized for diseases common to China, Japan and neighboring islands.

Explaining Marines, in moving forward, will come in contact with diseases rare on the islands they now occupy, flight surgeon Navy Lieutenant John M. Ellis, 36, Berkeley, Calif., assigned to a Marine night fighter squadron, administered shots to leathernecks for such things as cholera, bubonic plague and typhus, in addition to typhoid, tetanus and smallpox.

Just ask any Marine—the inoculation needle is the most accurate gauge of whether or not a move is in the making. (12Feb45)

UNDERTAKING MARINE

The Marine Corps tries to match men with duties close to pre-war occupations. It was a bit difficult to place Corporal Glenn A. Covington, 21, on the job most appropriate for him—he was an undertaker. So, he has been a clerk here in headquarters squadron of MAG 45.

However, on a recent trip to Fais Island, not long occupied by our forces, Corporal Covington had a chance to practice his peace time trade. The salvaging party was led by a native to a cave where the bodies of two imperial Japanese marines and a Jap civilian were found. Covington examined the bodies to determine how long they had been dead and came up with additional information—including souvenirs from their uniforms. They were the last Japs on the island.

The young Marine from Tulsa, Okla., entered the service in 1944. He had practiced his trade for three years before. (12Feb45)

SON TO SEE YOU

Electrician's Mate Second Class Morrel L. Beasley, stationed on a navy repair ship, had the surprise of his life recently. He was informed his son was aboard.

The 45-year-old resident of Houston, Texas, knew his son Marine Private First Class Bill Glen Beasley, 18, served with an aviation group somewhere in the Pacific. He never thought about his son being on the island visible from his ship.

The young leatherneck, who is also an electrician, knew the name of his father's ship. As soon as he learned the ship was in the lagoon here, he quickly arranged to board her. They had not seen each other in almost three years. (12Feb45)

ULITHI
FEBRUARY 12, 1945

There is much to tell, yet so little will pass the censor. Tonight will be my last night on this island. I am flying tomorrow to quite a distant spot where I will join other correspondents in another MAG. When we will shove off from there to our new island is anybody's guess. I think we can boil the possibilities down to three hot spots, or at least spots that are bound to be hot sooner or later. Diseases such as plague, cholera and typhus aren't all over the Pacific, and I have shots for all.

I have been in a state of confusion this past week, not knowing if I were coming or going or where or with whom. Orders quickly changed from staying with a squadron in this MAG to traveling to another MAG. Correspondents are moved around like checkers usually to places where there is the most news to report. I hate leaving because this is my first Marine outfit, and I've been with it several months. Pulling up and shoving off to a strange new spot with every face a new one is always a little unsettling, particularly not knowing whether it's by air or by sea. I've packed and unpacked so many times I am familiar with every spot on my clothes. I might even try to take a blanket. I think I have used one every night since I have been here, but the days are hot as hell.

Some of the boys gave me a farewell party, and out here they put them on in big style—or as big as the occasion can take. This occasion took a few cases.

If by air, I got a large bag made in the parachute loft which is big enough for my typewriter, paper, and enough clothes to last a year, doesn't take many, and I can travel light which is necessary when flying. I sent my seabag out with an outfit which I hope to run across in the near future.

I asked for a typewriter to be sent from DC, and it was in September. I haven't gotten it and don't expect it to arrive now. Somebody will make good use of the machine. They are scarce out here, and I can only hope mine will stand up a few more months.

Some of my stories have been published in the Chevron, Marine weekly newspaper with a wide circulation. I saw them in a copy that made it here. Also, a number of them have been in the clipsheet sent to all the papers. What I am sending out must be what they want, such as it is. I'm batting out three or four yarns at the last minute before I get squared away which will give me 162 or so since leaving.

When writing me, under MAG 31 just add the line Intelligence Section. I work closely with those men and I am sure to get my mail in the sweet bye and bye if not sooner. I'm pretty sure this will be my address for quite some time, and those you have written previous to receiving this letter will be forwarded.

Red saved clippings of stories his fellow combat correspondents published in the Marine Corps' Battle News Clipsheet, *which was distributed to newspaper editors by Denig's DPR. Clipsheet stories had no previous newspaper release. Only when headquarters received a clipping from the newspaper that reprinted the story was there any record that a story was ever published, or of how many times. Red had many general interest stories printed in the clipsheet.*

A great deal of insight is contained in the dispatch below concerning the relationship the marines established with the Ulithi natives. Written by Red's good friend and fellow combat correspondent Phil Storch, the two traveled together to Ulithi with MAG 45 and on to Okinawa with MAG 31.

ATOLL POTENTATE ENTHUSIASTIC AS PLANE WINGS OVER HOME ISLAND
BY SERGEANT PHIL H. STORCH, MARINE CORPS COMBAT CORRESPONDENT

Somewhere in the Pacific (Delayed)—Chief Mok, a Micronesian potentate, sat calmly in the back seat of a Marine Corps command car. He was smoking an American-made cigarette, and as he puffed at it he appeared thoughtful. He had much to tell his people.

The chief was clad in a Marine khaki shirt and a pair of shorts. His tousled hair was covered with a peak cap. On his feet, a pair of G.I. brown socks and shoes known as "boondockers" among the Leathernecks.

The chief had just returned from his first ride in an airplane. He had flown like a bird, and had seen what his islands must look like to the birds. His people had known he was going to fly and had gathered off-shore to wave to him as the plane he rode dipped past.

Piloting the plane in which the chief was a passenger was Major Menard Doswell, III, of Santa Barbara, Cal., commanding officer of the Marine "Red Devil" Torpedo Bomber Squadron.

Son Victim of Polio

Major Doswell had seen Chief Mok when the chief came from the island in this atoll, where the natives make their home. The chief had come here to see his son, a victim of poliomyelitis, who is receiving treatment at the hands of Navy doctors attached to the Marine Aircraft Group here.

When the chief arrived on this island, he wore nothing but the usual lap-lap. Taken in tow by the major, he was soon equipped with Marine clothes and he had something wonderful to look forward to.

The chief was very patient as Major Doswell took him into a tent to have him fitted with a harness and a parachute. He listened intently while instructions were given as to how to make use of the parachute in the event of trouble. Then he was taken to the Major's plane.

Knows Few Spanish Words

The chief is able to speak only a few words of English, and knows no other language, with the exception of a few Spanish words, than his native tongue. The soldier, interested in the language, is making a study of the chief's language and has thus far compiled a vocabulary of more than 200 words.

Although the chief is advanced in years, he was not worried about his adventure. Nor did he show any outward appearance of great joy. He was reserved, as dignified as he probably is among his people, and as dignified as anyone can be who is walking for the first time in shoes—boondockers, no less.

When they arrived at the plane, Technician Kasparoff climbed to the seat of the turret gunner. Major Doswell assisted the chief into the seat of the radio gunner, and then the Major climbed into the cockpit. Soon the ride was underway.

Chief Enjoys Ride

The chief enjoyed the ride. He told the Major soon after it was over. And at one point his enthusiasm got the better of his reserve.

Flying over the islands of the atoll, the Major picked out the one on which the natives make their homes and he dropped the plane low. Many of them were looking for this plane. They had been told Chief Mok was to ride. They waved.

The chief chuckled in glee as his people saluted him. He gave vent to a long string of excited languages. His face beamed. His eyes shown. What a story he'd be able to tell them when he got back to the island. Now he was in the command car. He was apparently phrasing that story to tell his people—a story that will join many other stories of native chiefs to be handed down from generation to generation. He was the first to fly!

SOMEWHERE IN THE PACIFIC
MARCH 2, 1945

Well, Big Brother, I suppose you know what tomorrow is, or I should say that you know what the third of this month was. On the eve of my 34th birthday, I can only hope the upcoming year will have at least part of it spent somewhere east of the Mississippi, but South Carolina is preferred. I am sitting on my sack somewhere I wasn't a month ago with the typewriter on a crude chair, said crude chair serving as the desk. It works better with the machine on top of the typewriter case. It is late, and I'm feeling all the years—but I should find my youth partially restored when I get home. This leaping to another milestone finds me at the half-way mark of what was said to be my tour of duty. Scuttlebutt has it, however, that the time is longer.

I want to thank you for the Readers Digest subscription you gave me for Christmas but since I have yet to receive a copy, would you please write Mr. Digest, or somebody, and ask to transfer the address to home. I'm asking because I will never see one out here, and I love to read them even a year or two back. So after I get home and in my green chair I can catch up with the opinions. I will be changing addresses so fast out here I fear the copies will go unclaimed. Thanks again for the thought and remembering I like the Digest so much.

I had the most pleasant surprise coming to this outfit. You see, I flew here, and stopped off at an island for the night. The Marines there were swell to me and one took me for a sight-seeing tour. He had a friend in the CB area and we stopped in at the mess hall where they were having late chow. They had ice cream (imagine that! But those CBs have ways) and we were invited to have a dish. So while munching ice cream and talking with men at the table I asked one if there was a fellow by the name of Bobo in his battalion. He said there was a fellow by that name in his battalion and took me to Bobo's tent. Bobo was not there—he had gone to the movie. So I sat in his tent and drank a can of beer while this CB looked for him. I had not finished the beer before Bobo walked in.

You guessed it—Gene. Both of us were happy as hell to see each other again after three years or more. Gene has been out here two years and is anxious to get home. We talked about everything and of our many mutual friends back in Anderson. Although he has been through some rugged places, he is none the worse off for his experiences and has quite a pictorial collection. For the most part he has been attached to the Marines, living and fighting with them.

So what with seeing Gene and the red hills on his island at the same time, I felt pretty much at home for the first time since coming out here. Yet, I was in the middle of the ocean and on a strange island where I thought I knew no one.

Marie writes that Buzz is looking more like his old man daily. She also wrote that Linda said to her the other day, "Mama, how about driving me to California so I can see my Daddy." Were I not supposed to be such a tough nut, I could choke up over that kid's innocence.

Thousands of fathers are undergoing the same experience as I am, and thousands of children are as lonely as Linda and Buzz for their daddies. I hope that number won't grow even by one, and I can cut it by one sooner than expected. Happy Birthday to me! By the way, the bush will be removed. I got Linda's message, "Please tell my Daddy to cut that off." So it is coming off because of the special request of my Sugar Baby. Well, this is about the crop.

PART 3

Okinawa

7. MAG 31 AND TACTICAL AIR FORCE RYUKYUS (I)

April 3–May 12, 1945

Securing Okinawa, the largest island closest to the Japanese mainland, was essential to the planned Allied invasion. "Operation Iceberg," the code name for the invasion of Okinawa, began Easter Sunday, April 1, 1945, after weeks of preliminary bombing.

MAG 31 arrived at Yontan Airfield on April 3 as part of Tactical Air Force Ryukyus, which included land-based army and marine aircraft. The original force was composed of two marine aircraft groups and a marine air warning group of the Second Marine Aircraft Wing. During the air support and defense phase of the Battle for Okinawa, the force was expanded to include two additional marine aircraft groups, totaling four—MAGS 14, 22, 31 and 33.

*TAF Ryukyus was commanded by Major General Francis P. Mulcahy, also commander of the 2ndMAW. He was succeeded in both positions on June 11, 1945, by Major General Louis E. Woods.**

From Ulithi, Red flew to Guam, next to Eniwetok, on to Kwajalein, and, last, Roi-Namur—boarding the Afoundria *with MAG 31. While on board, Red used radio information to put together a daily newsletter:*

* "90 Days of Operation Tactical Air Force Ryukyus, April 7–July 6, 1945," Claude R. "Red" Canup Collection.

FORE 'N AFT *TRIP X. NO. 36*
SOMEWHERE IN THE PACIFIC *S. S. AFOUNDRIA*

WELCOME TO OKINAWA!

Lovely Climate . . . Ideal Home Sites . . . Low Taxes . . . Sympathetic to Industry . . . Population 443,000 and Growing Every Day . . . 120 Square Miles . . . Under New Management. (Rotary Club meets Mondays at 12:15, Naha Commercial Hotel.)

Sample news release received on board AFOUNDRIA: Heavy Artillery Fire: Heaviest artillery duel of the Pacific war likened to major battles in the European theater blazed through its third successive day yesterday on southern Okinawa holding the 24th Army Corps. In this area, the main defense line, the Japanese in ravines and caves were fighting from pillboxes and blockhouses. One artillery officer described Japanese defenses as Okinawa's Siegfried Line. In spite of this, some gains were made. In the north the Marines gained rapidly. Many field pieces joined the army artillery, ship guns, and bombers in blasting the enemy's well fortified posts in the rugged country. A combined bombardment destroyed Japanese guns, emplacements, barracks, and small craft. In the north, the Marine 3rd Amphibious Corps moved ahead 2¼ miles to gain control of the pass of Motobu Peninsula against scattered, ineffective resistance. They were near Kushiboni and meanwhile infantry remained in the relative same positions two miles from Mathinato air dome and 4 miles from Naha, the capital of the island. 7 out of 10 Japanese raiding planes were shot down. (11Apr45)

MARINE AIRCRAFT GROUP 31

Colonel John C. Munn	Commanding Officer
Lt. Colonel Kirk Armistead	Executive Officer
Major Charles Kunz	Operations Officer
Captain Harry Martin	Intelligence Officer

Tactical Squadrons Attached to MAG 31

Squadron	Commanding Officer
VMF-224 (Fighting Wildcats)	Major Allen T. Barnum
VMF-311 (Hell's Belles)	Major Michael R. Yunck
VMF-441 (Black Jack)	Major Paul T. Johnson
VMF(N)-542 (Tigers)	Major Robert B. Porter

Tactical Squadrons Attached to MAG 31 (continued)

Squadron	Commanding Officer
VMB-612 (Devil Dog)	Lt. Colonel Jack Cram (correct as of 6 July 45)*

SHARE FIRST PLANE

Captain Ralph G. McCormick, 26, Detroit, Mich., and First Lieutenant John J. Doherty, 24, Seattle, Wash., flying with Hell's Belles fighter squadron, were the first pilots in their squadron to engage the enemy.

The two Corsair pilots shot down a Betty, twin-engine Jap bomber, attacking a carrier off Okinawa the first day the squadron arrived, the first kill by Okinawa-based pilots on the first combat patrol. The officers are credited officially with a half a plane each.

Captain McCormick is a graduate of Cooley High School and the University of Detroit. Lieutenant Doherty, a student when he entered the service, is a graduate of Kellog (Idaho) High School and attended Gonzaga University at Spokane, Wash. (15Apr45)

YONTAN AIRFIELD, OKINAWA
APRIL 16, 1945

We ran into one storm on the way here, and it was pretty rough. Often on the ship I wished that you could have been with me, for I know how much you enjoy playing sailor. Brother, you can have it. We were at sea quite a long time, stopping at a couple of places I can't mention, but I had already been to both. I saw more ships than ever before and just about every type we have. I'll bet you thought I was headed for Iwo since I left about that time from where the ships were gathering for that one.

After we pulled in here, we sat off Naha a couple of days before coming ashore. While there, we had a grandstand seat for some beautiful shelling by battleships, cruisers and destroyers. The big boys would pull up fairly close to our ship, drop anchor, swing into position, and let 'em have it. They were not far off shore, maybe five miles at the most. A few Jap planes would sneak through and dive for a ship. Our gunners on my troopship shot down one zeroed in on us. That one is now in the East China Sea.

* "90 Days of Operation Tactical Air Force Ryukyus, April 7–July 6, 1945," Claude R. "Red" Canup Collection.

Marines and tractors teaming up to rescue plane from the mud at Yontan Airfield, Okinawa, 1945. Photograph by T. Sgt. Charles V. Corkran, DPR with MAG 31. Claude R. "Red" Canup Collection.

Although the foot troops (Marines and Army) beat us ashore by a few days, those of us in aviation have had no picnic. Things have been rough, and a few nights I dared not leave my hole in the ground. It is a big hole, and sometimes I feel mighty small in it. There is not much top on top of it, and I can see the ack-ack fired at planes spotted by the search lights. It is some sight, one which you saw in the other war. I suppose, however, we've much more to throw at them than you ever dreamed of. Here we have the advantage of the fleet off shore, and those ships are not sparing the ammo. They've been a big help on the islands.

The rains came and I can't even describe the mud except it is ankle deep and like walking through a newly plowed cotton field after a rain. The mud may not be as red as at home, but tractors have had to pull planes out. It goes over the tops of shoes if you get off the packed mud roads and it seems to never dry out. There is something to be said for coral islands.

Our chow is not the best, but finally we've quit having to exist on K-rations. You know I have never liked stew or soup. Tomorrow I plan to eat with a CB outfit on the other side of the field. They're having steak and ice cream. Imagine that! Steak and ice cream always tasted better than stew and soup.

KIRKPATRICK ACES

Captain Floyd C. Kirkpatrick, 26, flying with the Black Jack squadron of the 2ndMAW, recently became an ace. Shooting down three enemy planes from his Corsair plus the two and a half kills from the Samoan area gives the pilot ace status.

He is a graduate of Klamath Union High School and attended the University of Oregon, commissioned April 1942. (17Apr45)

BLACK JACK'S WHITEAKER SCORES

Second Lieutenant Clay H. Whiteaker, a pilot in the crack Black Jack squadron, recently returned safely from a mission in which he shot down one Jap plane and shared a second with another pilot.

Graduating from West Lafayette High School in Lafayette, Ind., Lieutenant Whiteaker attended Purdue. He was commissioned December 19, 1943. (17Apr45)

EMERGENCY LANDING

Navy Lieutenant Clellean B. McAfee, Robertsdale, Ala., made an emergency landing on Yontan Airfield. His carrier-based Hellcat was hit by ack-ack while the 28-year-old southerner was artillery spotting in support of infantry. He is a graduate of Tri State College. (17Apr45)

LUCKY BIRTHDAY

Happy landing and lucky birthday gave dual reasons for Navy Lieutenant (jg) James E. Daly to celebrate today.

A carrier based pilot from Stoneham, Mass., Daly observed his 23rd birthday with an emergency landing on Yontan Airfield. Flying artillery observation over the island, his plane was damaged by ack-ack forcing him down here. Finding a handy airfield in friendly territory insured a very happy birthday for the young Navy pilot. (17Apr45)

PILOT SAVED

Second Lieutenant Edgar L. Rafferty and Private First Class Marvin A. Walker rescued a leatherneck pilot from a burning plane in the early phases of aerial operations on Yontan Airfield.

The Marines exposed themselves to the danger of exploding ammunition. Bombs and rockets nearby increased the risk they took. They were commended by their commanding officer for this action.

Lieutenant Rafferty is from Seal Beach, Calif., and Private Walker is from Hutchinson, Kan. (17Apr45)

ELDRIDGE SPLASHES FOUR ON PATROL

Four enemy planes on one combat patrol is the record of Second Lieutenant William W. Eldridge flying with the crack Black Jack squadron.

A resident of Hixon, Tenn., the Hixon High School graduate attended the University of Chattanooga before entering the service. (17Apr45)

THREE SPLASHES FOR MCGINTY

Second Lieutenant Selva E. McGinty, flying combat patrol in his Corsair recently bagged three Jap planes when his Black Jack squadron shot down 15 enemy bombers and fighters in 15 minutes in one of the greatest attacks in 2ndMAW history.

The 21-year-old-resident of Stillwell, Okla., attended El Reno (Okla.) Junior College and was employed by the Hamburger Inn before entering the Navy July 1942. He was commissioned August 1943. (17Apr45)

*Lieutenant McGinty became the nineteenth marine ace of the Okinawa campaign on June 8, 1945.**

LINE MARINES INSPECT PLANE

It doesn't happen very often, but Third Marine Amphibious Corps members Private First Class William J. Morrison, Jr., Delanco, N.J., and Private First Class Anthony J. Toscano, Brooklyn, N.Y., came down from the lines in

* "90 Days of Operation Tactical Air Force Ryukyus, April 7–July 6, 1945," Claude R. "Red" Canup Collection.

time to see firsthand what the enemy has been throwing at warships and heavy bombers which are supporting ground troops.

Rocket suicide planes, some in crates, were found on this airfield before the enemy was able to fly them. The crated planes were rushed to the United States for examination by technical experts.

The little suicide craft has an approximate wing span of 16 feet and carries an estimated load of 2,000 pounds of TNT sealed in the nose. It is propelled by three rocket tubes in the tail with five to six minutes duration. (17Apr45)

FLAG FADES

The area around Yontan Airfield is now occupied by the crack Hell's Belles fighter squadron instead of the Japs. Recently Lieutenant George Lee Newton, Memphis, Tenn., discovered a dugout still flying the fading flag of the Rising Sun at the front door—no one was home. (17Apr45)

COPPEDGE'S SPLASHES TWO PLUS NIP PLANES

Second Lieutenant Charles H. Coppedge, Halifax, N.C., had a personal score to settle with the Japs and wasted no time doing it.

The 26-year-old fighter pilot of the famous Black Jack squadron was shot down over Izene Island by enemy ack-ack. He bailed out, landed in the sea, and was rescued in a few hours by an LST. Even then the Japs stayed in his hair, two suicide planes crashing near the ship as it steamed toward Okinawa.

On his next patrol after returning to his squadron, Coppedge shot down two enemy planes and received credit with another pilot for sending a third down in flames. He was the only pilot of four to return.

A resident of Weldon, N.C., he attended Cowan College and was employed by a civil engineering firm working with the State Highway Commission before entering the service. He was commissioned October 1943. (17Apr45)

FIREWORKS OVER OKINAWA

Leathernecks of Major General Francis P. Mulcahy's 2ndMAW tonight saw one of the most brilliant displays of ack-ack thrown into Pacific skies by American batteries. The occasion was a Japanese raid on Yontan Airfield and also against ships in the harbor. The airfield is a mile from the beach.

When the Japs came over, batteries surrounding the field opened up. Soon other Nip planes were over the harbor, and guns from units of the fleet and cargo ships joined the attack. Together, the sea and shore installations threw up a blanket of fire. Several of the attacking planes were shot down.

Few bombs were dropped on the field. There also was little strafing. Thus Marines in their foxholes witnessed the fireworks in comparative safety. (18Apr45)

KILL BY NIGHT FIGHTERS

Second Lieutenants Arthur J. Arceneaux, Jr., Gramercy, La., and William W. Campbell, McCook, Neb., both shot down their first Jap plane on their first missions over Okinawa. The two Jap planes and pilots ended their flights in the East China Sea.

The night fighters, along with the day fighters, operating off Yontan Airfield since the early phases of the Okinawa campaign have accounted for over 30 enemy bombers and fighters in the first few days of patrol. Heavily armed Corsairs also supported leathernecks on the ground with strikes against Jap strongholds in the hills.

The lieutenants received several months of night combat air patrol experience on Ulithi with MAG 45 in the Western Carolines defending the fleet anchorage before the Tigers squadron transferred here with MAG 31.

Second Lieutenant Arceneaux is credited as the first pilot of his night fighter squadron to shoot down a Japanese plane from Okinawa. (20Apr45)

TWO FOR KAYSER

First Lieutenant Dale W. Kayser, 21, San Francisco, Calif., is the first pilot of the crack Hell's Belles fighter squadron to shoot down two Japanese planes in the Okinawa campaign.

The Californian, flying a Corsair off Yontan Airfield, which MAG 31 occupied a few days after leathernecks hit the beach a mile away on Easter Sunday, bagged a Hamp and Zeke—Jap fighter planes—on two separate patrols. He shot them into the sea.

He attended Orestimba High School at Newman, Calif., and his aviator wings were pinned July 1943. (20Apr45)

OKINAWA
APRIL 21, 1945

You probably know more about what is going on at the front than I do, or down South. I have met a number of correspondents and that is the reason I fell so far behind in my writing. They come first.

One of those little bastards—or somebody shooting at them—put a hole in my tent. When it rains here, it really rains and I haven't been dry since. The other night I said to hell with them and stayed in my damp sack. When the raid alert sounded, I hit the ground damn fast—blanket and all—for they strafed the airfield and laid down a string of bombs before I knew what was going on. I figured they wouldn't come back, got back in the sack under two blankets and was asleep when the next raid came. Again, I repeated the performance of the first raid except this time I cracked my head on a box. So there I lay, blood running down my forehead and my body pressed as close to the ground as I could get it. From then on, I was fully dressed and waiting for them. It gets cold here just like autumn at home; and even with my clothes and two blankets, I won't be too warm. I have slept with my clothes off once during the past couple of weeks or so, and then I didn't leave them off long.

It has gotten to the place now that I catch myself cringing whenever one of our own planes comes over at night. After all, there is no assurance that it is friendly. These Orientals are full of tricks and are turning the pages fast now pulling new ones out. Pretty soon they will be at the end of the book and we should be bothered with only air raids. That of course is plenty.

Don't let anyone kid you about life in aviation. Since we got here we have just about lived in damp, cold foxholes. Our positions have been well within mortar shell range and those damn Nips know it. So do the Kamikaze bombers. The boys are doing great, but don't let anybody tell you aviation is easy living with good chow.

Some of the pilots think I should bunk with them since they take up so much of my time. I could have a hell of a lot more comfort than I have, and could get all the liquor I want, and some of the guys want to know why the hell I don't take everything I can get. They don't realize that if I took those things it would piss off half of them.

What's wrong with the boys in Europe? Somebody is putting out a lot of bum information here. Twice already I have celebrated the end of the European war. I went over to one of the fighter squadrons and celebrated Russia's declaration of war against Japan with a pilot friend. We did it up royally only to find out the next day that it was nothing but scuttlebutt and that the war in Europe was not over and that Russia was not at war with Japan. Two nights later the pilot was killed. That was the biggest blow I have had here. He was a swell guy, real pal of enlisted men. Don't find many like him.

During my hops from place to place I have missed boxes and letters and my watch is traveling somewhere. No pipe yet, either.

B-29 AT OKINAWA

When Frisco Nanny made her unscheduled appearance on Yontan Airfield the Marines flocked around her like she was a USO show featuring Betty

Grable. Frisco Nanny is a B-29 and she limped to the nearest American base to Japan with two of her four engines on the blink. She was on a bombing mission from Saipan to Kyushu but turned back 100 miles from the target when the second engine knocked out. The first one failed 50 miles earlier. This was the first super fort landing on Okinawa.

"The strip is plenty adequate for B-29 landings," said Army Lieutenant Colonel William E. Robertson, Houston, Tex., plane commander. The giant bomber was flown here by Captain Robert Corday, Columbus, O. She was on her 12th bombing mission over Japan.

Engines were flown from Guam by Marine transport air group planes for Frisco Nanny's repair. The plane and other super forts have been bombing an airfield on Kyushu, which is the staging center for Jap raids on Okinawa. (23Apr45)

OKINAWA PRESS CLUB IS POPULAR

Marine Corps public relations personnel of MAG 31 on Yontan Airfield open the Okinawa Press Club to visiting war correspondents and photographers as well as transient pilots. The club's operators are combat correspondents James H. Driscoll, New York City, and Claude R. Canup, Anderson, S.C., along with combat photographer Charles V. Corkran, Flint, Mich.

During the shelling, bombing, and strafing of Yontan Airfield, civilian and service correspondents alike crowd into a "family size" foxhole in back of the press tent along with visiting pilots. Before leaving, visitors autograph and pose in front of the "Okinawa Press Club" sign. Visitors have included:

Sergeant Joe Donahue, formerly of the Naugatuck (Conn.) News.

Staff Sergeant James F. Moser, Jr., formerly of the Washington, D.C. Evening Star.

Second Lieutenant Milburn McCarty, formerly of the New Yorker Magazine.

Staff Sergeant Peter B. Germano, magazine writer, formerly of the New Bedford (Mass.) Standard-Times.

Captain William C. Brennan formerly of the New York World-Telegram.

Staff Sergeant Thomas P. Carson formerly of General Electric Radio Division, Chicago.

Private Roger Roberts formerly of Radio Station KLS, Oakland, Calif.

Captain Herbert Merillet, formerly of the Treasury Department, Washington, D.C.

Second Lieutenant Diggory Venn, formerly of the San Francisco Chronicle. (23Apr45)

Second Marine Aircraft Wing night fighter Herbert Groff (left) being congratulated by CBS correspondent Tim Leimert, Yontan Airfield, Okinawa, 1945. Photograph by T. Sgt. Charles V. Corkran, DPR with MAG 31. Claude R. "Red" Canup Collection.

BLIND DATE WITH BETTY

First Lieutenant Herbert Groff had a blind date with Betty. She was difficult to locate. When he finally found her, he stayed on her trail, kept the appointment, and returned to Yontan Airfield quite satisfied with the night's accomplishments.

Betty is a Jap twin-engine bomber, and Lieutenant Groff, who was flying midnight combat patrol, was vectored to her. She gave him the run around for 65 miles, but he caught her about 100 miles from Yontan.

"First time I saw her she was about 50 yards directly in front of my plane," explained the former school teacher of Summerfield, Mo. The first burst from his guns set the Jap bomber on fire and she went down flaming with her crew.

It was the first plane shot down here by blind control by a night fighter in MAG 31. Other night fighters of the squadron have planes to their credit, bagging them on dusk to dawn patrols.

Lieutenant Groff was promoted from second lieutenant the day he went up on his successful midnight patrol. (23Apr45)

DIFFERENT POINT OF VIEW

It's all in the way you look at a thing.

Our greatest invasion fleet may have been a thing of beauty to admirals, and it left a visible impression on the defenders of Okinawa. Shortly after D-day, a tired, mud-covered Marine stood on a hill overlooking the harbor filled with ships.

He remarked dryly, "Just think of all the champagne they wasted on the bows of them ships." (27Apr45)

MARINES LIKE PUNISHMENT

Found on Okinawa is a cousin of the man who cut off his nose to spite his face.

He is a mess sergeant with a fighter squadron on this airfield. He doesn't like to bother with ice cream, but somebody made a point of getting the freezer set up quickly in the galley.

"Just for that," coldly threatened the sergeant, "I'm going to feed them ice cream every day for two weeks until it runs out their ears."

The stuff he calls ice cream wouldn't pass for a reasonable facsimile back home. It's the kind that won't run out the ears—not at the end of two weeks, anyway. (27Apr45)

OKINAWA LIKE HOME

Despite all its drawbacks, this island has touched a soft spot in the hearts of Marines who have seen just about all of them from Guadalcanal on up.

This is the only one which really reminds them of home. Full of hills and valleys with their spring coat of leaves and flowers, many parts of the island could be removed to practically any state in the union and not look out of place.

But the comparison ends there. Even though Okinawa is not a tropical island, it is plagued with Oriental diseases and has too generous a supply of flies, fleas, and mosquitoes that carry malaria and were encountered in other Pacific campaigns. (27Apr45)

NOT ENOUGH JAPS

Being as close as they are to the Jap mainland, it would seem that fighter pilots of the 2ndMAW would be getting enough combat. They have been operating here less than a month and have shot down over 100 bombers and fighters. They still want more targets.

Night fighter pilots are grumpy and grouchy because day fighters come up with the dawn and crowd the field. Best time to flush a covey of bogeys is by the dawn's early light they say. The day fighters in turn claim that they are being denied kills by carrier-based planes, complaining that "not enough Japs are getting through to us."

Who would have thought? (27Apr45)

JUST A JOE BLOW

Mud in front of the press tent on Yontan Airfield was already ankle deep, and the rain kept coming. Crowding in the pyramid tent for protection against the elements, a dozen or so pilots and correspondents sat around making new friends and spinning favorite yarns.

Commando pilot 1st Lt. Tyrone Power being interviewed by Red Canup, Okinawa, 1945. Claude R. "Red" Canup Collection.

A Navy combat photographer sharing a box with an unshaven, mud caked Marine pilot turned to him and asked, "What did you do before coming into the service?"

"I made pictures," replied Marine First Lieutenant Tyrone Power, West Los Angeles, Calif., commando pilot and former actor. The inquiring photographer was Leif Erickson, also a former actor from Los Angeles. (27Apr45)

BUNK MATES

Marine boots who were caught with dirty rifles have been known to sleep with their M1 rifles at the command of hard-boiled drill instructors. That was considered by rookies as carrying things too far.

Drill instructors from Parris Island, S.C., to San Diego, Calif., would get a chuckle—a serious one—because of the sights here. With snipers roaming at night, Marines are certain of one thing before they hit the sack—they make sure their rifles are tucked in right beside them. (27Apr45)

LIZARDS SWAPPED FOR FLEAS

If circus flea trainers want to go in for the trade on a wholesale basis, they should come to Okinawa.

A combat photographer walked through a pine grove, and when he returned to his tent he discovered fleas on his pants from the knees down. Counting every one he picked off, he reported there were exactly 207.

His tent mates took his word for it. They fled at the count of one. (27Apr45)

COLONEL SAVES FACE

A Chinese war correspondent from Chungking has been of assistance to a Marine colonel from Seattle over the matter of a Japanese monument on Yontan Airfield.

Colonel Joseph P. Adams, Seattle, Wash., is the deputy commander in charge of naval air bases. Several times daily he had been asked by transient pilots the meaning of the inscription on the monument. "It has become very embarrassing when I admit I don't know," explained the Colonel.

Then Chuchiping arrived on Yontan. He is a war correspondent for Ta Kung Pao newspaper, Chungking, China. Colonel Adams' jovial face beamed when he saw Chuchiping. He showed the correspondent the monument and asked him to the translate inscriptions on the slab. Literal interpretation in

English, said Chuchiping, is that the stately monument is a memorial to fallen Japanese heroes.

Now, Colonel Adams waits for visitors to ask about the monument and then says quite proudly, "Let me explain the inscription to you." (27Apr45)

SIGLER IS NIGHT FIGHTER ACE

Captain Wallace E. Sigler, 24, became an ace today 15 minutes after midnight. The Brooklyn, N.Y., native who flew with the famous Wolf Pack squadron in the south Pacific in 1943 and bagged four Jap planes on his first tour in the Solomons, got Number Five while flying night combat air patrol over Okinawa.

It was his first mission over this island, and he had been up less than an hour when he was vectored to the enemy plane, a fighter known as a Tony.

"When I got on his tail," related the Captain, who also is executive officer of his night fighter squadron the Tigers, "I first saw him about 50 yards ahead. I chased him about five minutes and fired three bursts, the third one setting him afire. He was in flames when he fell out of sight."

Captain Sigler shot down the first four as a day fighter. He doesn't see a great deal of difference in hunting them by day or night. "It took more to make this one burn," he said, referring to his midnight kill. Although the moon was full, the Marine ace was never able to see the Tony pilot. The Japs had taken advantage of the bright moon light night to bomb Yontan Airfield, where Sigler's squadron is based. The plane he blasted out of the sky was returning from the raid.

Two of the five planes Captain Sigler has shot down were float bi-planes, and the others were fighters. He came back for his second tour of duty last September, and put in several months of night combat patrol in the Western Carolines prior to the Okinawa operation. Captain Sigler, Scarsdale, N.Y., holds the Air Medal for the first two enemy planes shot down June 5, 1943.

The Captain's stay here has been eventful from the beginning. A few days after landing, he was advised that he had become the father of a girl, born April 11. The baby has been named Jeanette.

He attended Dartmouth College, where he played lacrosse. (28Apr45)

INTERPRETER NOT NEEDED

When a leatherneck spent too much time turning the pages of a Japanese magazine, fellow Marines reminded him that he was wasting time—he could not read Jap.

"I can't read it, but I can look at the pictures." He replied.

It was a Jap movie magazine full of Marines' favorites—pin-ups. (28Apr45)

MABEY BAGS THREE

Marine Second Lieutenant Howard R. Mabey, 23, Hinsdale, N.Y., a fighter pilot stationed at Yontan Airfield and his plane crew have together relieved the Jap air force of three enemy pilots and planes. He gives accolades to his plane captain Corporal Eugene J. Neff, Buffalo, N.Y., for keeping the plane ready to fly on a moment's notice. Lieutenant Mabey came overseas last summer and had flown combat patrol in the Marshalls. (28Apr45)

RUSHFELDT BAGS THREE

First Lieutenant Collin Rushfeldt, 22, Albert Lea, Minn., recently got in the range of Jap planes off Okinawa and made the most of his opportunity.

In a 24-hour period, the young Corsair pilot in the Fighting Wildcats squadron knocked down three Jap planes—two twin engine bombers and one dive bomber—on patrol off Okinawa.

He attended Albert Lea Junior College before enlisting for flight training. (28Apr45)

CENTRAL HIGH SCHOOL'S PLANE SCORES

Second Lieutenant Marvin Bristow, of Houston, Tex., proudly flies a Corsair carrying a cockpit plaque stating it was paid for by the proceeds of war bond purchases by the students of Central High School, Bridgeport, Conn. The pilot made his first kill—a Jap Zero—using the plane.

Previously in bombing operations in the Marshall Islands, the plane had been credited with sinking three Jap ships. (28Apr45)

KUNZ AT YONTAN

Major Charles Kunz, Springfield, Mo., is the Operations Officer of MAG 31. He came to the Yontan Airfield an ace. This is Major Kunz's third major battle since the beginning of Pacific hostilities. In 1942 he participated in the battles of Midway and Guadalcanal, where he was credited with shooting down eight enemy planes.

Before moving into the western Pacific with his aviation unit, Major Kunz was commanding officer of the Marine fighter squadron Hell's Belles then operating in the Marshall Islands.

MAG 31 pilots have already engaged in nearly 4,000 combat sorties in almost 10,000 flight hours clearing the western Pacific skies of 120 enemy planes.

Major Kunz is a graduate of Monett High School and attended Southwest State College, Springfield, Mo. He was flying instructor with the Morgan Flying Service at the Springfield Municipal Airport before joining the Marines October 1940. (28Apr45)

FIGHTING WILDCATS COMMANDER

Major James W. Poindexter, 25, Stevensville, Mont., is squadron commander of the Fighting Wildcat Corsair squadron operating from Yontan.

Veteran of the war in the south Pacific, Major Poindexter assumed command of the squadron eight months ago when he came overseas for the second time. Since the beginning of operations here, his squadron has been credited with knocking down 40 enemy planes in the Ryukyu Islands area.

A graduate of Stevensville High School, Major Poindexter attended the University of Montana at Missoula before entering the Corps September 1940. (28Apr45)

ADDED EXCITEMENT FOR CARLTON

Downing a Jap Zeke while flying only 500 feet above the sea in the blackness of an Oriental night is exciting even for a night fighter pilot and Second Lieutenant Del W. Carlton admits he was a happy man when he landed his Hellcat on Yontan Airfield.

Flying with a squadron in the 2ndMAW, the 22-year-old from Emily, Minn., was on midnight combat patrol when he was vectored to the Zeke.

"I was flying at about 800 feet under an overcast sky 70 miles northwest of Yontan," Carlton related, "when I first saw the Zeke. He was 1,000 feet above and ahead of me. He must have spotted me at about the same time because he went into a steep turn. I had him lined up almost before I knew it and let him have three bursts. He was down low and did not flare until he splashed. The action lasted only a few seconds. It was over so soon I barely realized what had happened," gushed the young pilot.

Lieutenant Carlton received his wings October 1943 and was a student before entering the service. He is a graduate of Soudan High School and attended Crosby Ironton Junior college. (30Apr45)

BLAKENEY'S RECORD GROWS

Give Captain John W. Blakeney, III, credit for two Vals. Flying dusk patrol with the Hell's Belles squadron, the pilot shot down his second Jap torpedo bomber in the first three weeks of this campaign. The Captain was one of the first pilots in his squadron to have a Jap flag painted on his Corsair when he downed his first Val. (30Apr45)

COMMANDER RECEIVES CERTIFICATE

Marine Lieutenant Colonel Leo R. Smith, San Diego, Calif., Yontan air base commander, is proud of the tremendous expanse of this newly won airfield. Colonel Smith is former commanding officer of the Aces of Spades famous dive-bomber squadron which won its reputation on Guadalcanal.

The Colonel received an honorary membership certificate as an apprentice seaman in a Seabee unit based at Yontan Airfield, Okinawa. The Seabee unit certificate read: "This will certify that Lieutenant Colonel Leo R. Smith, USMC, having demonstrated ability in operating a cherry picker, qualifies as an apprentice seaman in the Seabees and is hereby awarded that rank in our unit." (30Apr45)

DOUBLE ZERO

Second Lieutenant Theodore A. Brown is holding his own with the fast pace set in combat patrols by squadrons operating off Yontan Airfield.

The 22-year-old native of Columbus, O., has shot two Zeros out of the battle for Okinawa. Flying a Corsair equipped with 20mm cannons, the former student of Ohio State University said the Zeros were no match for the F4U and its firing power. Most pilots return with the same general story: "When we hit them they just seem to fall apart."

Lieutenant Brown has been overseas since last winter. In addition to flying, he is assistant transportation officer of the squadron. (30Apr45)

CASE OF THE PROUD TEACHER

The professor came to Okinawa today, saw the great record his former students had chalked up against the Japs, and left proudly.

The professor is Marine First Lieutenant Eugene C. White, 27-year-old from Dallas, Texas. Now flying transport planes from the Marianas, he was formerly an instructor at the Marine Corps Air Station at El Toro, Calif.

The former students are fighter pilots of the 2ndMAW. The professor recognized six names on the group's scoreboard. The six former students had shot down 11 bombers and fighters in the first three weeks of operations off Yontan Airfield.

Leading the list is Second Lieutenant William W. Eldridge, Jr., 22, of Hixon, Tenn., with four planes. He bagged them in one afternoon's work when the combat air patrol ran into a swarm of Japs headed toward Okinawa. The raiding party was shot into the sea.

Professor White did not try to conceal the surprise plainly showing on his face when he saw Eldridge's name at the top of the board. It was genuine.

"I didn't think Eldridge would ever make a fighter pilot," confessed White. "He was the type that learns fast enough, but he just didn't seem to care. He was easy going and took very little interest."

White grinned proudly, and as an afterthought added, "But he seems to take plenty of interest in his work out here." (2May45)

SOMETHING NEW HAS BEEN ADDED—CLOTHES

The weather on Okinawa is just as unpredictable as the enemy—and it is causing more trouble than the Japs.

Pilots and ground personnel of the 2ndMAW were stationed in the Marshalls and Carolines for the most part before coming to the Nansei Shoto. Back there the weather was mild the year round. That is putting it mildly when, as a matter of fact, it was hot on those islands all the time.

In the Marshalls and Carolines the men were "dressed up" when they wore shirts. Shoes and shorts were the uniform of the day.

Some change in the climate was noted here when Marines came ashore the first of April. A khaki shirt felt comfortable during the day, and a wind-breaker helped cut the chill in foxholes during the night.

Then came the merry month of May and with it an east wind that blew in a cold rain. Quartermaster equipment was broken out quickly, and Marines were comfortable again—wearing long underwear, flannel shirt, utility jacket and a poncho. Not to mention woolen socks.

Also, came the latest mail from back home—letters reading something like this: "We have been enjoying mild weather for the past week. It has been real warm for this time of the year, but nothing compared to the heat you must endure on those Pacific islands." (2May45)

TURLEY LEADING THE LEADERS

First Lieutenant Norman A. Turley, 24, New Rochelle, N.Y., almost became an ace in less than a month of flying in the Okinawa theatre. Early in the campaign Turley broke into the scoring with a dive-bomber to his credit. Today, Turley bagged a fighter and another dive-bomber on the dawn patrol after coming in last night from the dusk patrol with a sleek twin-engine Jap bomber to his credit. As Lieutenant Turley puts it, "They get in our way and down they go."

Part of the 2ndMAW, his and other Corsair squadrons are cutting down the size of the Japanese air force daily. Practically every enemy fighter and bomber making passes at our ships are being intercepted by Marine fighters. In a 16-hour period, the Hell's Belles squadron, commanded by Major Perry L. Shuman, shot down eight bombers and fighters.

Jap planes are easy prey also for Marine pilots having a field day north and west of Yontan on dawn and dusk patrols. Equipped with 20mm guns, the Corsairs are making quick work of bombers and fighters alike. (4May45)

HAMNER'S FOURTH

Second Lieutenant Roland R. Hamner, flying with Hell's Belles squadron on Yontan Airfield, is shooting down his share of Jap planes.

The 22-year-old from Gastonia, N.C., was in a four-plane patrol this week that intercepted 11 Japanese planes 50 miles southwest of Naha. Disregarding odds of 11 to 4—about three per Marine—the Hell's Belles pilots engaged the enemy splashing eight sleek Tonys and three twin-engine Dinahs. Two of the Tonys and one Dinah were shot out of the sky by Hamner who had a dive-bomber already to his credit in the earlier mission. None of the enemy planes escaped, and the four Marines returned safely to Yontan after dark. (5May45)

BROWN FROM TEXAS IS ACE

Slender, boyish-faced First Lieutenant William P. Brown splashed four Jap planes—two fighters and two twin-engine bombers—on May 4. Those four planes, plus two single-engine bombers shot down less than a week before, made him an ace with one to spare.

When Brown excitedly detailed the four planes in one night to the intelligence officer, Captain Stuart W. Cragin, Greenwich, Conn., he said, "We were flying at about 9,000 feet 50 miles west of Naha, when we spotted the Japs just below us."

"How many were there?" inquired the intelligence officer.

"Eleven," answered the Texan from Kilgore.

"How many did you engage?"

"All of them!" Brown almost shouted. He was excited, bright-eyed—like a high school boy who had just made his first touchdown.

So with odds of almost three to one against him and each of his pilots, Brown's four-man team of Corsairs tackled 11 of the best planes the Japs are sending up these days—Tonys and Dinahs—the former a fast single-engine fighter, and the latter a reconnaissance plane which has been identified as possibly one of the carriers of the Baca, Jap piloted flying suicide rocket bomb.

Brown reported that the Corsairs turned easily inside the Tonys, which were extremely fast. At one point he was describing how he outmaneuvered a Dinah to send her down in flames.

"Where did you hit her?" he was interrupted.

"From stem to stern," he grinned.

But there were no shots wasted. The 11 Japs were splashed with 1,500 rounds, averaging less than 150 rounds per target. The Japs, flying in formation, were headed toward Marine airfields on Okinawa, and ships in the harbor.

All the Texan's planes were shot down on dusk patrols.

Lieutenant Brown's six top the scoreboard of the Hell's Belles squadron. The new ace was trained by his commanding officer, Major Perry L. Shuman, and came overseas with him last winter from El Centro, Calif.

Lieutenant Brown, who was commissioned at Pensacola, Fla., exactly two years after the start of the Pacific war, chose to fly with the Marines from that date "because I wanted to fly with land-based squadrons, and too, because the Marine aviators were doing such a good job at the time in the south Pacific." He volunteered another reason, explaining that "my instructor in pre-flight school was a Marine."

How did he feel while knocking down those four planes? "I got a hell of a kick, and the hell scared out of me," the ace confessed. (5May45)

SARK INITIATED INTO COMBAT

It is a long jump from Osage to Okinawa, and now that Second Lieutenant Thomas H. Sark is here he has found it more exciting than anything he had ever read about the Orient.

Shortly after landing on this Japanese island to fly with the Hell's Belles squadron, the Oklahoma native went on his first combat air patrol. He came back with a hole in the right wing of his Corsair big enough for three or four men to stand in. Ack-ack did it. Although he was 60 miles from his base, the Okinawa rookie brought his F4U back home without additional damage, only the left aileron worked.

Six hours after he landed, the Corsair was operational again with a new wing.

The next day's patrol was uneventful for Sark.

On his third mission, a dusk patrol, he was initiated into air combat. Flying with three other Corsairs, the four Marines, all young southerners just old enough to vote by the old standard, dived on a formation of enemy planes.

They streaked in and out of clouds until it was so dark that only silhouettes of the planes were visible. When the shooting was over, Nippon was short almost a dozen of its best aircraft with no damage sustained by the flying Marines' Corsairs.

Tom Sark, who admitted he was "just plain scared" when he was almost shot down on his first mission, showed he could take care of himself in the air. He splashed two Tonys, depositing them into the East China Sea with bursts of his four 20mm cannons. (5May45)

G-MAN GETS JAP PLANE

A former fingerprint expert with the Federal Bureau of Investigation in Washington is becoming a different kind of expert at Okinawa. He does not bother with minute details in dealing with Jap fliers. He simply has to spot an enemy plane, get it in the sight of his 20mm cannons and press the trigger.

Such is the Oriental career of former G-Man Jack M. Rothweiler, a first lieutenant fighter pilot who is flying with the Hell's Belles squadron. He shot down a dive bomber in a dawn patrol early this month when his division of Corsairs intercepted several enemy planes 50 miles west of Yontan Airfield. The Japs, flying Vals which are making one-way trips to this new American base and its attendant shipping, were headed straight toward our ships in that vicinity.

Lieutenant Rothweiler, who received his wings almost two years ago, is a graduate of Palmyra High School in Missouri and attended Southeast Missouri State Teachers' College at Cape Girardeau. (5May45)

AIR RAID ON YONTAN IN VERSE

Pharmacist's Mate Third Class Francis W. Tremblay, 20, Lebanon, N.H., has used poetry to describe his feelings about the constant air raids. He came into the service on his 18th birthday.

Air Raid on Yontan

The siren blew its moaning sound,
We crawled in the hole beneath the ground;

But here and there from sand bagged mound
Eyes peering toward the sky were found.

The moon, a yellow ball on high,
Made daylight of ground and sky;
And as the sounds of firing grew nearer,
Our fox holes to our heart grew dearer.

And in our holes we crouched with fear
As high above the planes grew near.
We shook, and yet it wasn't cold;
In the tense seconds men grew old.

Then suddenly we heard the sound
And felt the trembling of the ground.
The next one closer, then closer still,
And then an awful pause until—

A blinding sheet of flame ahead
The sky was painted gory red.
And sheets of flame came raining down
Into our fox holes beneath the ground.

And inches from the place we sat
The phosphorus crackled on the mat
Of straw we'd laid upon the dirt,
And yet we found no one was hurt.

Then further on another roar came;
Then silence except for the crackling flame.
And then we breathed a welcome sigh—
It was not yet our turn to die.

Heads silently rose above the ground
To see what damage could be found.
A blackened wreck that to a Marine
Once was home could be seen.

And holes and rips and rents
Could be seen in other tents.

We looked to see where the bomb fell
That made a life such earthly hell.

A hole in the ground, a lot of smoke,
We looked in silence; no one spoke.
We gazed like people in a spell
At where that fateful missile fell.

It had been a fox hole just before,
Water-filled, but now no more.
But where the bomb had just exploded
The walls with damp dirt now were loaded.

The owners stood by with ashen face.
Glad they'd been another place;
Praising He who rules all space,
And cursing them of another race.

What whim had God that spared their life?
Had not made widow of a wife?
So we picked shrapnel from our beds
And on the pillow laid our heads.

And slept ourselves a restless sleep,
Dreams of those who lonely vigil keep;
Waiting, waiting while we roam,
Waiting for us to come home.
Albert Tremblay, PhM3c, USNR (11May45)

FLYING BROTHERS MEET

Two brothers, both Marine pilots, met for the first time in six months today on Yontan Airfield. The Turley brothers—First Lieutenants Norman A. and James A.—are originally from Rochelle, N.Y. Norman, 24, Santa Barbara, Calif., flies with the crack Hell's Belles Corsair squadron. James, 26, is a transport pilot stationed in the Marianas.

Lieutenant James A. Turley, ferrying fighter planes to Okinawa, brought two of his brother's classmates from Corpus Christi's advanced flight school with him. First Lieutenant Floyd W. Johnson, 26, Minneapolis, Minn., and First Lieutenant H. Douglas Byles, 22, San Marino, Calif. The reunion gave the pilots an opportunity to celebrate the four Jap planes credited to Marine First Lieutenant Norman A. Turley. (11May45)

HELL'S BELLES, WHAT A RECORD!

Hell's Belles, a Corsair fighter squadron in MAG 31 based on Yontan Airfield, is making news on Okinawa. The squadron is shooting the Jap sky course much better than par.

The Corsairs in the squadron are first in the number of hours flown at Yontan in the initial month. They were up 500 hours over any other squadron on the field. And, they are first in the number of enemy planes splashed in the first 30 days of operation. The majority of Japs splashed by Hell's Belles are now at the bottom of the East China Sea 50 to 75 miles west and northwest of Naha.

Here's their score against the Japs in 30 days: Hell's Belles 41, Japs 0.

The squadron flew 3,141 hours on 975 combat missions including combat air patrol, escorts, protection for ships, and air support to ground troops pushing across the southern end of Okinawa. The pilots used strafing, bombing and rockets. Each pilot averaged flying 75 hours this month.

Planes from this squadron flew fighter escort protection for the transport that brought Admiral Chester Nimitz, Commander of the Navy, and General A. A. Vandegrift, Commandant of the Marine Corps, to Okinawa.

Hell's Belles' squadron statistics and the following box scores were prepared by Captain Stuart W. Cragin, intelligence officer, Greenwich, Conn., and Private Emerson N. Stewart, 27, clerk, Knoxville, Tenn.

Pilot	Jap Planes
Second Lieutenant William P. Brown, 21 Kilgore, Tex.	2-dive-bombers, 2-fighters, 2-reconnaissance bombers
Second Lieutenant Roland R. Hamner, 22 Gastonia, N.C.	1-dive bomber, 2-fighters 1-reconnaissance-bomber
First Lieutenant Norman A. Turley, 24 Santa Barbara, Calif.	1-twin-engine-bomber, 1-fighter, 2-dive-bombers
Captain Ralph G. McCormick, 26 Detroit, Mich.	1-dive-bomber ½–2-engine-bomber
Second Lieutenant Robert K. Sherrill, 24 Pecos, Tex.	1-dive-bomber
Captain Gilman B. Rood, 26 Burlington, Vt.	1-dive-bomber
Second Lieutenant Lawrence E. Whiteside, 21 Drumright, Okla.	1-dive-bomber
Captain John W. Blakeney, 24 Newton, Mass.	2-dive-bombers
Second Lieutenant Donald H. Clark, 21 Champaign, Ill.	2-dive-bombers

(table continued)

Pilot	Jap Planes
Captain Raymond F. Scherer, 29 Wilmington, Calf.	1-fighter, ½-fighter
Second Lieutenant Theodore A. Brown, 22 Columbus, O.	2-fighters
First Lieutenant John J. Doherty, 24 Seattle, Wash.	1-bomber, ½–2-engine-bomber
Second Lieutenant Thomas M. Kirby, 22 Jacksonville, Fla.	1-dive-bomber
First Lieutenant Billy Cooney, 22 Benavides, Tex.	2-bombers
Second Lieutenant Raymond Barrett, 22 East Orange, N.J.	1-dive-bomber 1-twin-engine-bomber
First Lieutenant Jack M. Rothweiler, 22 Palmyra, Mo.	1-dive-bomber
Second Lieutenant Charles E. Bacon, 21 Eustis, Fla.	2-fighters
Second Lieutenant Thomas H. Sark Bartlesville, Okla.	2-fighters

The squadron as a whole is credited with one twin-engine bomber, a Betty, which was "dated" by several pilots, all unable to single out the one who splashed her. (12May45)

MECHANICS ON YONTAN

"The engineering section deserves the credit."

That's what pilots of the crack Hell's Belles squadron say when compliments come their way. There are many compliments from high ranking officers. This squadron overcame numerous obstacles and won out over heavy odds to gain the distinction as the "hottest outfit" on Yontan airfield during the first full month of flying. Hell's Belles didn't have the largest number of planes that first month; but, it had more Corsairs available.

Ace Major Perry L. Shuman gives the engineering section the credit for the success of the squadron he commands. The Major knows his combat rookies and experienced pilots need the engineering section. This section is comprised mostly of rookies. Warrant Officer H. Gordon Strachan, 36, Albans, N.Y., squadron engineering officer, passes the credit along to Master Technical Sergeant Tom E. Robinson, 32, Chelsea, Okla. The non-commissioned officer in charge of the squadron engineering section took the group of new men and molded them into efficient mechanics who know a Corsair from propeller to tail.

The Hell's Belles pilots know their machines get not only routine maintenance; but, when the situation demands, the mechanics do emergency repairs quickly and thoroughly. Recently the need for more Corsairs in the air was radioed to the mechanics. Summoning off duty personnel, the mechanics changed out wings and propellers waving pilots to the cockpits of four planes as the last bolts were tightened.

This campaign has been rough on planes. Major Shuman is proud of the salvage work of his engineering section—taking from one plane to keep another flying. Prop changes in two hours and wing changes in two and a half hours keep planes in the air, and mechanics often working round the clock. Mechanics and pilots make quite a team eliminating the Emperor's air force. (12May45)

COONEY SPLASHES ANOTHER

The Jap plane started its dive on an American ship. Gunners shot streams of ack-ack. Smaller guns added more lead.

A Corsair suddenly flashed into view closing in on the suicide plane. Ship guns were silenced. The Corsair's 20mm cannons picked up where the gunners left off. A few quick bursts set the bomber on fire. The enemy plane splashed into the sea and exploded. Debris and flaming gasoline blew over the stern of the ship and caused slight damage.

The Corsair disappeared as suddenly as it had appeared. The bomber returned to Yontan Airfield. First Lieutenant Billy Cooney, 22, Benavides, Tex., climbed from the cockpit. Cooney is a graduate of Graham High School and was employed by the Sabine Transportation Company at Port Arthur before joining the service. He was commissioned May 1943 and became a Marine fighter pilot the same day.

"Billy the Kid" now has two planes to his credit. He also saved a destroyer escort. (12May45)

OKINAWA
MAY 12, 1945

It has been a long time between letters it seems—my correspondence I mean, but I can't remember what day it is, much less who I wrote last. I sent more stories out today and wrote cut lines for over two dozen film packs. They keep me on the go all day. Time flies here when something must be done in a hurry. So much is happening around here and so fast that the months on Ulithi seem only a dream—a pleasant one. And as far as Roi, I have done more in one day here than I did all the weeks I was there.

I don't know a hell of a lot about what is taking place a few miles to the south. All I know is that they are making a hell of a lot of noise and that the Marines were called down there to help. Those line Marines are a tough bunch and rugged as hell and have a lot of scores to settle with the Japs.

I am sending a lot of stuff out of here about Marine aviation, especially the Second Air Wing, and I hope it is being used. The pilots are doing a swell job. I am with the same night fighter gang I was with before.

I was over at Bill Couch's tent today. A bomb dropped nearby a night or two ago and there are about 100 shrapnel holes in the tent. Nobody was hit which is more or less a miracle since one boy had said to hell with the Japs and did not go to his hole when the siren wailed. I spent the last two nights under sandbags but am staying in the tent tonight and taking a chance on not having to get up. The weather is lousy for flying so I should be pretty safe. All our patrols are knocking them down right and left, yet they keep coming. This is the Jap's closest target and about the only one now so they will probably shoot the works at us as long as there are any works to shoot.

From the way you write, politics are about as rotten as ever. But why should they change? The people must change first. At the rear bases and aboard ship there was plenty of time to discuss the state of the nation. But out here nobody has time to discuss politics. There was much more talk about Ernie Pyle's death than Roosevelt's. Heard recently Il Duce got his. Well, well.

The 1946 tickets will be crowded with ex-service men. It undoubtedly will take more than being one of the ten million in uniform to be elected, and I'm afraid that the end in Europe will relegate this one to just a skirmish in the minds of the nation, especially on the East Coast.

How long do they say the Japs will fight? I thought, when Germany folded, the war over here might end before we finished wrecking Japan. Those Nips must have some common sense left and try to save something of the homeland. But maybe I don't know the Japs well enough. All I know is the picture here should discourage all of them. I dare say we have more on this rock now than they ever did, and we have just landed, so to speak. Now that I have seen the war on a big scale I do not wonder at the cost.

I am staying healthy despite all the reasons for not being so. I am not eating regularly and missing lots of sleep. I'm getting forgetful as hell and never know what day of the week or the date without asking someone.

I thought we were busy building up on Ulithi. That was like mowing the lawn and trimming shrubbery compared to this. Too much to be done and the place is too rough. But it is a beautiful island very much like our own state in spots.

Please tell the folks you've heard from me and that I am OK. Short of stamps now and not selling here yet. Gave a guy $2 to send stamps from Guam.

Too nasty out for visitors tonight so I will turn in. Do you think I have been in too many raids?

8. *BUNKER HILL* PILOTS

May 12–13, 1945

Bunker Hill, *a large* Essex-*class carrier, was damaged extensively by two Japanese kamikazes on the morning of May 11, 1945. Slamming into the flight deck, the suicide aircraft exploded thirty planes and twelve thousand gallons of fuel.* Pilots returning from combat missions were diverted to other ships for refueling and then to Yontan Airfield—the first step in reassignment.*

Always on the lookout for interesting stories, Red interviewed members of parts of two squadrons from the carrier that landed on Yontan. Among them was then Captain James "Zeke" Swett, already credited with downing sixteen and one-half Japanese planes—seven on one patrol.

BUNKER HILL VISITORS

Sunday, May 13, 1945, found the Okinawa Press Club tent crowded with transient pilots. Two days before, Jap dive bombers turned the flight deck of the carrier BUNKER HILL into smoking ruins. That left parts of two Marine fighter squadrons and a couple of Navy reconnaissance photographers with no place to land. The men found a haven here, stayed one day, and were leaving the next day aboard Commandos for a rear base and new orders.

These fliers, who have lived through so much hell in this war and who have seen so many tragic sights, were as gay as though they were spending the day

* Geoffrey C. Ward, *The War: An Intimate History, 1941–1945*. Directed and produced by Ken Burns and Lynn Novick (New York: Alfred A. Knopf, 2007), 374.

on the beach. BUNKER HILL pilots were in good spirits laughing and heckling each other. The ship was damaged but not sunk. There would be duty again on other carriers and other strikes against Japan.

These pilots experienced some close calls over Yontan itself. Long before the island was invaded and secured, carrier-based pilots reported the ack-ack over Okinawa was hotter than anywhere along the line. The "line" at that time was drawn from the Philippines and Formosa to Tokyo. But today, there was little talk about strikes against Okinawa—or strikes against any of the other Jap strongholds. That was a finished chapter to the pilots—it smarted too much.

While on Okinawa, BUNKER HILL pilots slept with their clothes on and their shoes handy like everyone else. This closest airfield to Japan is the target of at least one air raid every night. (13May45)

Bunker Hill *personnel identified by Staff Sergeant Canup from two pictures taken by combat photographer Charles V. Corkran, May 12, 1945.**

Members of *Bunker Hill*'s VMF 451 Squadron Landing on Yontan May 12, 1945.

Major Henry A. Ellis, Commanding Officer, Sacramento, Calif.
Major Herbert H. Long, Executive Officer, Miami, Fla., credited with 10 Jap planes.
First Lieutenant William E. Brown, Los Angeles, Calif.
First Lieutenant William G. Reavis, Greensboro, N.C.
First Lieutenant Charles H. Wade, Harrisburg, Ill.
First Lieutenant John S. Norris, Jr., Highlands, Tex.
First Lieutenant John N. Orr, Athens, Ga.
First Lieutenant Dewey J. Wamsgans, Flushing, N.Y.
Reconnaissance photographers with the squadron:
Navy Ensign Harold G. Packard, Columbus, O.
Navy Ensign Joseph P. Laurie, Patterson, N.J.

Thirty four Japanese planes were shot down by this squadron between Tokyo and Okinawa from February 16 until *Bunker Hill* was crippled by suicide bombers. They flew support for the Okinawa invasion.

* Photograph part of the Claude R. "Red" Canup Collection.

Members of *Bunker Hill*'s VMF 221 Squadron Landing on Yontan May 12, 1945.

Major Edwin S. Roberts, Jr., Commanding Officer, Los Angeles, Calif.
Captain Frank B. Baldwin, Lapeer, Mich., Marine Ace
Captain William N. Snider, Vicksburg, Miss., credited with 11½ Jap planes.
Captain James E. Swett, Executive Officer, San Mateo, Calif., credited with 16½ planes.
First Lieutenant Robert J. Murray, Medford, Miss.
First Lieutenant John E. Jorgensen, South Windsor, Conn.
First Lieutenant Walter Goeggel, Jr., Kirkwood, Mo.
First Lieutenant Ralph O. Glendinning, Avenel, N.J.
First Lieutenant Wes S. Todd, Wauwatosa, Wis.
First Lieutenant Clay D. Haggard, Durant, Okla.
First Lieutenant Eugene D. Cameron, Syracuse, N.Y.
First Lieutenant Fred E. Briggs, Roseburg, Ore.
Second Lieutenant George R. A. Johns, Bergenfield, N.J.
Second Lieutenant Robin Hood Adams, San Francisco, Calif.
Second Lieutenant Bill Bailey, Bloomfield, Ia.

This squadron, the Fighting Falcons, has 199 planes to its credit, 66 shot down between Tokyo and Okinawa.

BRIGGS OF *BUNKER HILL*

Life has had some exciting moments for First Lieutenant Fred E. Briggs, one of the survivors of the aircraft carrier BUNKER HILL. The flat-top's pilots, who were in the air when the ship was knocked out by Kamikazes, came to Yontan to spend the week-end before reporting to a rear base.

This was the first time Lieutenant Briggs had actually been on Okinawa but he had been over it. In fact, he had his most exciting moments on a raid over the island March 1, a month before the Marines and soldiers hit these beaches. On that day, he was on a bombing and strafing mission and destroyed two Jap aircraft parked on Yontan. One wing of his plane was hit, and he bailed out over Okinawa. Fortunately, he not only came away from the experience unharmed, but he was rescued by a friendly destroyer.

The morning BUNKER HILL was damaged, Briggs was in a division which had gone out on the dawn patrol. When he returned, he saw the crippled ship, some of the survivors bobbing around in the water. Pilots, who had them, dropped life rafts, and all dropped dye markers around survivors so that ships speeding to the scene could rescue them. Some circled overhead furnishing protection in the event the enemy attempted to return to finish the job.

While here, the pilot spent part of two days resting and looking over the airfield. The Japs were still in his hair, and he had to hit a foxhole when they sneaked in close enough to cause an alert.

Lieutenant Briggs' squadron participated in numerous carrier-based fighter sweeps over Japan, and his commanding officer Major Edwin S. Roberts, Jr., Los Angeles, received the Air Medal for leading the first Tokyo sweep of this nature. On that occasion, February 16, they silenced Radio Tokyo.

He was commissioned September 1943. He attended Oregon State College and played football and was on the track team at Seaside Union High School. (13May45)

PACKARD OF *BUNKER HILL*

Navy Ensign Howard G. Packard, 22, got an unexpected close-up view of Yontan. It is the job of the photographer to accompany Marine fighter pilots on missions and do reconnaissance aerial photography. He was on such a mission when BUNKER HILL was attacked.

"I never thought I would see Okinawa under these circumstances," he said as he rested at the Okinawa Press Club. Packard was over Yontan two days before the invasion.

Packard remembered the day his escort was attacked by 15 Jap planes near Amami Shima. Ten of the enemy were shot down.

The former student of Columbus St. Charles Seminary was commissioned in the Navy a year exactly before the big carrier-based fighter sweep over Tokyo and has made several flights over Japan proper and Okinawa. (13May45)

REAVIS OF *BUNKER HILL*

Marine pilot, First Lieutenant William G. Reavis, 22, Graham, N.C., was one of the survivors of BUNKER HILL.

He reported some of the pilots on patrol said they saw one bomber come out of nowhere, lay its eggs on the flight deck, bank and turn back into the ship for a suicide dive. The plane was crippled by Marine fighters close enough to attack it but could not be knocked into the sea.

Reavis has two Jap planes to his credit, splashing them during what he recalls as the most exciting combat experience he has had in the Pacific. "It was during the battle of the Inland Sea," he recalled. "We went over in force looking for the Jap fleet, or what was left of it in that area, and we found it. We also found lots of Jap planes which came up to meet us. A big dog fight followed, and I bagged a couple of Zekes. What with the flak, we had a hot time of it."

The North Carolinian has been on numerous searching parties and strikes with planes from BUNKER HILL and has hit targets on Japan proper. The former University of North Carolina student is a graduate of Greensboro High School where he played football. He was on the track team at the University. (13May45)

MARINE ACE SWETT REACTS TO *BUNKER HILL* BOMBING

"I just wish that we could have been there to do something about it before they did their damage," said Captain James E. Swett, Marine ace, after arriving here with part of his squadron. The Californian, 24, has 16½ planes to his credit but felt helpless when he saw the flat-top smoking. Earlier that morning, Swett led a division off the ship on patrol, and his wingman shot down a Betty, twin-engine bomber carrying a Baka bomb on this mission.

The fact the Japs can slip through occasionally on one-way tickets and get to ships steaming past their front door has yet to affect Captain Swett's preference for carrier duty to land base. Although, it was while flying with the land-based Fighting Falcons on Guadalcanal and Bougainville that he shot down 14½ planes—seven in one cluster—to write a new Marine Corps aviation chapter and be awarded the Medal of Honor, two Distinguished Flying Crosses, and Purple Heart.

The story of Captain Jim Swett, nicknamed "Zeke," in the south Pacific has made the rounds. Those were frustrating and demanding days for outnumbered American pilots—but the Captain's greatest thrill was not the "seven in one trip."

Asked about his most exciting moment, the Californian responded, "It was the flight over Tokyo on February 25. We went over the city and flew 103 miles inland of the island of Honshu. Do you have any idea how many Jap planes we saw on that little ride? Not a single one came up to welcome us, or at least I never spotted one."

Fighting Falcons and all carrier based squadrons of task forces that have terrorized the enemy in his front yard and right into his living room have flown over islands from Okinawa to Japan proper. All helped prepare for the successful Okinawa invasion.

Captain Swett was commissioned March 1942 and entered the service from San Mateo Junior College. (13May45)

ROBERTS, FIGHTING FALCONS AND *BUNKER HILL*

Major Edwin S. Roberts, Jr., is commanding officer of the Fighting Falcons. He led the first Tokyo sweep by carrier-based fighters on February 16.

"We knocked Radio Tokyo off the air that day and shot down a few of their planes," related the Major. But that was not his most exciting experience out here, although the Air Medal went with it.

His biggest day was when he led a three-plane shipping search over Kago Shima Bay at 1,500 feet. "There was lots of anti-aircraft fire, and we were attacked by fighters," he recalled. "We shot down six Japs." Major Roberts, on his first cruise with the Fighting Falcons, bagged two planes himself at Kago Shima, which is south of Kyushu.

The Fighting Falcons, one of the most famous squadrons in the Marine Corps, had been on two land-based tours before going aboard BUNKER HILL January 24. They were part of the 1stMAW in the Solomons, and also were at Midway. The Falcons have shot down 199 enemy fighters and bombers. After the first sweep over Tokyo, Major Roberts and his squadron were back in the vicinity twice. He led an attack on an airplane engine plant 100 miles north of Tokyo. He bombed and strafed the Japs on Yontan two days before Marines and soldiers hit the beach here.

He wants to get back into the fight soon, now figuring that he has a personal score to settle with the enemy. (13May45)

MURRAY OF *BUNKER HILL*

Experience came with a bang to First Lieutenant Robert J. Murray, Medford, Miss. He shot down a Kamikaze plane and returned from patrol to find his carrier had been hit by dive-bombers.

Asked about his most exciting moment, the former Boston College student surprised his listeners when he replied: "The day I heard my daughter was born."

The 23-year-old Mississippian was commissioned July 1943 and was captain of the football and basketball teams at Medford High School. (13May45)

ADAMS OF *BUNKER HILL*

Second Lieutenant Robin Hood Adams has had some experiences which would rival those of the hero of Sherwood Forest. After he became a flier, his most exciting adventure was his first combat air patrol off Okinawa. "We ran into a lot of Japs that day," he said, "and lots of them were shot down in flames." But Robin Hood is still looking for his first one.

The former enlisted man and plane captain revealed he never had a keen desire to fly and explained, "I had been overseas so long that I wanted to get back to the States. I figured that if I tried to become a pilot, I could go back and train. I don't regret the decision."

The former student of Kitsilano High School at Vancouver, B.C., had a close call on Midway. A bomb fell within ten feet of him and killed four men. (13May45)

TODD OF *BUNKER HILL*

First Lieutenant Wes S. Todd, Wauwatosa, Wis., has flown four fighter attacks over Tokyo—including the big attack on that city last February 16—doesn't count the Japs suicide attack on the carrier as his most exciting experience.

He shot down two planes March 18 over Kyushu, flaming one head-on and exploding the other with a burst from behind. He was hitting the Japs over Okinawa on Easter Sunday, the day Marines walked across Yontan.

This is the second cruise for the 23-year-old Lieutenant Todd, who was with the Hell Hawks on another carrier. The former Citadel, Charleston, S.C., cadet was commissioned in July 1943. He was a junior when he entered the service. (13May45)

ORR OF *BUNKER HILL*

When a couple of fellows from the same part of the country meet 10,000 miles from home, they begin conversing by brushing up on mutual acquaintances and outstanding events. War talk comes later.

Such was the case when First Lieutenant John N. Orr, stationed aboard BUNKER HILL, flew his Corsair to this base. Lieutenant Orr didn't care to talk much about the incident. He just figured the ship and all who came out alive were pretty lucky. As for his experiences out here, he recalled the day he shot down a dive-bomber was exciting. It was over the Kurai naval base, or in the vicinity.

"There was lots of ack-ack that day when the fighters went out looking for the Jap fleet," he said. "They strafed and shot rockets and, in general, disrupted the plans of the emperor's admirals for a long time." He has also flown over Kyushu and Okinawa numerous times and was flying support to Marines when they took this airfield Easter Sunday.

But the pilot, who was commissioned July 1943, warmed up more to the conversation when there was mention of Frankie Sinkwich and other University of Georgia players, and towns between Athens, Ga., and Anderson, S.C.—places like Royston, Elberton, Hartwell and the fishing streams in the mountains.

John attended Georgia before entering the service. He is a graduate of Athens High School and was captain of the football team in 1939.

While on Okinawa, the Georgian spent most of the time taking a busman's holiday—hanging around the airfield. To the carrier-based pilots, it was like a weekend off. (13May45)

9. BLACK MAC'S KILLERS

Yontan Airfield, May 1945

Lieutenant Colonel Marion Magruder, recognized as one of the few night fighter experts at the time, and his night fighter squadron, VMF (N) 533, wanted to flame Japanese planes. At the end of their cruise in the sedate Marshall Islands, the pilots requested an extension and duty on Okinawa. Approved, the squadron arrived six weeks after Yontan Airfield was operational. Their arrival provided a new source of stories for Red.

"BLACK MAC" MAGRUDER

Okinawa may seem like an out-of-the-way place for a Kentucky Colonel with the absence of mint juleps, fast horses, and beautiful women. The colonel is Marine Lieutenant Colonel Marion Magruder, better known as "Black Mac," and he and his men are a perfect fit for Yontan.

The Colonel commands a night fighter squadron, Black Mac's Killers, taking the name of the CO, and assigned operationally to MAG 31. The Hellcat pilots flew night combat air patrol around the peaceful Marshall Islands for the last 13 months before moving to Yontan Airfield six weeks after the invasion.

Life at best on the small coral islands they left behind was sedate, and the young night fighters had shipped overseas to become Marine aces. They were fed up with the monotonous and uneventful patrols night after night. They were practicing skills but not having the chance to use them.

With their scheduled overseas cruise completed and lacking the satisfaction of shooting down Jap planes, the squadron decided not to disband but ask the "old man"—the Colonel is only 33—to request Okinawa duty. This was granted and the squadron landed here practically intact with none of the original ambition to be Black Mac's Killers diminished.

When they arrived here, the squadron quickly gained the reputation of a "hot outfit"—not because they had made the headlines or really met the enemy. The Kentucky Colonel made the rounds and dropped a word here and there as he circulated about how good his boys could fly. Too, Black Mac brought along some original ideas about night fighting—some ideas so different that he laid himself wide open for unfavorable criticism in the event things did not pan out.

The medium-build, handsome Kentuckian, with black eyes that belie the strain of years of day and night flying, did not give a thought as to the possibility of having to hedge. To the contrary, he talked more and underscored some of his statements with the black and white clincher, "You can quote me."

A few days after arriving here the Colonel said, "We are going to operate a little different from some others out here." He had a gleam in his eyes as he explained his plans. Like the skilled magician who is about to perform one of those "you-can't-believe-your-eyes" tricks, he was satisfied within himself that all would turn out well.

"Give me ten days and I'll prove it," flatly stated Colonel Magruder whose plans are too secret to be mentioned. Of the other night fighter squadrons already operating on Okinawa, not one had approached the goal set by Black Mac.

Not waiting for the tenth day to check the records, maybe giving Colonel Magruder an out should he need one, early returns indicate he already has proven his point with the official facts. His Killers landed on May 10. On May 12, with only a Commando or two full of mechanics, radar, and radio technicians and a few ground officers, the squadron flew its allotted hours on night combat patrol.

Three nights later, one of the pilots made the squadron's first kill. On May 18, two Killers splashed a total of five Jap planes—four twin-engine bombers (Bettys) and a single-engine fighter. That one patrol alone established a Marine Corps record for night fighting for a squadron and a pilot. There was also another Jap plane shot down by a Killer that was not confirmed. Three days after Magruder had asked for ten days to prove his pilots, there were six Japs for sure and one probable.

Black Mac's Killers still have time as of this writing to shoot down Japs, but if they don't have any luck at all there will not be any finger pointing at the Colonel. He knows some things not in the book, but more important his fliers know what he knows.

Lieutenant Colonel Magruder literally wrote much of the book. He is one of the leaders in this newest area of Marine aviation. Thumbing through the pages back to the beginning. He was in Washington with the Bureau of Aeronautics in 1942 when word flashed from Guadalcanal that the Marines needed night fighters to intercept Jap bombers. The Rising Sun was shining in the middle of the night those days.

Night fighting was paying off for England at the time. The Colonel and four other aviation officers were sent across the Atlantic to learn all they could about night fighting to use in the Pacific. They studied British night fighting from the ground up to 20,000 feet and higher. They watched the Royal Air Force at work in the dark from January until July 1943. With a book full of data and a head full of ideas, he returned to the United States and was immediately made senior training officer of all night fighter training at the Marine Corps Air Station at Cherry Point, N.C.

Only the best day fighters were accepted from the beginning. Night fighters were instrument fliers vectored to the enemy by radio instructions from "controllers." They had to be the best shots as well. The first bursts from their guns were usually the only bursts that counted. Mistakes that could be corrected in daylight could mean plenty of trouble in the dark. Eighty percent of night flying is by instrument. Twenty percent is pilot's technique for handling the interception before contact is made, reading the scope, and knowing what to do next. The Colonel is the senior night fighter pilot in the Pacific. Higher ranking officers respect his knowledge, and his ideas and suggestions got their attention.

The first night fighter squadron of the Marine Corps went into action in the Pacific in August 1943. It landed on Bougainville. Black Mac's Killers, first night fighter squadron in Marine aviation to fly F6Fs, went to the Marshalls in April of the following year with their Hellcats. (19May45)

SPLASH TWO

Marine First Lieutenant Edward N. LeFaivre, night fighter pilot who bagged two planes on his fourth mission from this field, was afraid of only one thing as he chased the Jap bomber through the black night. "I was afraid I would lose her," he said.

The Baltimore pilot was flying midnight patrol last night and is believed to have shot down the Betty which created so much excitement on Yontan a few minutes before laying a string of bombs across the field and scoring a direct hit on a bomb-loaded Privateer. The Jap was streaking away when the night fighter was vectored to the Betty.

LeFaivre was flying at 15,000 feet. He swept around her for position and was flying 300 feet to the rear and starboard side when he fired his first burst knocking out the right engine. The wounded Betty lost altitude fast. At 9,000 feet the Hellcat pilot fired a long burst into the gas tank.

The bomber went into a steep dive. The pilot likewise put his Hellcat into a dive and catching the Jap who had leveled off at 1,000 feet. LeFaivre then dropped his landing gear to break his speed, fired another burst into the engine, and exploded the Betty.

This kill came less than a half-hour after LeFaivre shot down a Jap fighter known as a Hamp. The Hamp had been easier. It was intercepted about 60 miles north of Yontan, heading south at 14,000 feet. LeFaivre got a head-on vector and maneuvered to get on the Hamp's tail while it was climbing to 19,000 feet. Directly under the Jap, about 200 feet, the crack aviator fired a short burst into the Hamp's engine. The Jap nosed over; and, when he did, LeFaivre let him have it again—a long burst that exploded the Hamp. Only 100 rounds were needed for the kill. (19May45)

SCARED AND LUCKY

"I got pretty old sitting up there those last two hours of the patrol waiting and wondering if I would be shot down by friendly fire," sighed First Lieutenant Robert E. Wellwood, of Sheridan, Wyo. That helpless feeling countered any elation the 23-year-old pilot might have felt being told his shooting down of three Jap twin engine bombers set a new night fighter record.

The new record brought congratulations and commendations from ships at sea and high ranking officers on Okinawa. Wellwood appreciated all but could not acknowledge that the new record was the most exciting occurrence of the night.

A member of Black Mac's Killers crack night fighter squadron, Lieutenant Wellwood likened the last two hours in the sky to one of those nightmares in which you want to scream but nothing comes out or know something is about to grab you but you only run in place. He was at an altitude of thousands of feet surrounded by the blackness of the Pacific and had no idea where he was.

The record setting part of the night started at 9:45 P.M. when he took off from Yontan. "Just as soon as I had gained my altitude I was given a vector to 10,000 feet. That was about 30 miles northwest of the field. I picked up a head-on contact while climbing and closed in on the port side, coming up from behind on the dark side of the moon for protection from the light. I saw the Jap then. It was a Betty. One long burst was fired into the left wing gas tank, and the Betty exploded," explained the young pilot.

This was number one and required less than five minutes and only 50 rounds were fired from the 50 caliber guns. It was Wellwood's first Jap plane after more than a year of flying night patrol in the Pacific. However, it happened on only his fourth mission from Okinawa.

A half hour after the first Betty splashed in flames, the leading pilot of Black Mac's Killers made contact with another bomber. He was about 30 miles from the island and was flying at 15,500 feet. He swept around the Betty for position and leveled off, aiming at the pilot's compartment with the first burst.

The plane stayed on course seeming to have eluded damage. But the flashes from the Hellcat pilot's guns gave him away. He was spotted by the top turret gunner who opened up on him. One shot hit the tail of the night fighter plane, but the others went wild.

After the first burst Black Mac's Killer made another pass and fired from above and behind the Betty, setting the portside engine on fire. During that time the Jap gunner continued to fire . . . and continued to miss. The Betty then tried to shake him off, pointing her nose toward the sea and diving fast. Wellwood stuck with her, easily following the flight by the fire blazing from the port engine.

The fire went out in about 15 seconds, but the Wyoming flier kept the range and fired another short burst into the fuselage. That sent the Jap into a spin from which the Betty never recovered. He followed her down to 7,000 feet, pulled out and was notified that the Betty had disappeared from the controller's screen. That was number two.

Bob then climbed back up to 14,000 feet, and shortly before 11 o'clock he made another contact and visual on another Betty still in the area. "The sky must have been full of them," he said.

He closed in from three miles behind, maneuvering 300 feet behind and below the Jap. Before he could fire, the Jap spotted him, made no effort to fight back and disappeared in a hurry in a steep dive. It was a successful evasion.

"I didn't have time to get sore about losing that one before another popped up," Wellwood recalled. "It could have been the same Betty because I was still down to about 10,000 feet from the chase when I made contact.

"This one was a tail vector; and, I was losing altitude keeping on the Jap because he was dropping down for greater speed on the way back home," continued Bob.

Just as Bob was closing in on the Jap one of our warships picked her up and began throwing everything at her except the anchor . . . Bob was right in the middle of it . . . and his plane was shot up by ack-ack before he could pull away.

"That was the scariest time I have ever had in my entire life," confessed Bob. His Hellcat's port wing was hit, the tail and fuselage took a share of the flak, and his engine absorbed a few pieces. The radio was knocked out, and the air speed indicator would not register.

"The plane was in such bad shape and the engine running so rough, I decided to give up the chase and return to the base," he reported. "I was not sore about losing that Betty. I was too thankful that I came out of the ack-ack alive."

Before he had gone two miles, Bob picked up another bogy. He couldn't pass it by. After chasing it about ten miles at high speed he closed in and got a visual above and behind. "I believe it was the same Betty because I saw her pull to the right to get out of the ack-ack same as I did," he said.

By the time Bob closed in on the Betty, he had no idea where he was. It was getting darker, too. But, he maneuvered into position and fired a burst into the pilot's compartment. It was perfect shooting but also gave away his position, and the Japs returned the fire—but not much because the Betty went into a steep dive. Bob followed her down as she vanished into the darkness. He did not see her again until she hit the water, flames shooting up with the splash. That was number three.

"I was feeling good about it all then," said Bob, "but suddenly realized I was lost. I had no idea of my position—and I could not use the radio. I climbed to 10,000 feet and saw a light far to the south. I didn't know who or what it was—I headed for it. Then the darn thing went out."

Wellwood, gravely concerned about the condition of his engine, decided to circle until some of his own squadron pilots came along. He still had radio reception and "sort of froze in my seat" when he heard one of his own pilots being directed to his position sent out to shoot him down.

"I was scared all over again," grinned Bob by now amused over the incident as he related his story. "I followed the approach of the other Killer over the radio. I didn't want to turn on my lights for fear it would be a dead give away to any Japs in the vicinity. I just circled around, waiting and praying that my buddy would identify me before it was too late. When he got within a 1,000 feet or so, I flashed my lights . . . still hoping and praying."

"After what seemed like a lifetime he recognized me, reported me as friendly and brought me back to the field which had been told to prepare for an emergency landing. I made it all right, and I felt pretty lucky."

Lieutenant James E. Smurr, Columbus, O., the fellow squadron pilot sent out to shoot down Lieutenant Wellwood, confirmed him to be friendly. "I guess I'm as glad as Bob that I recognized him as a friendly plane," Jim said. He laughed and added, "After all if the Japs couldn't shoot him down, I doubt if I could have either."

In addition to firing a very small amount of ammunition to splash the three bombers and setting a record for shooting down three planes in one night, Bob might well have been flying his Hellcat on an A-coupon because the whole trip required only 250 gallons of gas. Wellwood enlisted in 1942 and was commissioned in 1943. He received a private flying license while in college at Brigham Young University. (19May45)

MARINE CORPS HISTORY MADE

Marine Corps aviation history was written here last night, but Lieutenant Colonel Marion Magruder wouldn't advise that the story be given to the printers for a while because he is convinced that another chapter may be written any day.

First Lieutenant Robert Wellwood set a record for individual night fighting when he shot down three Japanese bombers on one mission.

First Lieutenant Edward LeFaivre splashed a Jap fighter and bomber during the same midnight patrol to couple with Wellwood's three for a Marine night fighter squadron record for a night's work.

No other single engine Marine night fighter squadron has come close to those figures. The Black Mac's Killers fly Hellcats.

"I wouldn't take a thing away from those kids," said the Lexington Kentucky Lieutenant Colonel, "but I have a squadron full of crack night fighter pilots—the best. And they're liable to come up with a better record any night."

The two pilots made history on their fourth mission from Yontan. (19 May45)

OKINAWA
MAY 21, 1945

A Marine lieutenant colonel, senior officer in night fighting out here, has a night fighter squadron which has been here for only a short while and is setting records right and left. He is colorful as hell. It makes news every day. Good news. The Colonel doesn't give a damn what he says about generals or anybody else. He brags and he lives up to it. His pilots are probably the best night fighters, or among the best, in the business. He says so, and they have the records to prove it. Things have been popping around here so I haven't been able to talk with him lately about his boys "piling up so many records it will take an adding machine to figure up the total."

He is good copy and took a liking to me when I went around to talk with him one day. He is the kind of fellow I don't have to sandwich "sir" in between every word and talk to him just like one of the boys. We're just a couple of men who have jobs to do and we can be of help to each other. That's how we are dealing.

As I said, the Colonel and I got along fine. I have talked with two-star generals and admirals and buck privates, and they're all alike as a rule—there are exceptions, of course. Going into a colonel's tent or a major's tent and not bothering to be soldiery at all requires delicate diplomacy.

BY DAY ONLY FOR WILHIDE

The Wilhide brothers, Andrews, N.C., who had met here for the first time in 28 months, were separated before their day-and-night combination against the Japs had time to materialize.

Second Lieutenant Wilfred Wallace Wilhide, 21, had been flying with a day fighter squadron of the 2ndMAW three weeks. His brother First Lieutenant Robert Maurice Wilhide, 23, arrived the second week in May with the night fighter squadron Black Mac's Killers. On May 15 on his second patrol, Bob shot down a Jap twin-engine bomber.

On May 17, Bob went up on patrol and got on the tail of a dive-bomber making a run on a ship. He closed in fast and opened rapid machine gun fire on the bomber. Intent upon shooting down the plane before it could damage the vessel, Bob failed to pull out of the flak. He never returned to his base.

Grief-stricken, Wally went up on dusk patrol May 20. His division intercepted five Jap bombers. Wally raked one of them with a long burst from his guns sending the plane down in flames. The Jap was spotted at 5,000 feet just as it started a dive for an American destroyer. Wally knocked it out at 1,000 feet over the water.

"That one was for Bob," the elder brother said later and added, "I hope that I can get lots more for him." Of Bob's loss, Wally said, "You can't sit up there and watch them dive on our ships no matter if there is ack-ack. It just doesn't seem right not to try to do something.' (21May45)

101ST MISSION FOR MOORE

Flying his 101st combat mission since coming overseas 14 months ago, First Lieutenant Richard M. Moore, New York City, made his first contact with the enemy. A Japanese night fighter went into the sea.

The night-fighter pilot flying his sixth combat air patrol was on a midnight hop when he intercepted the Jap at 11,000 feet 30 miles northwest of Ie Shima.

Pulling behind and to the right of the twin-engine fighter, Lieutenant Moore fired a burst into the starboard engine, flaming out the front of the plane and shattering the right wing. "I slid over and raked the fuselage with the burst and started the fire," said Moore.

The Jap began losing altitude in a lazy spiral. The resident of New York fired another burst into the left engine flaming it. The short burst into the Jap's tail was just for good measure before the plane splashed into the sea.

"It was damn exciting," grinned the pilot who had waited over 13 months for this opportunity. (28May45)

JAP BIRTHDAY PRESENT

First Lieutenant Robert S. Hemstad celebrated his 22nd birthday by shooting down a night fighter in the Japanese Imperial Air Force.

The plane was bagged on his sixth mission from this base and was splashed 30 miles northwest of Ie Shima. He intercepted the Jap at 14,000 feet and fired five bursts into the Irving before it went spinning down in flames and exploded.

"It was simple," said the pilot from Minneapolis, Minn.

The flyer was born in Duluth and commissioned August 1943. (29May45)

WHAT STOKES CAME FOR

First Lieutenant Jay Arthur Stokes shot down a Jap fighter on his 11th mission from this field. The 22-year-old from Brigham, Utah, intercepted the Jap as it was leaving the Okinawa area heading toward Kyushu at 4:40 AM. The night fighter fired only two bursts and got direct hits. The enemy plane exploded in midair. (10June45)

EVERYTHING'S JAKE FOR BAIRD

Captain Robert Baird, South Gate, Calif., was "pretty excited" over shooting down his first enemy plane, a Jake.

On his 11th mission from Okinawa, the Captain bagged the Jake in the Pacific darkness 30 miles northwest of Ie Shima. After intercepting the enemy, Captain Baird closed in to 150 feet behind and below and fired three bursts, the second one flaming the engine. The Jake tried to climb, turn, and dive away but was not successful—exploding when it hit the water.

Captain Baird had previously flown in the Gilbert, Marianas, and Marshall Islands. The pilot has a brother Jesse in the Navy. (10June45)

10. GIRETSU ATTACK ON YONTAN

May 24, 1945

*The six bombs dropped northeast of Yontan Airfield and seven more north and west of MAG 31 headquarters, plus continuous waves of bogeys that provided diversionary tactics for the Japanese, paved the way for a new dimension in Pacific warfare. The giretsu attack on Yontan (giretsu roughly translates as "act of heroism") occurred a short time later. It was the first Central Pacific airborne attack. The Japanese successfully belly-landed one suicide plane carrying troops close to Yontan's control tower. Early the next morning the last of the Japanese troops was shot a quarter of a mile behind MAG 31 squadron headquarters. Successful in the eyes of the Japanese, sixty-nine Americans died, nine U.S. planes were destroyed and twenty-nine damaged at a cost of only five Japanese planes.**

After Red's death in 1999, a copy of Robert Sherrod's History of Marine Corps Aviation in World War II *was found among his papers. In the margins of pages 404 and 405, the former USMC combat correspondent had written "Canup covered attack." This claim is corroborated in a September 1, 1945, letter to Brigadier General Robert L. Denig, where Red noted, "Night fighters I covered re-wrote the record books, and I wrote the stories of the only eye-witness accounts of the airborne suicide attack on Yontan."*†

* Robert Sherrod, *History of Marine Corps Aviation in World War II* (Baltimore: Nautical and Aviation Publishing Company of America, 1987), 404–5.

† Claude R. "Red" Canup Collection.

Site of the May 24, 1945, giretsu attack, Yontan Airfield, Okinawa. Claude R. "Red" Canup Collection.

EYE-WITNESS REPORT

(Note: This eye-witness account of the attack on Yontan airfield by airborne suicide squadrons from Japan was told to Sergeant Claude R. Canup, a Marine Combat Correspondent, by Marine Sergeant Leroy D. Hall, Devils Lake, N.D., a tower operator on duty during the raid that started the night of May 24 and ended sometimes before dawn the morning of May 25.

The Japs came in five planes, one belly landed on the airfield, about 250 feet from the tower, with a dozen or more Japanese soldiers destroying 9 planes, damaging 29 and flaming over 70 thousand gallons of fuel. Another crashed on the field with two Japs spotted. Maynard Kelley was the only Marine causality. Eighteen were wounded.)

I was the first one to see the Japs of the suicide squadron after their bomber made a belly landing on the northeast-southwest runway, and I fired at the last member of the party to be seen alive on the field several hours later.

There were three of us in the tower that night. We had full view of all three runways and the entire field. Two bombers had come over between 9:10 and

10:05, flying high, dropping their bombs and getting away, just out of reach of the ack-ack.

At about 10:30 the ack-ack opened up again, the red tracers zooming just over the tower. We ducked behind sandbags and then looked out to see if we could spot the plane. I didn't see her until she burst into flames about 500 yards away. It was coming in at tree-top level, headed for the north-south runway but exploded 300 yards from the tower. The next morning I saw several burned and mangled Jap bodies in the debris.

The second twin-engine bomber came in a couple of minutes or so behind the first. I just glimpsed it as it glided through the light of the exploded plane. Its engines were cut and it made a belly landing on the northeast-southwest strip skidding to a stop 100 yards or so away from the tower.

I snatched up a pair of field glasses and trained them on the bomber. At about the same instant it stopped, I saw two men sneak from the blind side of the plane and crouch, joined quickly by five or six more. I yelled to Marines close by, who had just come out of dugouts, that Japs were on the field. They grabbed rifles and took up positions on a road just off the field. Some other Marines hid under the tower.

The Japs, bunched together, spread out and slowly walked away from their bomber toward our planes across the runway. Walking slowly in a crouch, they had taken only a few steps when Marines opened fire. The Japs hit the strip and began firing tommy guns and rifles toward the men and the tower. They kept crawling. Two turned toward the tower and the others made for the planes. It was a bright, moon-lit night. We could see clear as day.

When the Japs started shooting at the tower, we got in a hurry. I got my rifle and joined the men in the road. By this time three of our Commandos were burning. A Jap threw a small fire bomb at another plane. The bomb hit the fuselage. The plane burst into flames.

It was almost like day-light by then, and 30 or 40 of us were on the road firing at the Japs maybe 50 or 60 yards away. The anti-aircraft guns were trained on the field. We had lots of stuff turned on the Japs. We could see them sneaking around burning planes. One Jap was shot, and when he fell the other two threw hand grenades at us. We ducked for cover.

In the confusion, the Japs fired at two or three fighter planes and ran back across the strip toward their wrecked bomber. We opened fire again. They got near the middle of the field and paused as if picking out more planes. We shot several of them as they ran into the shadows.

During this time, two more bombers tried to come in but were shot down in flames. Three or four Japs got out alive when a plane crashed on the other side of the field. Fires were started in that direction. By this time garrison troops had arrived, and the shooting soon stopped except for sporadic bursts from all over the area.

At daybreak I counted four Jap bodies—two by their bomber, one near a destroyed Commando, one near the front of the tower. That could have been the one Lieutenant Maynard Kelley shot before the Japs shot him. The member of Black Mac's Killers was the duty officer in the tower when it all started.

Seven or eight men stood looking at one of the Jap bodies. A lone Jap suddenly dashed from the ruins of a Commando, stopped, and threw a grenade at them. All were wounded. Several of us shot the Jap. He set off a grenade under himself, and the explosion lifted him four or five feet. I didn't see another Jap alive after that. (26May45)

MAYNARD KELLEY

Maynard Kelley never thought about being afraid. The night the Japs sent a suicide squad to Yontan, Kelley was already on duty in the most dangerous place on the field. The 22-year-old Marine was in the radio tower the night of May 24, 1945, when a troop-loaded plane crash landed almost in front of him.

One of the tower operators on duty with Lieutenant Kelley that night, Marine Staff Sergeant Robert N. Dietrich, Cincinnati, was nearby when the duty officer with MAG 31 was killed. This is Sergeant Dietrich's account of the incident:

"First Lieutenant Kelley was in the tower during the bombing that preceded the suicide squad landing. 'I'd give $50 to be up there and able to get a shot at those guys,' the Lieutenant exclaimed when it started. Several minutes later, when three enemy bombers appeared over the field at one time, he exclaimed louder, 'The ante has just been raised. I'd give $75 to be up there right now!'

"About that time ack-ack was seen firing at a low target just east of the field. It was a plane. Lieutenant Kelley yelled, 'What the hell?' Another plane made its approach and landed just opposite the tower. Thinking some of the crew would still be alive, Kelley grabbed the field glasses. When he saw six or eight forms getting out of the plane, he grabbed his .38, repelled down the ladder, and hurdled into the jeep. We saw the Japs headed straight for the jeep, and we hollered for the Lieutenant to come back.

"About that time the first plane set on fire by the Japs almost went up in their faces. Our guys stopped the jeep, and Lieutenant Kelley jumped out to run back to the tower to alert his squadron by telephone. The Japs were heading our way showering the tower with gun fire.

"Lieutenant Kelley started firing his revolver at the slinking forms, and shouted, 'I got him! I got that one!' Things were happening all over the field by that time, and several of the guys headed in the Japs' vicinity. They hollered they wanted the spotlight from the tower thrown in the general direction of the enemy.

"Lieutenant Kelley hurriedly scaled the ladder knowing he would be a target for the Japs. A shot struck him in the chest. He turned on the spotlight and still had his finger wrapped around the trigger when he was removed from the tower."

Lieutenant Kelley lived with his grandparents in Seattle and received his commission and wings in 1943. After duty at Jacksonville, Fla., and Cherry Point, N.C., he shipped overseas with Lieutenant Colonel Marion Magruder's "Black Mac's Killers" and had flown only a few times since his squadron landed on Okinawa in May. He was buried in the Marine cemetery. (30May45)

The Associated Press article below, documenting USMC combat correspondent Claude Canup's own account of the May 24–25 giretsu attack on Yontan Airfield, Okinawa, appeared in the Anderson Independent *on May 29. (Reprinted with permission granted from the* Independent-Mail*)*

CANUP SEES JAP SUICIDE ATTACK
ANDERSONIAN IN THICK OF FIGHT DURING INCREDIBLE ENEMY EFFORT

GUAM, Sunday, May 27—(AP)—Japanese fanaticism reached almost unbelievable heights in the Thursday night-Friday morning 18-hour attack on Yontan airfield, Okinawa, and shipping offshore, today's Navy communiqué said.

In an almost incredible display of suicidal tactics, the Nipponese tried to crash-land several plane loads of airborne troops on Yontan airfield Thursday night. One of the enemy troop planes succeeded in landing at Yontan and its personnel did some damage.

An estimated 200 enemy aircraft made the heaviest attack on American airfields and offshore naval units since May 4. They damaged 11 light U.S. ships, one of them heavily, and destroyed nine aircraft on the ground, Pacific Fleet headquarters said.

There were 15 Japanese aboard the plane that succeeded but only eight scrambled out with grenades, side arms and machine guns. They went into a quick huddle then headed for American planes and the radio tower.

"The Japs came out of their plane, then spread out cautiously and approached our planes across the runways," said Marine Sgt. Claude Canup, Anderson, S.C., combat correspondent who witnessed the attack.

"They had taken only a few steps when the Marines opened fire. The Japs hit the deck and began firing, but kept crawling toward the radio tower."

While the Japanese succeeded in setting American planes afire, all were killed or committed suicide when they were wounded.

(Sgt. Canup, known here as "Red" Canup, was sports editor of *The Independent* and managing editor of *The Daily Mail* prior to entering the Marines. His sports column was widely known throughout the state.)

The Giretsu attack began with Japanese diversionary tactics—bombs dropped near Yontan and the radar screen filled with bogeys. Radar picked up two to three bogeys at a time before the first low flying Sally approached Yontan and was shot down by ack-ack protecting the field. Several Japanese survived long enough to fire gas dumps. Three other enemy aircraft loaded with suicide troops headed for the airfield were shot down.

On patrol that night, Lieutenant Colonel Marion M. Magruder's "Black Mac's Killers" are credited with shooting down five Japanese planes.

LIEUTENANT SMURR'S SHOW

Night-fighter pilots based on Yontan had been splashing Jap bombers and fighters in every direction from the island. All had fallen too far at sea to be visible to ground personnel on the field until First Lieutenant James E. Smurr, Columbus, O., went on his ninth mission of this campaign. He gave them a show.

While the Japs were bombing Ie Shima and landing suicide troops on Yontan, they were also losing other bombers to our night fighters. One of them, a Betty loaded with bombs earmarked for Ie Shima, didn't reach the target. Lieutenant Smurr, 22, intercepted the Betty flying at 18,000 feet on its way to the neighboring island. He hit her with one burst that gave away his position. The Japs opened up with guns from the tail and turret, red tracers cutting the blackness all around Smurr's Hellcat.

The Japs were slow in finding the range, and Smurr shot a killer burst with only two of his four guns working. With the Japs still firing at him, he flamed the Betty. The plane crashed on Ie Shima in full view of his squadron personnel and others on Yontan. The men who saw the flaming streak crash heard about the feat over their radios at about the same time. They cheered. The show for the men below was something new in night fighting here.

It was the following day when Smurr received congratulations from his squadron. Yontan was having too much trouble with the Nips to bring in its night fighters. Smurr's Hellcat and others landed on another field on the island.

Lieutenant Smurr has a brother Private First Class John A. Smurr with the Eighth Marine Field Depot in the Marianas. (26May45)

LONG TIME COMING FOR TRAMMELL

Tom Trammell had been in the Marine Corps since the summer of 1938, and since December 7, four years later, he had been looking for a chance to avenge Pearl Harbor. His day came the night the Japs had planned a field day in this campaign.

The enemy sent out one of its biggest raiding parties the night of May 24. Twin-engine bombers were directed to Ie Shima, 19 miles from Okinawa. That night was costly to the Nips. Numerous bombers and converted transports were shot down over the two islands and into the sea. A night fighter squadron from Yontan bagged five bombers, and credit for one Betty went to First Lieutenant Thomas B. Trammell, Brunswick, Ga.

The former enlisted man who became a commissioned officer and pilot on June 15, 1943, intercepted the Betty before it reached Ie Shima. There was no question about her cargo as she burned and exploded at 10,000 feet after several bursts from his gun.

The good-natured Trammell was wearing a big smile when he returned to his squadron the next morning from a nearby field where he had landed during the raid on Yontan.

"It took me a long time to make contact," he grinned, "but I finally got one!" (26May45)

SALLY MISSED HER DATE BECAUSE OF DELLAMANO

Albert Dellamano, who was never in an airplane until he enlisted for combat flying, shot down two Jap bombers and a fighter off the northern tip of this island the night of an aerial attack on Yontan. One of the bombers, a Sally, was the same type—loaded with demolition experts—the Japs successfully glided onto this airfield on May 24, 1945 under the cover of darkness. First Lieutenant Dellamano, night fighter from Brookline, Mass., was on his seventh mission and his first contact with the enemy since being transferred to Okinawa from the Marshall Islands. His bag of three planes on a single mission equals the Marine Corps record established a week before by First Lieutenant Robert E. Wellwood, Sheridan, Wyo., of the same fighter squadron.

The 23-year-old Dellamano made his first contact with the enemy at 9:45 PM. The plane, a twin-engine bomber referred to as a Betty, was intercepted eight miles off the tip of Okinawa flying at 13,000 feet headed toward this base. After being vectored to the Betty and picking it up by the sight of his naked eye, Dellamano closed in from behind and fired a burst into the starboard engine making it glow. The Betty went into a dive, with the night fighter sticking close and firing several more bursts, each one finding its mark. The bomber was burning freely after the third burst and splashed into the ocean with an explosion. Dellamano fired his last shots into the plane at 6,000 feet. The Betty never attempted to put up a fight.

Less than a half-hour later, two miles farther from the island, the former Watertown Arsenal employee, got on the tail of a Jake, twin-float reconnaissance plane. The Jap was flying at 11,500 feet with Dellamano 300 feet behind and slightly under him. The first shots started a fire on the right float, and the Jake lost altitude quickly. After two more bursts, the plane was enveloped in flames. It fell and was almost destroyed by the time it hit the water.

Then came Sally. The bomber was intercepted 15 miles north-west of the island, a half-hour after the Jake was destroyed. It was headed toward Yontan. Dellamano was 300 feet below and behind the Sally when he sent a stream of 50 caliber incendiary bullets into the right wing root. He saw pieces of the plane fly through the air, some hitting his Hellcat. The wing blazed, but the night fighter's fire was not returned. Sally started falling and wound up in a 45 degree dive. A few more bursts were fired into her setting more fires. "She hit the water hard, setting up a tremendous explosion," Dellamano recalled. He paid a compliment to Captain Jack Wilson, of New Orleans, saying "The ground controller did a marvelous job on all three splashes." (30May45)

11. MAG 31 AND TACTICAL AIR FORCE RYUKYUS (II)

May 15–July 7, 1945

This chapter contains Red's dispatches from Yontan until June 30, at which time the MAG relocated to the newly constructed Chimu Airfield, twenty miles north of Yontan Airfield. The summary of TAF accomplishments for the first ninety days on Okinawa is found at the end of this chapter.

COLONEL JOHN C. MUNN

Landing on Okinawa in early April as commanding officer of MAG 31, Colonel John C. Munn's 22 years of military service in several South American countries and throughout the Pacific had prepared him well for the island.

Following his graduation from the Naval Academy, Nicaragua in 1928 was his first duty station. The young Marine officer returned to the States September 1929 serving at Camp Rapidan and Quantico until assignment to the Pensacola, Fla., naval station, receiving his wings there March 1931. His next assignment was the West Coast as an officer of the expeditionary force at San Diego from April to September 1931. He then joined VMS 14, first Marine squadron to serve on a carrier.

For the next five years he had sea duty aboard carriers SARATOGA, LEXINGTON and LANGLEY. The leatherneck was again assigned to Quantico for a year as utility pilot and another year as assistant operations officer.

June 1938 found the Colonel in South America as naval attaché to Colombia, Venezuela, and Panama, with added duties as attaché to embassies in Peru and Ecuador. March 1941 Colonel Munn returned to the States, joined a squadron based at Quantico, and also served aboard YORKTOWN on neutrality patrol.

At the start of the Japanese war he was rushed to the West Coast again to serve as intelligence officer for the 1stMAW commanded by Major General Roy S. Geiger. August 1942, he sailed for the south Pacific and Guadalcanal. His assignment lasted from September 1 until April 1, 1943. Immediately upon his return from the Pacific, the Colonel took command of MAG 11. In July of that same year he was transferred to Washington as Assistant to the Chief of the Aviation Section, Plans Division, Marine Corps Headquarters.

On March 6, at Rio-Namur, Kwajalein atoll, Marshall Islands, Colonel Munn assumed command of MAG 31. The MAG, on alert for the Okinawa campaign, shoved off that month aboard a dozen ships. Colonel Munn's Corsairs and Hellcats arrived Yontan Airfield, Okinawa, April 3, 1945, and made the first kill by Okinawa-based fighters on April 7.

The Colonel still calls Prescott, Ark., home but has seen little of his hometown since arriving in Annapolis in 1923. (9May45)

ERASE A BOMBER

Second Lieutenant Lloyd J. Parsons, a night fighter based on Yontan Airfield, is a quiet, easy-going middle westerner now living in Pasadena, Calif. Bagging his first plane in the second month of flying here may change that.

Lieutenant Parsons was vectored to the twin-engine bomber about 30 miles southwest of Naha. In the darkness of the Oriental night, Parsons was little more than 100 feet from the Jap when he first spotted the bomber. The Jap apparently saw the night fighter below him at the same moment. He attempted to maneuver his plane into a better position to fight off the Hellcat. It was too late by then. Parsons, on his tail and slightly under him, opened his guns and set both engines on fire.

Parsons was so close that oil from the bomber splashed on his windshield as he slashed across the path left by the flaming bomber. As he watched the plane splash into the sea, the Marine pilot said it was a "beautiful, yet pitiful sight." He added also that it made him feel very good. (15May45)

A HALF FOR AN ACE

Captain Raymond F. Scherer, Wilmington, Calif., is looking forward to his next engagement with the Japs. With any luck at all, he will become a Marine ace then.

In three meetings with the enemy, the Hell's Belles fighter pilot has knocked down four planes and shares another with a fellow pilot. It probably will be a whole when he does bag his fifth, but the way the Captain looks at it, that will be the Japs' tough luck.

Flying in the dusk patrol last night as the leader of a two man section, Captain Scherer, who already had one and a half fighters to his credit, knocked down three dive-bombers between here and Formosa. Three were spotted about 80 miles from Naha, and the Californian, handling his Corsair like a toy, fired bursts of his 20mm cannon into two of them while his flying mate took care of the third. He was so close to the second one when it exploded that his plane streaked through smoke and flame. Part of the fabric of his victim caught on the Captain's plane.

The Corsair was slightly damaged but far from being out of commission. A few moments later he spotted four dive-bombers attacking a destroyer but had to share three with more Corsairs that had reached the scene.

Captain Scherer is now ranked the second highest man in planes downed by the Hell's Belles squadron, operating on Yontan Airfield. Scherer, 29, received his wings in 1943 and is a former student at Loyola University, University of California at Los Angeles and the University of California. (15May45)

KNIGHT OF THE CLOUDS

Second Lieutenant Wayne H. Knight, flying with the dusk patrol between here and Formosa, shot down a Jap dive-bomber which was heading toward an American destroyer. It was his first plane, the 46th for his squadron in the second month of flying from Yontan Airfield.

Knight, who was flying wing for a fellow Hell's Belles pilot, splashed one of three dive-bombers that were intercepted about 50 miles southwest of Naha.

The 21-year-old fighter pilot from Lebanon, N.H., left the University of New Hampshire to take flight training. He received his wings two years ago and had been stationed in the Marshalls several months before his squadron joined this campaign. (16May45)

THE BETTER FOR SPLASHING

Hellcats, the 2ndMAW's night fighters, are getting new bolts of trained "lightning" in their wings for combat air patrol and night strikes.

Previously equipped with only 50 caliber machine guns in the wings, the Hellcats now are sprouting a couple of 20mm cannons. Not all of them have "grown" the additional firepower, but, until that happens, it is probably just as well for the Japs not to know the "haves" from the "have nots" in this respect.

Night fighters are used principally for defensive work in the Pacific, but now that more of them carry the 20's, they are going on strikes against the enemy on other islands in the shoto. Too, they are equipped with rockets, the silencers of gun emplacements. Strafing with 50's and 20's, and bombing with rockets in the dead of the night can do more than just break down the morale of the enemy—and, that is what the Hellcats are accomplishing when they disappear into the darkness off Yontan. (17May45)

MISSION ACCOMPLISHED IS BEST WAY TO GO

While flying squadron Marine mechanics can perform what amounts to "mechanical miracles" in the field, sometimes they are confronted with problems which require more tools and a better equipped shop. It is then the service squadron, the backbone of every Marine aircraft group, receives the engine. It is the job of the service squadron to do the job too big for the flying squadron's engineering sections to handle, yet not large enough to necessitate a trip back down the line. The service squadron serves two to six tactical squadrons assigned to an aircraft group.

Time is required to set up a well equipped shop in the field, and the first few weeks of this campaign found only limited repair facilities—but, with what they have had to work with, plus plenty of ingenuity, plus the dire need for all available aircraft to be in the air, the Marine mechanics have done commendable work—both in flying squadron's engineering sections and aircraft group service squadrons.

"The only time an engine has to be transported back to fully equipped shops or factories," explains Commissioned Warrant Officer Grant M. Senour, engineering officer of a night fighter squadron, "is when it has to be disassembled for repair due to damage, or when it is worn to the point of requiring a complete overhauling job. And by the same token, an engine is never pushed aside to go to waste. We either repair them or send them back."

Of the largest number of engines shipped from the forward areas, it can be written on the packing crates—"mission accomplished." (17May45)

NUMBER 3 FOR BACON

"I've got to get another Tony to shut them up!" said Marine Second Lieutenant Charles E. Bacon, Eustis, Fla., after he returned to the base from a dawn patrol. The 2ndMAW pilot, with two Jap fighters to his credit, made his third kill of the campaign the "easy way" in the eyes of teasing fellow Hell's Belles squadron pilots. His third victim was a Willow, a trainer plane which the Japs must have found at the bottom of the barrel. It was carrying a bomb estimated to be a 500 pounder.

The 21-year-old Hell's Belles squadron member splashed the Jap 60 miles southeast of Naha. Two bursts from his 20mm guns into the fuselage sent the Nip diving. The Willow leveled off 10 feet above the water, tried to shake his pursuer with sharp skids and turns at low speed, and then suddenly banked and splashed. Several Willows have been shot down here recently. The pilots bagging them usually get the unwelcomed nickname of "Willow Killer." His first two planes bagged were Tonys. Lieutenant Bacon is a graduate of Eustis High School. (19May45)

VANISHING AMERICAN

Tokyo Rose, the Japanese radio comedienne, would have given her left eye for this one had it happened on Guadalcanal instead of this close to home:

When a Jap bomb scored a direct hit on a fully gassed and bomb-loaded bomber here the other night, the explosion threw a book 200 feet from the plane.

It was Zane Grey's The Vanishing American.

The novel was picked up the next morning by Marine Second Lieutenant Roswell V. Dobbs, aerologic officer, of Seattle, Wash. (20May45)

RAIN ON OKINAWA

A couple of 2ndMAW privates, attached to a fighter squadron, became so sick of the mud on Okinawa that they put down their feelings in rhyme and verse.

Leatherneck poets are Private Lester D. Boddye, Fairbury, Neb., and Private Joseph A. Bologna, Detroit, Mich.

"Rain On Okinawa"

Sahara is a lonely place.
Where pangs of thirst are all to face.
But in another land that's wet
Other fates are to be met.

The land is washed with a reddish water
A blood of muck and recent Jap slaughter.
There is mud that saunters through the door
Silently slushing the sunken floor.

The constant patter on the tent
Is enough the hardest skull to dent.
Wait: A lull in which to look.
Oh! Outside now there flows a brook.

The rain again begins to fall
He builds a dam, the water to stall.
But this is work that is all in vain
For who is man that can stop the rain.

To wile away the eminent time,
The lad for books, doth tread the slime.
There is no path on which to tread,
For travel now one needs a sled.

Thru slush and gathering muck
He stumbled and fell and up with a jerk
A ghost and appalled in drenched shoes he stood
Dripping features 'neath sodden hood.

For there he beholds a battered box
Filled with books and molded sox.
For the lid on the box was protection meek
The books and sox with water did reek.

Madly he fumbles through the lot,
Eagerly scanning each novel's plot.
Searching in vain for an interesting story,
To release his mind from the mess so gory.

The roar of the break from his solace did wake,
For the dam had been broke to a fast running lake.
Anger mingled with surprise in his look,
As he noticed the water fast filling his nook.

With a shovel and pick and a vow on his lips,
He promised himself no more of these trips.
Once off the ship at war's glorious end,
To hell with the seas and the water they send.

(20May45)

DECOYS

The open field at the end of one of Yontan's runways is bombed frequently by the Japs. The two fighter planes parked closely together make a great target. Nobody bothers to move the planes. They are bullet-riddled and shrapnel-ized.

The planes were left by the Japs when they vacated the airfield. (21 May45)

LOWMAN'S FIRST

Captain John Lowman, Jr., was thinking more of getting out of the anti-aircraft fire after he shot down his first Jap plane than of the sensation that comes with splashing a bogey.

When he returned to his base here and told his story he did not have to elaborate to make his audience understand. Captain Lowman, on his second Pacific cruise, lives in Smithfield, Mo., and on his latest patrol intercepted a Jap dive-bomber that had made a run on a destroyer and was heading for the airstrip at Ie Shima.

He chased the Jap two miles toward the island and let him have a long burst at 400 yards as the bomber started diving for the airfield. It was after sunset and anti-aircraft batteries on the island had opened up on the raider. Lowman's guns sent the enemy splashing into the sea off the end of the runway, and the Captain quickly ducked out of range of the ack-ack.

The fighter pilot, who was in charge of a squadron that landed on Roi in the Marshalls D-plus-three, February 1944, holds the Purple Heart and the Presidential Unit Citation. (21May45)

LOOS' TOJO

Second Lieutenant Billie E. Loos, Carbondale, Ill., has broken into the scoring circle of pilots on Yontan Airfield. The former University of Southern Illinois student shot down his first enemy plane on dusk patrol recently.

The way Loos describes the incident, it was quite simple. He was flying north of Okinawa when he spotted Tojo below him. He went into a dive, pulled out level with the Jap and opened up with his 20mm guns. The plane immediately began smoking, rolled over, and splashed into the sea.

Lieutenant Loos, 23, is a graduate of Murphysboro High School and was employed in the Carbondale office of the Illinois Central Railroad Company before entering the service. (21May45)

TWO AT A TIME

Jim Keegan had to wait a while to show what he could do when he tangled with the Japs, but when the time came he left no doubt as to how true he can shoot and also how well he can handle his Corsair.

The East Port Chester, Conn., resident, First Lieutenant James F. Keegan, was up on dusk patrol when his big moment came. His division spotted five Jap fighters and engaged them.

Keegan scored hits on the first one he tackled, but it eluded him. The next Jap was not so lucky. A long burst into the Tony set it afire and it splashed into the sea. The third one he fired on went down without a fight after taking a burst of 20's.

Now that he has a head start, the 21-year-old hopes he won't have to wait as long again before making contact with the enemy.

He attended Greenwich High School before taking flight training and came overseas last winter to join his present squadron, then flying in the Marshalls. (21May45)

ARCENEAUX SCORES AGAIN

Marine Second Lieutenant Arthur J. Arceneaux, Jr., 21, Gramercy, La., set a trap for a Jap plane on the dusk patrol and proved himself an air strategist as well as a good marksman.

The pint-sized graduate of Luther (La.) High School, who would look more at home in a campus jalopy, is a Marine night-fighter pilot. He already had one plane to his credit, bagged shortly after his unit began operating here, and now, through quick thinking, he is credited with half of another.

A section leader, Arceneaux and his wingman spotted a Jap reconnaissance float plane loaded with bombs and headed for Ie Shima, which was then under an air raid. "Arcy" was above the Jap, and peeled off to dive, but was observed before he had a chance to fire. The turret gunner opened up on him as the Nip climbed to escape, but the night fighter got in one burst from directly above that broke the right pontoon, setting it and the right wing on fire. When the Jap found cover in a cloud, the wingman was directed to "sit up there on the cloud and wait for the bogey to come out." Arcy was waiting below the cloud to cut off that avenue of escape.

The Jap came out above the cloud and Second Lieutenant Gordon Coles, Pendleton, Ore., the wingman, was in a position to let him have it. A long burst from the tail to the cockpit started a fire on the left wing, knocked the bogey out of control, and it cart-wheeled into the water, exploding into several small fires when it splashed.

The battle, which had started at 4,000 feet, ended with this knockout burst at 1,000 feet.

The raider, identified as a Jake, was intercepted 35 miles north of Ie Shima, heading south. (21May45)

"I JUST YELLED"

When Marine Second Lieutenant Gordon L. Coles, Pendleton, Ore., shot down his first Jap plane he was so excited that he couldn't remember what to say over his radio. "I was yelling while I was chasing him, and when I saw him splash I just hollered that I got the ———!"

Everybody in the squadron was glad Coles splashed one. He is the kind of guy everybody pulls for. While this was his first completed kill, he shares a reconnaissance twin float plane, shot down minutes before, with another pilot. With the first one, the Oregonian waited for the Jap to come out of a cloud.

The second one was different. Darkness had settled and Coles was flying at 5,000 feet north of Ie Shima. When he contacted the Jap, the night fighter was below and to the rear. He opened fire and kept up a stream of bullets until he was within 150 feet of the Nip spreading fire from stem to stern.

The Jap plane, called a Jake, went into a glide, and Coles followed the Jap down giving him three more bursts at 1,000 feet. The Jake exploded upon impact with Coles following him down.

"I was so excited," the 23-year-old from Pendleton explained, "that I almost got my feet wet." (21May45)

MIDNIGHT PATROL

Marine night fighters, assigned to intercept enemy fighters, bombers and airborne suicide squads have one of the most lonesome and dangerous jobs in this war.

They fly alone. On these dusk to dawn combat air patrols, the pilots depend on the radioed voice of their controllers. The instrument pilots can on occasion find the enemy as they visually scan the sky, but the enemy is also scanning. Which plane is downed often depends on which pilot spots the other first.

Night fighters have set new squadron and individual records in the Ryukyus. Shooting down over 35 raiders in less than two months, two of the kills were by Lieutenant George Collins, of New York City. The 25-year-old pilot, flying over 100 missions as a night combat flyer, agreed to share a night experience from his Hellcat (F6F) cockpit. To help us understand how these men think, how they act and how they pass the hours alone in the sky, he chose a patrol during which he downed his first, a Jap Kate.

- - - - - - - - -

Lieutenant Collins has been given the false code name of Eightball Seven for this four hour mission. Here is his story:

Hello, tower, this is Eightball Seven. Request clearance to taxi down for takeoff position. Over.

"Hello, Eightball Seven. This is tower. You are cleared to taxi. Out."

Another and final check of instruments and switches is made as the Hellcat rolls down the runway.

Hello, tower. This is Eightball Seven. Request clearance for takeoff. Over.

"Hello, Eightball Seven. This is tower. You are clear for Number One takeoff. Good luck. Out."

The throttle is pushed forward, eyes on the instruments, and I pray that there's nothing in my way,

Now I can see the ships at sea, the outline of the airfield, the tents silhouetted against the water in the background. It is midnight. Most of the camp is asleep. But to the south brilliant, red gun flashes. There is no sleep where the enemy is making his last ditch stand. Only the eternal sleep of the dead.

Hello, control, this is Eightball Seven. Airborne over field. Request instructions for combat air patrol. Over.

"Hello, Eightball Seven. This is control. You will patrol north sector. Report to control on that sector. Out."

Signal lights are switched off. Only the dim instrument lights are on now as the Hellcat gathers speed northbound.

Hello control, this is Eightball Seven on station. Have you any business for me? Over.

"Hello, Eightball Seven. This is control. We have no business in the area just yet. Please orbit area. Out."

Orbiting . . . Around and around . . . Reading instruments, peering into the darkness . . . Thinking . . . A half-hour passes, 45 minutes and then an hour drags by . . . This seat gets harder and harder . . . Not much room to move into a more comfortable position . . . Wonder if the Nips will try to come tonight? . . . Just my luck for them to wait until I'm below, as usual. A hundred missions and not a kill—what a record! . . . Wonder what's doing in New York now? . . . Let's see, 1 AM here . . . 3 PM back there . . . 3 PM yesterday . . . I'm flying here this morning, they're working back there yesterday afternoon at the same time . . . What a cockeyed world! . . . They've just finished lunch yesterday afternoon, and here I am almost ready for breakfast tomorrow . . . Um, I should have brought my umbrella. Clouds are moving in at 4,000 and it looks like rain . . . I knew I shouldn't have left my wash hanging on the line . . . Whe're the

Nippers . . . I could use a bogey now . . . A hundred missions, and here I am flying less than 300 miles from Japan—and not a bogey . . . What a war!

Hello, north control. This is Eightball Seven. Do you have any business for me? Over.

"Hello, Seven. This is control. Do not have any business for you. Is this Collins? Over?"

Yes, this is Collins. Over.

"Hello, George. This is Doc. How is everything going up there?"

Everything's okay up here, except for a few clouds getting in my way. How is everything with you?

"All's well down here. Do you know if I got any mail today?"

Didn't see any for you. She probably doesn't love you anymore.

"Oh, no. She must have broken her arm and will write later."

Doc, I'm going to climb a few thousand to get above this layer of clouds. Let me know when you have any business. Out.

Ah! Much nicer up here, but maybe it's because I can't see who might be next door. Any rate, half the period is over so I'll break out one of those delicious tropical chocolate bars. Funny thing about candy, if this can be called candy without kicking the word too much, back home when I could get the real stuff I never cared for it. Now these bars taste just like steak—and are about as tough.

Better make sure the radio checks okay up here . . . Nice thing a radio—and an easy chair and a long, cold one . . . Just press a button and out comes the best music in the world—but up here I can only get Doc . . . But there'll be a day . . . Let's see—three months, five days, two hours and 26 more minutes more out here. That is, if my relief is on time . . . Wonder where the fellow who will take my place is from—Texas, I guess, or the middle west . . . I should have joined the Army and gone back after 25 missions . . . On second thought, I'll stick to the Marines.

These Oriental nights are the tops . . . Misty, a quarter moon breaking in the background, with the outline of the shore below . . . In the next war, I'll advocate for one hostess with every F6F . . . It seems lighter up this far even on the blackest nights than down in the Carolinas . . . Wonder if other guys have noticed it . . . Or maybe I'm developing cat eyes . . . But I can't see a bogey . . . How the hell am I going to face my brother when he starts telling me how many the Army shot down over Europe? . . . There must be something up here . . . My mother should have made me eat carrots instead of so much spinach . . . Oh, well, if you can't see them you can't shoot them, I hope that means if they can't see me, they can't hit me . . . Ho, hum, half hour to go—round and round . . . They should take a picture of me in action! . . . This seat is harder than the bleachers at the stadium . . . Wonder what the Yanks will do this year?

. . . Maybe I can get back in time to help root them into the series . . . Three months, five days, one hour and about 14 minutes. That will be the day—what th'? . . .

"Hello, Eightball Seven. This is north control. Heads up. There are enemies in your vicinity. Believe them to be low. Expedite dive. Out."

Here we go—400 per and yet it seems like a crawl . . . Um, wonder what happened to my stomach. Must have left it back there . . . The guns check okay . . . Now turn on the gun sight and keep that finger against the trigger, ready to push . . . Better level off about here.

Hello, control. This is Eightball Seven at 3,000 feet, directly north of base. Do you have any more information about enemy raid? Over.

"Hello, Seven. This is control. We have information that one enemy plane seems to be headed for Yontan. Go get him. Out."

The throttle is open, eyes looking ahead, trying to spot an object in the blackness . . . Can't see a thing . . . There he is! . . . Coming right at me, about 300 feet away. Hell, I can't get into position this close to give him a burst . . . I'll do well to keep him from ramming me . . . This looks like his round . . . Nothing to do now but a fast shunt (night fighter lingo for any maneuver to get out of the range of fire) . . . Whew! That was close . . . Somebody must have been praying mighty hard for me then . . . If he fired at me, I don't seem to be hit.

Hello, north control. This is Eightball Seven. Your boy was almost creamed. I'm now looking around for the bum who tried it. Over.

"Hello, Eightball Seven. The guy who just missed you seems to be headed from base now. Try out that way. Out."

So he's headed for home. This would be one way of seeing the night life of Tokyo if I had enough gas . . . Wish my stomach would catch up with me . . . Good thing the flight surgeon isn't getting a beam on my heart now . . . Too much excitement for such a short time—and rotten luck . . . First I see and he's got the advantage . . . What a dud I'm turning out to be . . . Probably have to extend my cruise to get even one.

There he is! A dive-bomber not more than 500 feet off the water and streaking northward. A quick dive now and maybe this will be my round. Um, he sees me but that's too bad for now—for one of us. He's turning toward me. Now's my chance while he's turning. A long burst. There goes part of his right wing. Your mistake! He's rolling over on his back. A perfect target for another burst. I'll glue this finger on the trigger until he flames! That does it! There he goes into the water! So long, chump.

That was easy. Nothing to it. So that's how you splash a bogey. And what a pretty picture. I should be an artist and paint that!

Control. This is Eightball Seven. Splash one Kate. Over.

"Hello, George. This is Doc. Congratulations. Guess you're no longer a virgin. Out."

I didn't know I could feel so good up here. Even the seat is soft now. Wait till the folks hear about this! What the heck? Just 15 minutes of gas left. I've got business elsewhere.

Hello, Doc. This is George. Very low on gas. Request permission to return to base. Over.

"Hello, George. This is Doc. Permission granted. Return to base. And say, don't forget to put your wheels down! Out."

Wonder if I'll be able to sleep after the first one? Never knew anything could be so simple. Maybe getting him out of the way will end the war a minute or two sooner . . . Glad he didn't get to the base and wake up the boys. Then I know I couldn't sleep.

Hello, tower. This is Eightball Seven over base. Request clearance to land.

"Hello, Eightball Seven. This is tower. Clear and Number One to land. We have a strong cross wind from the right. Out."

I'll double check everything to make sure that my elation does not overcome my flying sense . . . Easy does it . . . The good earth again.

- - - - - - - - -

Lieutenant Collins was warmly greeted and congratulated by his mechanic. Reaching operations to store his flight gear, to his amazement he found Major General Francis P. Mulcahy, commanding general of the 2ndMAW, had left a message, "Well done!"

The pilot, who had served as an enlisted Marine for several years before receiving his commission and wings, admitted the next afternoon that he was unable to sleep until late in the morning. He explained, "I was as wide awake as a kid on Christmas morning—and just as excited." (21May45)

TWO FOR COLLINS

Second Lieutenant George J. Collins, the Bronx, who studied for the priesthood and then became a Marine, shot down a Jap fighter on dusk patrol to give him two splashes in the Okinawa campaign.

His second splash was a Tony, which he spotted out of the corner of his left eye as it became silhouetted briefly against a moonlit cloud. He went in fast on the Jap, and one long burst, starting at 500 feet, set the Tony afire. The plane blew up immediately, forcing Collins to bank sharply to dodge the explosion. He had fired 180 rounds into the Tony, scores of them into the engine.

Lieutenant Collins, who joined the Marine Corps in 1938, served as an enlisted man for five years. He received his wings and commission November 1943. He was educated at St. John's College, George Washington University and

William and Mary Extension. He was 25 years old on Okinawa's D-day plus one. (25May45)

"JUST CALL ME JOE"

A first lieutenant, adjutant of a Marine night fighter squadron, admonished leathernecks with a bulletin board notice reminding them to refer to officers by rank.

That night a Jap air-borne suicide squad landed on the airfield.

A guard jumped into the adjutant's fox hole, and exclaimed, "Lieutenant, Japs on the field!"

The adjunct just as excitedly replied, "Don't refer to me as a lieutenant. Just call me Joe!" (26May45)

SOREIDE AND DORRELL SPLASH THREE EACH

A North Dakota rancher's son, who has been riding horses since he was six years old, proved last night he can do better than fair in a Corsair. In his first contact with the enemy, the Hell's Belles squadron member shot down three Jap planes—and he won't be old enough to vote until August 28. Flying as his partner was Second Lieutenant Richard F. Dorrell, 23, Morgantown, W.Va.

Second Lieutenant Carl E. Soreide, enlisted for flight training just three months after graduating from high school, was flying wing on another day fighter pilot on the dusk patrol when they intercepted a half-dozen dive-bombers only six miles from several of our destroyers. All of the bombers were shot into the sea before they had a chance to strike.

"The dive bombers were flying six abreast in a combat line," related Soreide. "My partner and I were meeting them head on. He peeled off and went down on them from the left, and I tackled them from the right side. They broke formation, and I opened up on the first one I contacted about 800 feet from above and to the side. My second burst was a level one which set him on fire. He splashed into the sea without firing a single shot."

When Carl pulled out of his dive after following his first victim down far enough to see that he would not escape, the young day fighter found himself on the tail of another bomber for a perfect shot. He fired a quick burst immediately setting the plane on fire. It plunged into the sea without so much as a staggering maneuver.

"I was feeling pretty good by this time," Carl said. "I pulled up, turned to the left and saw a couple of other Jap planes. They were about a mile to the west so I went after them. The Japs were coming my way. They saw me and separated. I made a pass for the one that chose to go north."

The Jap who Soreide picked out was only interested in getting away. He made a sharp turn to the left, Carl duplicated the maneuver and was in position to fire. One burst had the enemy plane in flames. The Jap went into a wingover and fell a thousand feet into the water.

"I didn't get excited until I got back to the base," he said. "My partner got three, too, so we had plenty to celebrate." It was Soreide's 43rd mission from Yontan—his first contact with the enemy.

Second Lieutenant Richard F. Dorrell, 23, of Morgantown, W.Va., was equally excited. He related he was about ready to return to the base when all the planes were spotted. He has been flying with Hell's Belles night fighter squadron since last winter.

The boys had done more than shoot six Jap bombers into the sea. From one of the ships, apparent targets of the dive-bombers, came a message of thanks; and, as the Corsair pilots raced for Yontan in the gathering darkness, their radio sets picked up this message from one of the destroyers, "Our commodore sends personal congratulations!"

Dorrell attended the University of West Virginia. In addition to flying Corsair strikes from this base, he is squadron parachute officer. (26May45)

PINCH-HITTER

A dogfight in the black of the night with a Jap dive-bomber is not unusual for night fighters. Having a battle with a Nip that turns on his tail light is really unusual. Splashing the Jap because of his mistake is very satisfying.

Second Lieutenant Gordon L. Coles, 23, Pendleton, Ore., a night-fighter pilot, was on combat air patrol as a pinch-hitter. He was zeroed in on a bogey that dropped flares in the vicinity of U.S. ships. The Jap, Coles believes, was being directed by an enemy ground station. The dive-bomber not only evaded the night fighter but got on his tail three times. Neither the Marine nor the Nip ever got close enough to fire during the dogfight.

Circling, diving, and evading from 5,000 to 500 feet, the Jap exited. Coles went down 4,000 feet searching the skies. Spotting a bomber circling with an activated tail light took the Lieutenant so much by surprise that he radioed the base before flying closer for a better look. The radio squawked, "Not friendly! Not friendly!"

Coles immediately swung into the circle with the Jap. The first burst was shot from 300 feet, the 50 caliber bullets hitting behind the engine. Fire spread from wing tip to wing tip. The blazing dive-bomber splashed with a tremendous explosion.

"I leveled off after following him down," said the pint-sized Marine night fighter. "When he exploded the blast lifted my plane 100 feet. I felt like somebody had kicked me."

All bagged in a seven day period, the flier now has two and a half planes to his credit in this campaign. "I don't know why the Jap turned on his tail light," explained Lieutenant Coles, "but it was a big help to me. I might have lost him!" (26May45)

HOLLOWELL FLIES WING ON A BETTY

Flying wing on a Betty, prized medium bomber of the Imperial Japanese Air Force, was the biggest thrill ever experienced by First Lieutenant Morris M. Hollowell, a night fighter. The 26-year-old resident of Churchland, Va., was flying night combat patrol when he intercepted the Jap at 14,000 feet 65 miles northwest of this base.

"After firing a burst on each side of the Betty, starting small fires under both engines," the Virginian pondered, "and the bomber not bursting into flames, it made me wonder what went wrong. The other pilots told me they usually sent them down flaming with two bursts. I raked the bomber from about a thousand feet and sent it into a mild spiraling dive. She still didn't burst into flames. The crew not shooting whetted my curiosity."

"I moved closer to her left wing," grinned Lieutenant Hollowell. "I could see the pilot and another Jap working frantically. Now and then a light would flash on and off in the cockpit. I don't think they saw me. The most thrilling sight I saw was the rising sun on the fuselage and wing. That got me more excited than seeing the two Japs."

"I dropped back and fired a long burst into the bomber's tail while the plane spiraled and dived. My last burst went into the fuselage and right engine. Down to 1,000 feet I pulled out and watched her finally splash. Both engines had been burning since my first two bursts." (28May45)

OKINAWA
MAY 28, 1945

I was up and down a half-dozen times last night running to a dugout and went to sleep once sitting on my helmet—wonder I didn't dream I was in the head!

From the news, I suppose you have a definite idea what we're catching here now. The Japs are throwing all they have left into this campaign. Where the hell they are getting it all beats me.

The actual raid isn't as bad as standing around in the blackness wondering if and when one of the little bastards might drop out of the sky either in a glider, bomber, or parachute. Sleep is out. I try to catch a nap during the day, but news is breaking faster than hell. I can't sit around and watch it go stale—tramped around in the mud all afternoon rounding up pilot stories.

I'll go now and get some sleep. Meanwhile, you might pass the word around the usual circles that I am safe and well, feeling chipper and crazy as ever—if not more so. I'm glad that a year overseas hasn't affected me in the least. Some guys get a little batty in the belfry. I keep telling them I have been skipping around in circles flapping my arms since I was a kid!

AEROGRAPHERS TO JAPAN

Ready to take off for a strike against a Jap-held island far to the north, a dozen rocket-laden Corsairs were taxied back to their area. The strike had been called off. The weather had closed in on the target.

A weather report grounded Thunderbolts fully loaded and gassed for a mission to Kyushu. Before the planes could be taxied off the line, another weather report relayed from plane to ship to air base put the planes in the air and on schedule. The weather was perfect at Kyushu, and the target was standing out like a sore thumb. Marine aerographers were on the job.

Flying in Privateers with Navy search crews combing the waters around Japan for shipping, these enlisted weathermen bring word on the weather to the base or radio the information if the need is immediate. Weather reporting is an important and exciting job here entailing more than storms forming or fronts coming. These aerographers have learned to spot enemy ships and planes, fire tommy guns at 500 feet, and on occasion cut loose on the Nips with .45 automatics.

The aerographers do not make long range forecasts. Their observations are usually for 12-hour periods and never more than 36 hours. Spot weather coverage is used immediately by operations officers planning strikes. Full reports are turned in at the end of each flight by the aerographers. Reports, notes, and charts are compiled with those of other observers. From the collected data, forecasts are made for ships, planes, and weather stations as far away as Saipan.

Often when the weather closes in on Okinawa, the sun is shining brightly over Japan less than 400 miles away. Thanks to spot reports being radioed, the aerographers let our bombers and fighters know what to expect beyond the clouds.

The four Marine aerographers in the Marine aircraft group on this field are Sergeant John W. Scarborough, 31, Houston, Tex.; Private First Class Harold R. Beaver, 37, St. Joseph, Mo.; Corporal Charles W. VanAmburg, 19, Barnhart, Mo.; and Sergeant Paul D. Sauder, 21, Crabill, Ind.

These men have flown within 40 miles of Tokyo, flown non-sop to Vladivostok, and flown over smiling, flag waving Korean natives. The aerographers fly with Army and Navy observers sweeping the Pacific and East China Sea keeping officers informed and saving light bombers and fighters from running into storms that would blow them out to sea. They are the advanced men of the air arm—the men behind the weather man. (4June45)

AIR MEDAL FOR MCCORMICK

Captain Ralph G. McCormick, a fighter pilot, stood ankle deep in mud here today and received the Air Medal "for meritorious acts" during the initial phases of this campaign.

The 26-year-old resident of Detroit, Mich., is a division leader in a Corsair squadron which is leading other units on Yontan in the number of enemy planes knocked down. The Air Medal was pinned on the rain-dampened shirt of the Captain by Colonel John C. Munn, commanding officer of the Marine aircraft group on this field.

Presentation was made in the presence of the entire flight personnel of the squadron, and Colonel Munn praised the work of all pilots in this campaign declaring that "It is the best flying I have seen in 15 years."

Captain McCormick is a veteran of Guadalcanal. (6June45)

AIR MEDAL STAR FOR SHUMAN

Major Perry Shuman, a Marine ace in the early phases of the Pacific war in the Solomons, is still flying against the Japs at the new base and has received a star in lieu of a second Air Medal.

Major General Francis P. Mulcahy, commanding general of the 2ndMAW presented the star to the commanding officer of a Corsair squadron leading other units of Yontan in the number of enemy planes shot down.

Major Shuman is also holder of the Distinguished Flying Cross for shooting down six Jap planes on his first cruise. He led a flight patrol in June 1943 that intercepted a formation of enemy planes over the New Georgia area, and in the ensuing action personally shot down three Zeros. Again in July, he attacked a superior number of Jap planes and shot down two fighters in flames and possibly a third. His sixth was also bagged in July.

The Marine ace, a former professional swimming instructor, assumed command of his present squad in December 1944 stationed in the Marshall Islands and led it to Okinawa shortly after the airfield was secured.

Major Shuman has a brother William J. Shuman, a lieutenant in the army air force. (6June45)

SERGEANT HICKS AWARDED SECOND PURPLE HEART

Staff Sergeant James H. Hicks has been awarded a gold star in lieu of a second Purple Heart for wounds received as a result of enemy action in the Asiatic-Pacific area. Hicks, 23-year-old resident of Houston, Tex. was on the flight line the night of April 15, 1945, when the Japs bombed and strafed Yontan. Wounded in the hip by a piece of shrapnel, he was away from his post only a few days for recovery.

Almost two years ago, Sergeant Hicks was wounded in almost the same place. July 26, 1943, he was a gunner in a torpedo bomber and shot down off Munda. He and the pilot were both wounded, and the radio gunner was killed. The wounded men were in the water six hours before they swam to the nearest island.

The Marines were discovered after three days by natives. On July 30, 1943, a canoe trip to a PT boat stationed at Rendova saved their lives. The aviators flattened themselves on the bottom of the natives' boat. The natives covered them with palm branches for the long trip in open sea since Jap artillery fire had the water covered day and night.

Hicks is in the ordnance section of a Marine fighter squadron. (6June45)

RICHARDS RECEIVES AIR MEDAL

Major Samuel Richards, Jr., Bates, Ark., holder of the Distinguished Flying Cross for shooting down two enemy planes in the Solomons campaign, today has been awarded the Air Medal.

His squadron was one of the first to begin operating on Yontan, and is leading others on this field in the number of enemy planes shot down with more than 60 to its credit.

He has been flying since June 1941 and is an alumnus of Arkansas Tech. (6June45)

PURPLE HEART FOR SERGEANT GRIFFIN

A wounded ankle kept Sergeant John Griffin, 19, Hickory, Miss., off the job for only a few days after the April 15, 1945, night bomber raid on Yontan Airfield.

The Purple Heart was awarded to Sergeant Griffin "in the name of the President of the United States and by direction of the Secretary of the Navy" for wounds received as the result of enemy action that night.

Sergeant Griffin, an ordnance officer, rearms machine guns and loads bombs and rockets on Corsairs. (6June45)

TWO ON TEST

A 2ndMAW pilot today downed two Japanese planes while testing a Corsair. Second Lieutenant Raymond M. Barrett, 22, flying north of his base, was breaking in a new engine when he downed an enemy aircraft. Forcing the Jap into the sea without firing a round, Lieutenant Barrett chased the plane causing the Jap to make violent turns and lose control when his right wing dragged the water.

Barrett, East Orange, N.J., downed a second Nip plane with several short bursts exploding the bogey and adding another to the bottom of the sea. This brought Barrett's total kills in the Okinawa campaign to four.

The Lieutenant, flying combat air patrol over the island, is a graduate of Wardlaw High School and attended Springfield College at Springfield, Mass. (8June45)

65 TO 0

One Corsair squadron of the 2ndMAW wound up two months of combat air patrol on Okinawa today with a score of 65 to 0 against the Japs.

The fighter squadron, commanded by Major Perry L. Shuman, has averaged better than a plane a day since its first mission here April 7, without a single loss to enemy action, according to Sergeant Claude Canup, a Marine combat correspondent. (8June45)

DFC FOR BROWN

Marine Second Lieutenant Theodore A. Brown, 22-year-old fighter pilot from Columbus, Ohio, is authorized to wear the Distinguished Flying Cross "for heroism and extraordinary achievement while operating against the enemy."

He was cited by Major General Francis P. Mulcahy, commanding general of the 2ndMAW for his missions from Yontan, particularly on April 26 when, reads the temporary citation prepared in the field, Brown "by skillful flying and expert marksmanship, succeeded in shooting down two Zekes on one flight. His courage, determination, and skill contributed materially to the success achieved by the squadrons and his conduct at all times was in keeping with the highest traditions of the United States Naval Service."

Yontan had been soaked by days of rain, yet in spite of bad weather the Corsair pilots slowed down little from their missions. This drew the commendations of generals and admirals in this theatre of operation. (9June45)

TWO FOR PECOS KID

Second Lieutenant Robert K. Sherrill, 24, Pecos, Tex., is keeping up with the field. At the end of two months' flying on Okinawa, the "Pecos Kid's" squadron had a record of better than one enemy plane per day, and Sherrill came through with a couple of them, bagging his second recently. He shot down his first in late April.

The Jap, dead-set on reaching his target, continued on a straight course, until his craft was hit, and neither fired at Sherrill nor attempted evasive actions. He was shot into the sea 20 miles southwest of the island of Kume. (11June45)

KAYSER EARNS SECOND AIR MEDAL

First Lieutenant Dale W. Kayser, 21, San Francisco, Calif., has been presented a star in lieu of a second Air Medal "for meritorious acts" while flying combat patrol in the Ryukyus. The Californian was the first pilot in his squadron to be credited with two enemy planes, shooting down fighter aircraft on two separate missions in the early phases of the campaign. (17 June45)

BROWN'S SEVENTH

Things are happening fast for Bill Brown, former Austonio, Tex., student.

Back in April, shortly after his squadron arrived here, Second Lieutenant William P. Brown, Jr., 21-years-old, shot down a couple of enemy planes.

Early in May he bagged four more on a single mission to become a Marine ace. Shortly after that Major General Francis P. Mulcahy presented him with an Air Medal. A couple of days ago the former student at Texas A and M shot down another Jap, his seventh.

Something else exciting also recently happened to the ace. First Lieutenant Brown's promotion came through shortly after he was credited with six planes.

He received his wings December 1943. (12June45)

THE MAJOR IS AN ACE

Major Robert B. Porter, Los Angeles, Calif., became an ace the hard way. He started his string two years ago in the Solomons shooting down three Japanese planes as a day fighter pilot. The two he shot down here recently as a night fighter completed the five kill requirement. Commander of a night fighter squadron on the island, Major Porter shot a Betty (medium bomber) and a Nick (heavy fighter) on a single midnight patrol mission.

He bagged the Betty as it headed toward Kyushu from a bombing run in the Ryukyus. Several bursts sent her flaming into a cloud where she disappeared. The Nick was easier. The twin-engine fighter disintegrated a few hundred feet above the water after two bursts from the Major's guns.

"They are harder to get at night," the Californian explained. "Day and night interceptions are different. One slight error at night, correctable in the day light, may not only result in losing the enemy but giving away your position. Avoid allowing the Jap to attack is the best advice I can give—keep control." (17June45)

KANSAS AIRMAN IS POET

T/Sgt. Charles F. Newcomb, Pittsburg, Kan., wrote the following:

Killer by Night

You climb into your airborne mount,
Oh, rider of the night!
You warm her massive engine,
And see that all is right.

When at last you're sure she's in the groove,
You taxi to the strip,
And rev her there in readiness
For another night trip.

The watchman in the tower hears
And gives the go-ahead.
You return the well-known "Roger"
So he'll know that you have read.

Now down the runway, flying man,
The end is there in sight.
Give her all the gas she needs,
Then off into the night.

You climb the angels pre-assigned,
To orbit till you're needed.
Now G.C. has a bogey man,
So, to that spot you're speeded.

Your schooling re-asserts itself;
You find you're very cool.
Japs go mad, but not this lad.
You'll show them you're no fool.

You pick him up and hone right in.
He makes a good bull's eye.
You expect evasive action,
But the sucker doesn't try.

From the darkness like a flash,
You guide your demon plane!
She spurts forth from her fifties
A deadly, fiery, rain.

His mount is staggered, wounded, stopped.
It falls a ball of fire,
And hits the inky water there,
A blazing funeral pyre!

Your exultation wells within;
You nearly choke with joy!
The work is done, the battle won,
You've splashed one more Jap boy.

The mighty demon's in her stall,
Her massive engines still.
But there'll be other nights for her.
She can, she did, she will!

And in his foxhole, tent, or shop,
Each man will glow with pride.
For he sent his workmanship with you,
Upon that midnight ride.

[not dated]

ALWAYS A GRANT

One of the Grant brothers of Alabama can usually be found taking part in most any operation out here. Occasionally the brothers' paths cross—all five Grant brothers are in Marine Corps aviation.

The paths of two of the Grant brothers in the Ryukyus campaign crossed on Yontan today. Technical Sergeant Braxton E. Grant, stationed with MAG 22 on Ie Shima, thumbed a ride to Okinawa to see First Lieutenant Hubert D. Grant, with the Tactical Air Force here.

The other three Grant brothers are "somewhere in the Pacific." Corporal James C. Grant is with an air warning squadron in the Western Carolines; Technical Sergeant Odis L. Grant is with operations of the 1stMAW; and Private First Class Henry E. Grant is with a fighter squadron that shipped out recently.

The Marines are from Repton, Ala. (19June45)

CORPSMAN WOUNDED

A Marine corpsman, Pharmacist Mate First Class James R. Freeland, 23, Los Angles, Calf., has been awarded the Purple Heart "for wounds received as result of enemy action" in a bombing raid on Yontan the night of April 15.

Freeland, who was educated in France and lived there several years, was wounded in the leg by shrapnel while on duty at MAG 31's sickbay. It was a slight injury and he continued on the job.

This is the second cruise for the corpsman who enlisted in the Navy February 1942. He served on Guadalcanal in 1942 with the First Marine Division. (20June45)

WOUNDED IN ACTION

Master Technical Sergeant John E. Sullivan, 21-year-old resident of Tonawanda, N.Y., has been awarded the Purple Heart "for wounds received as result of enemy action" during a bombing raid on Yontan Airfield the night of April 15.

Sullivan and other Marines were on duty in the engineering section of MAG 31 when the field was bombed. The men ducked for cover under the jeep in which they were riding. Sullivan was hit by a piece of shrapnel, but was not seriously injured.

The medal was awarded by Marine Major Joseph A. Gray, Mishawaka, Ind.

Sullivan enlisted in the Marine Corps June 1941. (20June45)

BROTHERS TOGETHER AGAIN

Marine Private First Class Edward W. Clifton, Altoona, Ala., who is stationed with a night fighter on Yontan, was getting a pass to permit him to look up his brother when the squadron office telephone rang. The call was from Corporal John P. Clifton, First Marine Division, who was trying to locate the younger half of the Clifton Marine team.

The boys had last seen each other in April 1942. (20June45)

The following article, dated June 20, 1945, appeared in an Anderson newspaper. (Reprinted with permission granted from the Independent-Mail*)*

"ALL WE KNOW IS WHAT WE READ IN THE PAPERS"

Red Canup, former editor of *The Daily Mail,* now a Marine combat correspondent, is in the thick of fighting on Okinawa. Red writes: "Okinawa is quite a spot. It is a big island not nearly as full of disease as first believed, and the weather is not too bad if you like it on the hot side. You know more about what is going on over the island than we do. Because all we know is what we read in the papers.

"I received an armful of *Daily Mails* a few days back. I brought them from the post office just like I used to bring in stove wood. There were that many. And were they put to good use. Not only were they enjoyed by fellows who had never been to Anderson, but I managed to get a few copies to a couple of Marines from our town. We got a kick out of the weekly questions. Particularly the one pertaining to what should be taken off the ration list. Gasoline came in first.

"If anybody ever wonders about what is happening to all the gasoline, they should see the air traffic over Yontan. And this is one of our latest air base additions out here. We've been sending fighters up to Japan from here, as you probably read weeks ago. But this is only the beginning of the end. Some of the guys think I am rock happy by this forecast, but it is my guess that the war will be over Thanksgiving."

PROPROFSKY RECEIVES PURPLE HEART

Private First Class Thomas F. Proprofsky has received the Purple Heart for "Wounds received as result of enemy action" during a bombing raid on Yontan Airfield. He is from Detroit, Mich.

The ground crewman was wounded the night of May 24 when Japanese suicide troops staged an air-base Giretsu attack on the airfield. He was back at the job the following day.

Young Proprofsky, who is in Hell's Belles squadron, attended Cleveland High School in Detroit and was a machinist in the Plymouth Motor Company before joining the Marine Corps November 1943. (20June45)

4TH OF JULY ON YONTAN

The Fourth of July on Yontan, in terms of fireworks, is most any night since 2ndMAW Corsairs and Hellcats put this former Jap airfield to good use.

A sign, erected at the air field here, reads: "WELCOME TO YONTAN EVERY NIGHT A 4TH OF JULY."

Air raids on Yontan have not been as intense recently as they were during the first two months of the operation, but the field is close enough to Japan—350 miles—and important enough to make it a prize target for high-flying medium bombers that carry enough gas for a return trip, or the obsolete dive-bombers that come in loaded with explosives and are definitely on a one-way trip.

But it is the defensive part of a bombing raid that makes for a Fourth of July. Giant searchlight fingers pick out the bombers and keep them spotlighted while large anti-aircraft shells burst around, or score a hit, to send a flaming plane spinning to the ground. And when the attackers come in low enough, it is even more exciting and colorful, with thousands of red tracers streaming up from the small A-A batteries.

Flares and phosphorous bombs dropped by the enemy also make for brilliant colors and excitement in the dead of the night, and it was on that score that a corpsman here wrote these lines in his poem titled "Air Raid on Yontan:"

> "A blinding sheet of flame ahead, the sky was painted gory red, and sheets of flame came raining down . . ."

Captain William L. Thompson, Jamaica, N.Y., ordnance officer, remarked simply the first time he saw the welcome sign, "The Fourth of July displays back home will never touch a real raiding picture." The Captain is a former salesman and golf promoter for A.G. Spalding and Brothers of New York City and recruited in Minneapolis and Chicago several months in 1943 and 1944 before he shipped overseas.

One thing is certain—Marines who sweated it out on Yontan during the most intense air raids of the Okinawa campaign will not be too receptive to fireworks hereafter—even on peaceful Fourths of July. (20June45)

LIEUTENANT HARRY TRICE'S DOUBLE OR NOTHING

It was double or nothing for Second Lieutenant Harry L. Trice, Dallas, when he made his first contact with the enemy. It came out double.

On his third combat mission, the Lieutenant and his wingman intercepted a medium bomber carrying a Baka bomb, one of those under-slung TNT-laden one-man suicide tricks the Japs use against shipping.

The bomber had a seven-man escort. Other Corsairs went after the fighters who turned tail and fled. Trice and his wingman went after the bomber, a Betty. The Jap tail gunner put the wingman out of the fight, but the Texan put the Jap gunner out of the fight—silencing him. With the gunner out of the way, Trice pulled up behind the bomber, fired another long burst, and watched her flame and hit the water about 50 miles northwest of Yontan. The Baka bomb was jettisoned into the water as soon as the Corsairs gave chase.

"It was my biggest thrill," said Lieutenant Trice in describing the air battle. He received his commission in April 1944.

He is a graduate of North Dallas High School and attended Southern Methodist University and worked with an insurance agency before entering the service. (23June45)

SOUND THE ALARM

A plane identified as unfriendly by radar on Yontan Airfield triggers the Chrysler-Bell victory siren. Powered by an eight-cylinder industrial engine, the siren can be heard for two miles with the throttle open.

One Marine described the volume of sound screaming from the siren as being like "two supermen shouting in your ear at once." Another Marine declares the siren to be so loud and the sound waves so strong that he is lifted out of his sack. This Marine sleeps about 50 yards from the siren.

Yontan is so close to Japan that enemy bombers target the airfield an average of two alerts every night. (23June45)

M-1 VS. HABU

Snakes on Okinawa are plentiful and deadly. Private First Class Dennis Kincaid, 26, Detroit, Mich., and Sergeant Roy E. Johnson, 23, San Diego, Calif., recently killed one of the largest found so far on Okinawa.

The Habu was a 63-inch specimen, whose length was measured by comparing the reptile to an M-1 rifle. The snake is Okinawa's counterpart to North America's rattler.

Kincaid, who discovered and helped kill the snake, attended Wade High School in Toledo and was a welder at the Cadillac Motor Company before enlisting May 1944. He had previously served with the Marines.

Johnson was a rigger at the Kaiser shipyards in San Francisco and attended school at Nashwauk, Minn., his former home, before enlisting May 1943. (26 June45)

MAN FROM DIXIE, YA'LL

This story is making the rounds here.

A Marine F4U pilot's rich southern voice drawled lazily, excitedly out of the loudspeaker as he contacted his controller.

"Here comes three bogeys, and I'm a-going after them."

Moment's silence.

"Spa-lash one."

Ditto silence.

"Spa-lash two"

Then, "Spa-lash three."

"Well, what do you know? Here comes fo' mo.'"

Silence.

"Spa-lash fo.'"

Short pause.

"Spa-lash five."

His drawl still belying excitement, the new Marine ace said: "Here come eight mo."

He added quickly, yet calmly, "You better send mo' boys up here, or you're gonna lose a hell of a hot pilot 'cause I'm coming home." (27June45)

A copy of the dispatch below, cut from the Marine Corps' Battle News Clipsheet, *published by the DPR, was found among Red's personal WWII papers. Previously unpublished dispatches of general interest were made available to newspaper editors across the country through the clipsheet. Whether the dispatch was ever published is not known.*

MARINE, OKINAWAN FIVE-YEAR-OLD SEAL FRIENDSHIP WITH CANDY BAR BY SERGEANT ELVIS LANE, MARINE CORPS COMBAT CORRESPONDENT

Okinawa (Delayed)—The five-year-old found in a damp cave by a Marine patrol was three feet of dirty rags, flea bites and wide-eyed fear.

Marine PFC William C. Vasiliou of Long Island, N.Y., strolled by. The next moment, the Marine's rifle rested against a tree and the youngster was in his arms. "The kid's hungry," Bill Vasiliou said, opening a box of rations. "How about some food, Joe?" The youngster managed a weak smile. The Marine passed over a chocolate bar.

The boy's tiny fingers finally tore off the wrapper. He offered the Marine half. Bill shook his head. "Just ate, Joe," he said.

A hurt look crowded the boy's face. He put the candy down.

"Here, kid, I'll eat half—we'll go 50-50," the Marine said quickly. As Bill ate, a smile spread over the boy's face. He bowed, and commenced eating.

"Now, Joe, you're going to get a bath—a Saturday night bath—and some clean clothes," the Marine said. It's strictly Bill's business how he procured the new clothes. An hour later the youngster gleamed with cleanliness.

When told he couldn't keep Joe, Bill only said: "Just let me take him to the stockade."

The boy sensed something was wrong. He nudged his head against Bill's shoulder. Inside the stockade, the Marine handed the small fry to an Okinawan woman.

Joe broke loose and wrapped his arms around the Marine's legs. Bill didn't know what to do, but suddenly he saw a box of rations in the corner. "Food, Joe," he said, pointing. "We go 50-50."

The boy raised a tear-stained face. He looked where the Marine had pointed. Slowly, he grinned. He ran toward the corner, Bill walked rapidly out of the stockade, never once looking back. He stopped before the guard.

"Tell Joe I'll be back to see him—when the fighting's over."

AURORA LEATHERNECKS

You can't tell a fellow who is 9,000 miles from home that this is a small world but circumstances here today belied the distance.

Two Aurora, Ill., Marines, who had just met for the first time in ten months, were waiting for a photographer to show up, and were joined by two more.

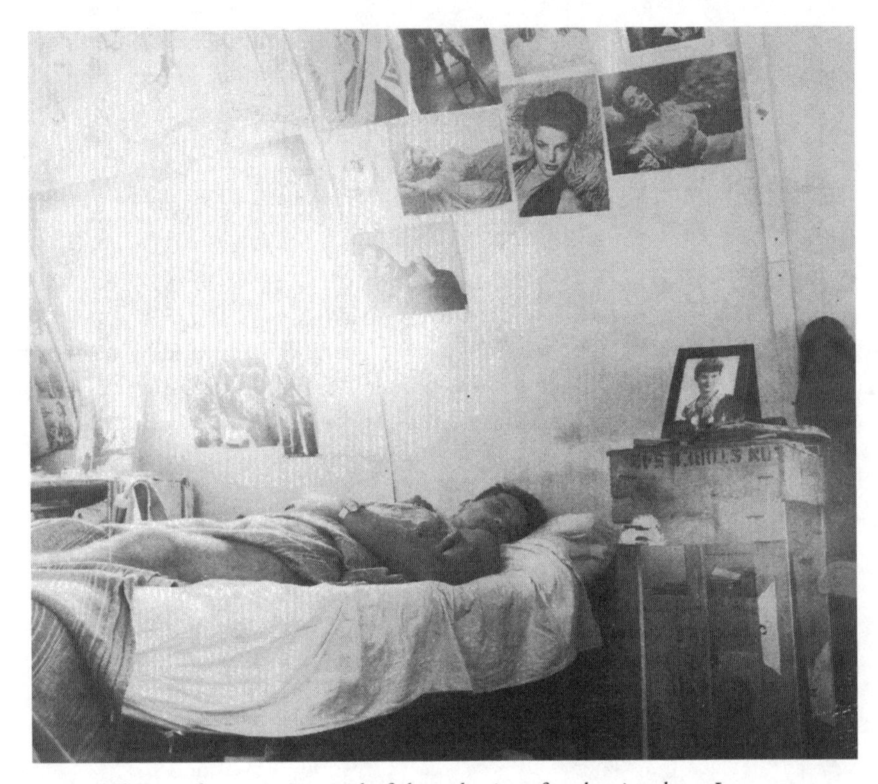

1st Lt. Del W. Carlton, MAG 31 night fighter, sleeping after shooting down Japanese aircraft, Yontan Airfield, Okinawa, 1945. Photograph by T. Sgt. Charles V. Corkran, DPR with MAG 31. Claude R. "Red" Canup Collection.

Private First Class Francis W. Breese and Aloysious O. Pawlowic were surprised when Sergeants John J. Komes and Joe L. Becker joined them. All four were acquainted before they became leathernecks. They are stationed on Yontan Airfield with three different Marine aircraft groups.

Pawlowic and Breese were brought together by pot luck. Of the tens of thousands of men on this island, Breese asked a total stranger if there was a fellow by the name of Pawlowic in his outfit. The stranger knew Pawlowic and lived two tents from him.

Pawlowic and Breese worked at Independent Pneumatic Tool Company, became Marines April 1944, were in San Diego boot camp together and were separated just before shipping overseas. Their serial numbers are as close as ham and eggs, and they were promoted the same day.

Pawlowic, 35, is the father of five children. Breese, 27, has three children.

Sergeant Komes, true to the Corps, married Sergeant Edna M. Komes of the Women's Reserve. She is stationed at the Marine Corps Air Station, El Centro, Calif. He attended Sacred Heart and East High School and worked with Lyon Metal Products, Inc.

Sergeant Becker, 20, is a graduate of Marmion High School. He enlisted August 1943.

The Marines are looking forward to meeting in Aurora—to talk about the time they met on Okinawa and talked about Aurora. (27June45)

CARLTON'S SECOND

Dog fighting with a midnight raider at 11:30 pm was a new experience for First Lieutenant Del W. Carlton, 22, Emily, Minn. The 2ndMAW pilot, flying combat patrol, intercepted the single float plane 60 miles off Yontan.

"The moon was so bright," explained Carlton, "that when he discovered I was after him he took evasive actions giving me quite a time for a couple of minutes." One burst from Carlton's guns shot off the float and two more flamed the plane. It blew up before hitting the water. This was the second plane shot down by the night fighter. Two nights before Carlton destroyed an enemy landing barge at an island north of Okinawa.

He received his wings October 1943. (28June45)

OKINAWA
JUNE 30, 1945

When you receive this letter there is no telling where I will be—it is probable that the troops nearest to Japan will be shuffled, and I don't know of anybody closer than my outfit.

Earlier tonight, one of those sons-of-a-bitches slipped in and caught me 30 feet from my dugout. I didn't know I could move so fast—must not be nearly as old and tired as I thought.

If he dropped anything, it was out at sea. It's just that diving sound that gets you . . . everyone is jumpy now, even when it's only a jeep backfiring.

ACCOMPLISHMENTS OF TACTICAL AIR FORCE
THREE MONTHS PERIOD ENDING 6 JULY 1945

Most publicized of Marine Major General Louis E. Wood's Tactical Air Force, Ryukyus, during the campaign has been the destruction of 611½ enemy planes in aerial combat at the loss of only four to the Japanese airman.

In the three months of action ending today, Second Marine Aircraft Wing pilots accounted for 495½ and 301st Army Fighter Wing fliers were credited with 116. The half score is because a TAF pilot teamed up with a carrier-based Navy fighter to split credit for a kill on June 6.

Corsairs of Marine Brigadier General William J. Wallace's fighter command grabbed the lion's share of the spoils with 437½ kills. Army Thunderbolts were second with 113. Marine Hellcat night fighters shot down 56. Army Black Widow night fighters bagged three. Marine Avenger torpedo bombers splashed two.

Achievements of the four groups making up Second Marine Aircraft Wing were: MAG-33, 225; MAG-31, 188½; MAG-22, 73; and MAG-14, 9, in combat only three weeks.

Best hunting was during May when 276 Jap aircraft were knocked down. Seventy-five were in one day, May 25, and 141 in a five-day period May 24–28. Kills were counted on all but 10 days of the month. In April, 148 were destroyed; in June 176½; and in the first three days of July, 11. Diligent search, even over Kyushu, revealed no airborne enemy opposition on July 5 and 6.

Complete statistics on close air support of the ground forces and the bombing of enemy installations throughout the Ryukyus and in Kyushu have not been compiled as yet. On the support phase, several "well dones" from Admirals Nimitz, Halsey and Hill and Generals Buckner and Stillwell have credited TAF with aiding mightily in the conquest of OKINAWA.

In April, fighter bombers alone hit target areas with 151 tons of general purpose bombs, 114 fire bombs, ranging in weight from 800 to 1300 pounds, and 2929 five-inch rockets. The totals for May were: 141 tons of bombs, 340 napalms and 3676 rockets. Sorties for the 90 days period totaled 33,510. A one day record for fighter sorties was set on June 20 with 697. The largest fire bomb strike was on June 14 when 64 Corsairs seared enemy positions on the southern tip with 19,220 gallons of jellied gasoline.

Other highlights of the campaign:

April 7—Yontan Airfield operative.

April 9—Kadena Field operative.

April 12—First big kill, 15 planes splashed.

April 13—First strike in support of ground troops.

April 16—Marine 2nd Lt William W. Eldridge, Jr., Hixon, Tennessee, bags four bogies in one engagement.

April 21—Marine 1st Lt Herb Groff, Belle, Mississippi, scores first night fighter kill.

April 22—Three pilots of Marine "Death Rattlers" squadron VMF-323 become aces with 16 kills in as many minutes—Major Jefferson D. Dorrah, Hood

River, Oregon, six; Major George C. Axtell, Jr., Baden, Pennsylvania, five; and 1st Lt Jerry O'Keefe, Biloxi, Mississippi, five.

May 4—Best hunting for Leatherneck pilots, 60 bogeys.

May 10—Marine 1st Lt Robert R. Klingman, Benger, Oklahoma, scores kill by chewing tail off Jap with propeller in three passes.

May 11—"Death Rattlers" shatter one month operational record for Marine squadrons with 90½ shoot-downs. Previous record of 85½ set over Rabaul in 1943.

May 16—Marine 1st Lt Fred Folino, Cleveland, Ohio, tallies TBM kill by using rockets.

May 19—Marine 1st Lt Robert E. Wellwood, Sheridan, Wyoming, gets three night kills in one hop.

May 22—MAG-22 planes fly first combat missions.

May 24—Marine 1st Lt Albert F. Dellamano, Brookline, Massachusetts, ties Wellwood's Hellcat record; first kill for Thunderbolts.

May 25—Record one-day score, 75; best Army day, 34; "Death Rattlers" break six-weeks operational record for Marine squadrons with total of 105½. Old record of 104½ set over Rabaul 1943.

June 1—"Death Rattlers" add four aces for total of 12 in seven weeks smashing old mark of 10 in 18 weeks over Rabaul in 1943.

June 8—1st Lt Selva McGinty, Oklahoma City, Oklahoma, becomes 19th Marine ace of campaign.

June 11—Marine Major General Louis E. Woods succeeds Marine Major General Francis P. Mulcahy as Commanding General TAF.

June 21—First P-61 kill by Lieutenant Shephard.

June 22—Captain Robert Baird, Los Angeles, California, becomes first night fighter ace in Marine aviation history. Marine Captain Ken Walsh, Washington, D.C., Congressional Medal winner at Guadalcanal gets his first over Okinawa, his 21st. Marine 1st Lt John W. Leper, Hopkins, Minnesota, exhausts ammunition trying for third kill of day and deliberately crashes into foe, then bails out safely.

June 30—Marine 1st Lt C. S. Stitt, night fighter from Steubenville, Ohio, bags Command's 600th bogey. The kill was also 30th night interception for Lt Col Marion Magruder's red hot Hellcats.

July 1—Corsairs escort B-25 in first medium bomber attack on Kyushu from Okinawa bases. It was first time Mitchells have been over Jap homeland since Doolittle's famed carrier raid three years ago.

July 1—Operations began from Awase and Chimu fields.

July 2—Major M. R. Yunck, New York City, New York, and Captain J. P. Lynch, Hyde Park, Massachusetts, become 20th and 21st Marine aces of campaign.

July 5—Thunderbolts fly cover for Okinawa-based B-24s making their first land-based attack on the Jap homeland. It was the most powerful strike of the TAF campaign, being made up of 47 B-24s, 25 B-25s and 102 P-47s.

RESTRICTED, source unknown*

* "Accomplishments of Tactical Air Force: Three Months Period Ending 6 July 1945," restricted handout, Claude R. "Red" Canup Collection.

12. CHIMU AIRFIELD

July 1–September 7, 1945

On July 1, 1945, MAG 31 relocated to the newly constructed Chimu Airfield. Seabees carved the airfield from Okinawa's rough terrain and, located twenty miles further north than Yontan, their new home made the MAG again the closest American unit to Japan.

For the first time since arriving on Okinawa, the MAG had time to settle in and build floors and porches for tents, mark off a softball field, and enjoy the newly constructed enlisted men's mess hall. The Japanese surrendered six weeks after the MAG arrived on Chimu.

During an evening meal a few days after the enemy surrendered, Colonel John Munn made an announcement—the aircraft group was headed for Japan for the initial occupation. Colonel Munn volunteered the group to be the first U.S. military occupants, destination Yokosuka naval base near Tokyo Bay.

Included in this chapter are two newsletters, The 31-Magazette *dated August 17 and August 20, that provide interesting and little know information—such as the instructions General MacArthur gave the Japanese envoy meeting with him in Manila. Also included is the Presidential Unit Citation that the 2ndMAW received, an excellent summary of their activities on Yontan.*

LUCKY OR UNLUCKY 13

Second Lieutenant Joseph L. Driscoll, Dorchester, Mass., is like a lot of people when the number 13 comes up. He's not sure whether it brings luck or misfortune—even considering what happened the other day.

Lieutenant Driscoll was one of an eight-plane sweep over Kyushu. All the sudden the high flying Corsairs plunged into a formation of 20 Zekes flying

Staff Sergeants Canup, combat correspondent, and Charlie McDade, combat photographer, swapping war stories under the newly constructed tent porch at Chimu Airfield, Okinawa, 1945. Claude R. "Red" Canup Collection.

above a layer of clouds. A free-for-all dogfight was raging when 20 to 30 more Jap fighters materialized. The odds were better than five to one against the Marines. The leathernecks sent eight flaming and smoking to the ground before all returned safely to their base 350 miles away. Driscoll's first engagement with the enemy left him emphasizing "how lucky we were to get out."

"That was your 13th combat mission, Joe," another pilot remarked.

"No! Don't say that," Driscoll exclaimed. "It must have been 12th or 14th—anything but the 13th." Although it was pointed out that the mission was completed and was a success, the flyer still didn't like the number 13.

Lieutenant Driscoll has two brothers Army Captain James Driscoll and Army Private Francis Driscoll also stationed on Pacific islands. (4July45)

CHIMU AIRFIELD, OKINAWA
JULY 4, 1945

I have not unpacked my gear since moving as I am waiting until our living quarters are finished. There are two other grunts with me, and we are building a floor and deck for our tent.

I have been kept busy trying to beat out a few stories and pass as a carpenter too. Building anything here is quite interesting. It has so many angles. In the first place, there is nothing with which to build. We had to take timber from native houses, felled trees, and beg for a few pieces of wood, nails, etc. . . . and appropriate by moonlight.

After getting my latest picture of Buzz I understand now why everybody raves about the lad. He is much bigger, handsomer and looks older than I had imagined him. Always proud of the rascal, I am now even prouder. It's a shame I can't be there to enjoy him, but when this war is over hopefully I can have the pleasure of watching him grow and amount to something—and that I will be able to give him a helping hand now and then. He should make a fine man.

The other guys are hammering and sawing now so I had better drop a period along here and do my part.

REDHEADED MARINE COMMANDER IS ACE

Major Michael R. Yunck, commanding officer of the Hell's Belles, had to come to Japan to finish off the requirement to become an ace.

Almost three years lapsed between the three planes he shot down in the Solomons and the two he recently bagged over Kyushu. "We had just passed an airfield about 15 minutes before we connected with the Japs. They were flying a beautiful formation," Major Yunck explained. "We went down to engage them so quickly that I doubt if they saw us before we were right on top of them. About the time we tore into them, we saw another formation of 20 or more coming in. Our eight planes accounted for at least eight of the enemy during the dogfight before we got out. All of our pilots returned safely."

The first one shot down by the Major was eliminated in a hurry. The Jap was trying to climb above the Marines when he came into the sight of Major Yunck's guns. One burst sent the enemy down in flames.

The second one was not so easy. "My wingman had gone after a Zeke," clarified the Major, "and I was alone. I saw two bogeys in loose formation and went after them. They separated and went for a hole in the clouds, but I closed in on the nearest one and got in a long tail shot." The result of that kill was observed as the clouds rained debris from the Nip's plane.

The Major said he found the Jap pilots over Japan were not as aggressive as those he fought on Guadalcanal. The 26-year-old holds the Silver Star and the Presidential Unit Citation. He is from Oklahoma City, Santa Barbara and New York City and attended the University of Michigan and the Naval Academy at Annapolis.

Shot down off Santa Isabel Island in 1942, the Major was returned to Tulagi in a 16-man native canoe. They traveled 60 miles in open sea. (4July45)

KALAMAZOO KID

The "Kalamazoo Kid" was almost apologetic for his excitement when he saw his first plane with red meatballs painted on the wing and fuselage. But he need not have because he kept cool enough to shoot it down—right on the emperor's side doorsteps. The Kid was on his 15th mission, his second trip over Japan, and his first engagement with the enemy.

"We were fighting all over the place," First Lieutenant Fredrick W. Edison explained. "In a flash I was on the tail of a Zeke and set him afire with one burst. After that I felt pretty cool and went after another one. He dodged into the clouds."

First Lieutenant Edison, who was educated at Kalamazoo's Central High School, is now a resident of Detroit. (4July45)

THE PRESIDENTIAL UNIT CITATION

The most concise account of the Second Marine Aircraft Wing's crucial role in the Okinawa victory can best be found in the Presidential Unit Citation awarded the unit: *"For extraordinary heroism during the period April 4 through July 14, 1945, bearing the entire burden of land-based aircraft support during the early part of the Okinawa Campaign, the Second Marine Aircraft Wing established facilities and operated its aircraft under the most hazardous field conditions with a minimum of equipment and personnel. Undeterred by either the constant rain during April and May or by heavy enemy artillery shelling and repeated day and night aerial bombing of the air strips, the unit succeeded in carrying out highly effective aerial operations against the enemy from Kyushu to the southernmost islands of the Ryukyu Group, flying picket-ship and anti-submarine patrols, fighter sweeps, day and night fighter and bomber strikes, reconnaissance and search missions, escort missions, and minesweeper and photographic plane cover, in addition to paradrop missions to move essential supplies to our forces. Blasting night and day at the enemy's dug-in infantry and artillery positions and executing some of the most successful night fighter operations of the Pacific War, the unit furnished close air support for our ground forces, shooting down 495 Japanese planes during this period. A gallant fighting unit, complemented by skilled officers and men, the Second Marine Air Wing played a major role in achieving the air superiority essential to our success in the Okinawa operation."**

* Henry I. Shaw and Benis M. Frank, Jr., *Victory and Occupation,* vol. 5 of *History of U.S. Marine Corps Operations in World War II* ([Washington, D.C.:] Historical Branch, G-3 Division. Headquarters U.S. Marine Corps, 1968), 887 (appendix N).

MECHANIC MIRACLE MEN

The miracle men of this war are the field mechanics. Workshops are shielded areas of tarp roofs and bare ground floors. Working not by the clock but against time, these Marines keep the Corsairs ready to scramble.

The factories that make the aircraft send representatives into combat zones to watch mechanics working on planes in the worst of conditions with unbelievable timetables. Chance-Vought Division of the United Aircraft Service Corporation and the Pratt and Whitney Division, which makes Corsairs, both are represented here.

The representatives are in awe that the miracle men accomplish all they do with conditions in the field mechanically the worst possible—dust and mud. With new problems coming with each island hop, the aviation mechanics have adjusted to every climate change.

The mechanics work into the night to ready planes for dawn strikes. With escaped Japs hiding in the hills overlooking the airstrip, the mechanics are constantly guarded—and often the guard is a mechanic.

Major Michael R. Yunck, commanding officer of the Hell's Belles squadron of MAG 31 praised the Corsair's "reliable engine" and said the F4U is a "rugged ship." The "trouble shooters" from the factory are stationed on Okinawa for the present and said, "Our trips into the field to observe Corsairs in combat are doubly helpful. We bring new information to the mechs and pilots. They in turn pass on discoveries made under conditions we could never duplicate in our factories." (12July45)

IT COMES OUT RIGHT HERE

"Are they keeping you busy?" inquired a young Marine as he stepped into the tent.

"Huh?" grunted Staff Sergeant Claude R. Canup, a Marine Corps combat correspondent, as he glanced up from a typewriter.

"I happened to see your sign out front and just dropped in to look around," said the visitor.

"Sure. Come in and have a seat," the correspondent invited.

"What do you work with?" the correspondent was asked.

"Work with? Oh, we work with typewriters."

The young man's jaws sagged as he stared unbelievably at the little portable typewriter.

"That's something new, ain't it?" he wanted to know.

"Oh no, I just keep it cleaned up a bit. This machine has been on more than half-dozen islands," the correspondent replied.

"What about the electricity?" questioned the stranger, looking about noticing the absence of wires in the tent.

"This is one of the old-type models," he was told. "You know, the kind you work with your fingers."

"Let me see how it works," the guest challenged.

The correspondent typed a couple of lines. "See?"

"I mean," insisted the visitor, "show me how you press pants on it."

"What the hell are you talking about?" demanded the correspondent. "Maybe you've been out here too long."

"You'd better get on the ball yourself," exclaimed the visitor, "because the sign out front says 'Okinawa Press Club.'" (19July45)

MARINE ACE TAKES TONY FOR A SPIN

A Japanese Tony, painted to look like an American plane and piloted by a Marine ace, was almost shot down over this island.

"I was pretty worried," admitted Major Charles M, Kunz, 26, Monett, Mo., pulling himself from the enemy fighter he had been testing.

The Major was flying the lone Tony near Yontan field when a Hellcat pilot zoomed down on it. The Major's escort delayed on takeoff arrived just in time to identify the plane as friendly. "I was in a tight spot," explains Major Kunz, "because the cockpit is too small for me to wear a parachute."

The Marine ace has eight planes to his credit and is holder of the Navy Cross, Distinguished Flying Cross, Air Medal and two Purple Hearts. He has flown practically every type of America's best fighters including the F3F, Wildcat, Buffalo, Hellcat, Corsair, Thunderbolt, and Mustang. He was flying a Brewster Buffalo at Midway in June 1942 when he shot down two planes. Flying a Wildcat at Guadalcanal, he bagged six more, three on one hop.

The Major reports the Tony is best handling of the planes. Its landing speed is slower, it is lighter on the controls, and it is more maneuverable than the heavier, faster American craft. He likens the Tony to the army's P-51 but it doesn't quite come up to the Mustang. "It is speed that counts now rather than maneuverability," he said, "and our planes have the edge on speed."

Major Kunz is operations officer of MAG 31. He formerly commanded the crack Hell's Belles squadron now operating on Okinawa. (26July45)

THE HARDY BOY

Second Lieutenant Irving B. Hardy, who is doing all right as a night fighter pilot, has no post-war worries. He is looking forward to a baseball career, possibly with the New York Yankees. Hardy is a right-hander and already has received contract offers.

The 20-year-old shot down a Betty, twin-engine Japanese bomber, on his 11th mission from this base. It was No. 1 for the young flier who had flown patrol over the Palau and Ulithi atolls, and he sent it flaming into the sea 50 miles west of Naha on the midnight patrol.

More interested in talking about his future plans than going into details over the splashing of the Betty he revealed, "Al Gettel, Yankee pitcher, is a good friend of mine," He and Gettel pitched for Kempsville High School and were on the same team one year. "Al was a couple of years ahead of me," explained the leatherneck, who also is a pitcher. He hurled a no-hit game for his high school in 1941, and was extending his academic and athletic careers at William and Mary College when he joined the service.

If he doesn't like professional baseball, the night fighter will try his hand with a dance band. He is a trombone player and admits he probably is better with it than the baseball.

As for the Betty, Hardy "pitched" it three perfect strikes, setting the engines afire with the first two. "The third burst was for good luck," he said. (31July45)

HE HAD A HUNCH

Shortly before 11 PM, Marine Second Lieutenant William E. Jennings prepared for midnight combat air patrol. Leaving the operations building, he hollered to the other pilots, "I'll get one tonight. I've got a hunch."

Four hours later, the 21-year-old from Greenwood, La., intercepted a Tony. For months he had practiced every move for the big moment. The instant the radar scope picked up the Tony nothing happened as planned.

"I couldn't be positive at first that it was an enemy plane," the red-headed former Greenwood football captain explained. "Once he began taking evasive actions, gunning the ship, and speeding toward Kyushu I was sure."

Jennings' Hellcat chased the Tony. "It was dark," he said, "and I gave him a quick burst at 50 feet, swinging to the left to avoid an explosion or flying debris. I was flying wing on him for a moment. The pilot was in full view and frantic. My first burst had fired his engine and seeing me flying beside him had him trying to get away. I got on his tail again and fired another burst. The canopy flew off when his steep dive started. He was burning and I saw him go all the way to the water."

The very brief engagement took place at 10,000 feet just off the coast of Jap-held Tokuno Shima. Jennings' bogey was the 18th kill for his fighter squadron. On his eighth mission, the pilot related he felt "just like he did when he scored his first touchdown." (10Aug45)

NOTE OF DISTINCTION

The following story was filed from Okinawa, September 1, 1945, by Staff Sergeant Claude R. Canup, a Marine Corps combat correspondent, formerly of the Anderson (S.C.) Independent.

A young redheaded Marine night fighter pilot who calls his shots destroyed the last Japanese plane to be shot down by the powerful 2ndMAW in the Pacific War, the last Japanese plane of the war to be flamed. Japanese planes, refusing to accept defeat, attacked after the Japanese surrendered and were shot down.

Holding the distinction is 21-year-old Second Lieutenant William E. Jennings, Greenwood, La. It was his only victory of the war, and the 511th by Okinawa-based leatherneck pilots.

Jennings, whose football frame fills the cockpit of his Hellcat, made his historic kill close to the midnight hour on August 8. He shot the Tony down off Tokuno Shima. (1Sept45)

USMC combat correspondent Claude R. Canup dispatched stories of the first planes shot down by these MAG 31 pilots as captions accompanying combat photographers' pictures. As the war gained momentum, combat photographers and correspondents coordinated efforts to release as many Marine stories to hometown newspapers as possible. This list was compiled by the editor from picture captions.

MAG 31 Pilot	*Hometown*
Major Robert C. Hammond, Jr.	*Utica, Miss.*
Captain Frank Mick	*Milford, Dela.*
First Lieutenant Donald A. McMillan	*Alder Manor, Wash.*
Second Lieutenant James B. Bender	*Worcester, Mass.*
Second Lieutenant William W. Campbell	*McCook, Neb.*
Second Lieutenant Wm. H. Donovan, Jr.	*Wadley, Ga.*
Second Lieutenant Thomas A. Gribbin	*Glen Cove, L.I.*
Second Lieutenant Charles L. Kline, Jr.	*Englewood, Colo.*
Second Lieutenant Hyman S. Kovsky	*Russell, Ky.*
Second Lieutenant Elmer E. Luther	*Maitland, Mo.*
Second Lieutenant Gene R. Mauldin	*Albany, Tex.*
Second Lieutenant Denver V. Smiddy	*Flint, Mich.*
Second Lieutenant Clifford B. Troland	*Vancouver, Wash.*
Second Lieutenant Lowell L. Truex	*Columbia City, Ind.*

(list continued)

MAG 31 Pilot	*Hometown*
Second Lieutenant Robert H. White	*Grand Prairie, Tex.*
Second Lieutenant Hal E. Winner	*Thune, Neb.*

A YEAR LATER

Marine Master Technical Sergeant William B. Bates, 23, Nacogdoches, Tex., recently received the Air Medal for which he had been recommended a year before.

Bates, non-commissioned officer in charge of the communications department of a night fighter squadron earned the medal "For meritorious achievement while participating in aerial flights as a radio gunner attached to a Marine scout bombing squadron operating in the Solomon Islands and Bismarck Archipelagoes areas from September 1, 1943, to August 10, 1944."

He flew 48 strikes against the Japanese, and since then has had a furlough at home. He recently returned from the West Coast to join his present squadron.

Bates attended Stephen F. Austin Teachers College and enlisted January 1942. (11Aug45)

MARINE AIRCRAFT GROUP-31'S NEWSLETTER "THE 31-MAGAZETTE"

(Published Under Jurisdiction of Group Recreation Office, PFC Bud Prather, Editor)
August 17, 1945

Jap Peace Envoys Will Be at Ie Shima Tomorrow

General of the Army Douglas MacArthur will deliver surrender terms to the Japs Friday in his Manila Headquarters, close by the hallowed shrines of Bataan and Corregidor. He issued instructions to the Japs Wednesday to send their surrender envoy to Ie Shima, an island near Okinawa, in a green-cross-marked plane. From there the envoy and aides MacArthur ordered to accompany him will be transported to Manila in an American aircraft.

Earlier in a note addressed directly to Hirohito, MacArthur informed the beaten Japs he had been designated Supreme Allied Commander of All Forces in the Pacific, and was empowered to "arrange directly the Jap authorization for cessation of hostilities at the earliest possible date."He also gave detailed instructions for the official designation of a Tokyo radio station as the medium for further communications with his headquarters in English. For MacArthur it is a personal triumph which will have widespread significance in the "face saving" Orient. When the Japs tossed in the sponge, MacArthur was poised as Commander of all Allied Forces in the Pacific for an "on to Tokyo" drive. His brilliant campaigns in the southwest Pacific had fulfilled his "I shall return" pledge to the ill-equipped, sick and starving American and Filipino troops he left behind at Bataan and Corregidor on orders of the late President Roosevelt. MacArthur ironically chose as the recognition signal from the Japs envoy plane the word "Bataan." The white painted aircraft with green crosses visible at 500 yards, MacArthur instructed the Japs must be in an unarmed type Zero model 22 L-2 D-3, which must leave the Sata Misaki Airfield on southern Kyushu Island Friday morning. It must circle at one thousand feet or under any cloud layers until joined by an escort of P-38 fighter planes and then land on an Ie Shima Airfield marked with more green crosses. Six hours advance notice of the readiness of the envoy's plane to leave Kyushu must be given by the Japs. One of General MacArthur's first demands on the Japs will be for the speedy release of Lt. Gen. Jonathan Wainwright and other American prisoners.

MacArthur's Final Dispatch

While turning to the task of imposing surrender terms on the beaten Japs, MacArthur Wednesday issued his final communiqués of the war. In the first, it was disclosed that the American planes had damaged 20 Jap ships in the final sweeps over the empire's home waters, and had shot down 17 enemy planes. Some patrolling for observation will continue, he said. His final communiqué, number 1228, announced the completion of formal communiqués from MacArthur's headquarters, which began from Melbourne, Australia on April 21, 1942.

Hirohito Explains

Emperor Hirohito told his people Wednesday that Japan had surrendered to escape obliteration by atomic bombs, then accepted the resignation of the cabinet that lost the war and an empire built by a half a century of conquest. Hirohito broke all precedents in speaking by radio, and Domei Agency pictured the entire nation as prostrate on the ground and weeping as the people heard from his lips of the first defeat since Japan embarked on the Road of Conquest in 1895. Japanese broadcasts reflected the bitterness and frustration of the leaders who chose on December 7, 1941, to wage war on the Mightiest Industrial Nation of the Earth. War Minister Kobeichika Anamy, the only general in Premier Kantano Suzuki's cabinet, committed suicide, said Domei Agency dispatch. He was reported to have opposed the first peace overture. "The enemy has been employing a most cruel bomb, the power of which to do damage is indeed incalculable, taking a toll of many innocent lives," said Domei today.

Hirohito told the people to "beware" of outbursts of emotion which may engender endless "complications" or internal strife.

Medals Awarded to VMF (N) 542

Lt. Arthur Arceneaux, 542 night fighter pilot, was awarded the Air Medal yesterday by his commanding officer, Major R. B. Porter, in an impressive ceremony at Hill Field. The ceremony was held in conjunction with a troop inspection. Lt. Arceneaux's medal was awarded for shooting down a Jap plane, a Zeke, at night.

At the same time, M/Sgt. John Rohrback received the Purple Heart for wounds received at Guadalcanal in November 1942.

In a fitting tribute on Victory Day, Major Porter complimented the night fighter squadron as a whole for outstanding work performed under trying conditions and called upon the personnel to maintain their high standards for the work still lying ahead.

What War's End Means

The war's end will mean for the United States: Discharge of five million persons from munitions, perhaps seven million unemployed by Christmas; cancellation of billions in Army and Navy contracts; release of over five million men from the Army in 12 to 18 months; limiting of the draft to the 18–26 year old bracket and a cut in draft calls from 80,000 to 50,000 men per month; end of manpower control by the war Manpower Commission; end of gasoline rationing, although some food rationing will continue for months; return to store shelves of scarce articles.

Japs Don't Know War Is Over

Japanese suicide planes crashed into American troops in the Ryukyus yesterday, and other Jap airmen strafed at the U.S. Third Fleet in defiance of Japan's unconditional surrender. At least two American soldiers were wounded when the bomb-carrying Kamikaze aircraft dived into Iheya Shima, 30 miles north of Okinawa in the darkness 12 hours after President Truman's peace announcement.

A few minutes after Admiral Halsey's Third Fleet, 100 miles off Japan, received Admiral Nimitz's "cease fire" order, Japanese planes which had been reluctant in wartime to tackle the ships began to appear. Within the next few hours, Halsey's anti-aircraft gunners knocked about 16 Jap aircraft into the water, said a press correspondent with the fleet.

A Tokyo broadcast following reports of Jap aircraft operations against American forces indicated that the Jap's imperial staff may be having some difficulty fastening peace restrictions on its diehard men.

Paper Drive Collects

Celebration of the end of the war with Japan brought an all time record amount of paper cascading into the streets of New York. In the twenty four hours ending at seven A.M. Wednesday, the Sanitation Department cleaned up 4863 tons of paper. The American Legion Convention in 1937 when 2500 tons of paper were thrown into the streets had tops until Tuesday.

Don't Stuff Yourself

Just because the war is over, don't expect to go out and get all the beefsteaks and sugar you want. There is still a worldwide shortage of food, a shortage this country has promised to help meet. The removal from rationing of meats, butter, margarine, other food fats and oils and sugar may be months coming. In the case of sugar and fats and oils, lifting of rationing may be possible by mid-1946.

Gasoline, all blue point coupons for fuel oil and stove oil went off rationing Wednesday. The blue point system covered canned fruit, vegetables, and such products as catsup, chili sauce, and grape juice.

Length of the War

How long have the wars lasted? Our war with Japan lasted 1346 days after the Pearl Harbor attack on December 7, 1941. The European war lasted 2075 days after Hitler's legions struck Poland September 1, 1939. For the Chinese, peace came after 2946 days of uninterrupted warfare with the Japs beginning with the Marco Polo Bridge incident of July 7, 1937.*

DINNER IS SERVED

The men in Major General Louis E. Woods' 2ndMAW had many surprises from the first week of the campaign in April until the Japs threw in the towel some five months later. The surprise today had the enlisted guys laughing and the officers grinning.

First lieutenants, second lieutenants and warrant officers dished out food and kept bread, water, and coffee on the tables for privates, corporals, and

* The newsletter is part of the Claude R. "Red" Canup Collection.

sergeants. What fun for a private to yell "Hey, Mess!" at a commissioned officer —and him come running. Officers serving at the opening of the new enlisted mess hall surprised the leathernecks and they "ate it up." Explained First Lieutenant Clark Campbell, mess hall officer from Elizabeth, Pa., "We just wanted to surprise the boys. They've been through a lot and have done a great job!"

Here's the gauntlet the enlisted Marines ran at the serving table:

The squadron adjunct, First Lieutenant David Zenoff, Laguna Beach, Calif., spooned out salad.

First Lieutenant Elbert F. Veuleman, Birmingham, Ala., transportation officer, served peas.

Top job went to First Lieutenant Charles H. Forejt, communications officer, Mt. Pleasant, Pa. He served steak.

Intelligence Officer William N. Burks, Jefferson City, Mo., served French fries—more rare than steak on this island.

The maintenance officer Albert H. Trowell, Grosse Farms, Mich., handed out bread, butter, and cookies.

Keeping the tables supplied were Warrant Officer Jerome G. Perrone, head of the quartermaster department, New York City; radar and radio officer First Lieutenant John C. Thompson, Decatur, Ga., and Commissioned Warrant Officer Grant N. Seneur, Seattle, Wash. He is the squadron engineering officer.

The eight officers thought it "a lot of fun." The diners did, too. Their favorite question during the meal, "Why, lieutenant! What did you do to pull mess today?" (21Aug45)

NO GAME

War's end did not solve the mud problem on this island, so Marines at the outdoor movie asked no questions when the following announcement was made between reel changes:

"All baseball games have been cancelled. The field has been turned into a gravel pit."

Earlier a Marine sick bay had been moved when blasting Seabees discovered it had been set up on a vein of coral. (21Aug45)

CHIMU AIRFIELD
AUGUST 21, 1945

All are happy the war is over, but few of us here shouted. To us it means moving again, possibly to Japan for a bloodless invasion. Those of us looking forward to an early return are sweating. None of us correspondents know when we will go back or for that matter how. Since I am under orders from D.C. any movement of large groups may not affect me. There are all sorts of rumors among the correspondents about how and when we will be released.

I have had some pretty good stories cut to pieces and some things cut out of my letters by the censors that certainly would have been no aid, comfort or information to the enemy even if he were able to get hold of them. If he did, there wasn't a thing he could have done about the information because the Japs were so helpless that our battle wagons could lay a few miles off Tokyo coast and lob in the shells. If you remember I long ago predicted that the Japs would throw in the towel come Thanksgiving . . . 10:15 AM to be exact.

Marie wrote about how you all got together to hear the war's end broadcast. Too bad the wireless, as the British call it, fouled everybody up so often. It was the same here inasmuch as we depend upon stateside broadcasts for our info. It didn't really matter—we felt it would be over soon and the day made no difference. The night it was supposed to have been over, however, we had a long alert and a bomb-laden Nipper was splashed off the coast—and the same routine of blackouts.

This has been a Navy and Marine show for the most part, coupled with Army aviation. The Marines took the stepping stones. The Marines carried the load on this joint operation. The Navy knocked out the Jap navy, and Navy and Marine pilots did the most in clearing the skies of the rising sun. But we don't get to apply the clincher. Figures.

MARINE AIRCRAFT GROUP-31'S NEWSLETTER "THE 31-MAGAZETTE"

(Published Under Jurisdiction of Group Recreation Office, PFC Bud Prather, Editor)
August 20, 1945

Japs Land at Ie Shima

Local receivers were all tuned to the frequency on which the Jap emissary's plane was scheduled to make contact with the tower at Ie Shima Sunday. Monitors were rewarded by hearing the Jap ship, using the call "Bataan 1," make contact with the tower, and heard the landing procedure broadcast. They landed at about 1235 Sunday, and were presumed to have boarded a waiting American transport for the trip to Manila, where they will be met by General MacArthur, who will be flanked by an honor guard of 30 men, all over 6 feet tall. The Jap plane followed a strict landing procedure, landing directly behind a P-38, while the rest of the escort circled overhead.

Date at Manila

The Japanese, their dream of empires smashed and their once arrogant armies surrendering, will learn at Manila today the cost of capitulation. Weather permitting, two unarmed Japanese planes, painted white and marked by green crosses, were scheduled to take off at six A.M. Sunday for Kisaruzu Airfield, southeast of Tokyo. Aboard were to be a representative of the Imperial Government and at least three officers from Japan's army, navy and air forces who will get their surrender orders at a historic conference today from General MacArthur. The Japs messaged their plans and itinerary to MacArthur, who had grown impatient at their delays, and had sent them a peremptory note to quit stalling and comply with his orders at once. The Japs did not say so but over Satano Cape, on the southeast corner of Kyushu, their planes were to be picked up by 36 lightning fighters, which will ride herd on them to an airfield at Ie Shima, west of Okinawa.

More Jap Sneak Attacks

Personnel connected with the Army bombers on Okinawa were burning with indignation over the second attack in two days on their reconnaissance planes over Tokyo. In the second attacks Saturday, two big U.S. bombers were set upon by 14 Jap fighters. The bombers shot down two of them but not until one aerial photographer had been killed and two crewman wounded.

Later News

News picked up as this paper is being prepared says that the Japanese peace envoys landed as scheduled at Ie Shima, and were transferred to two American transport planes, and were flown to Manila.

Don't Want to Go Over Again

Troops of the 95th Division are sending telegrams to Congress and newspapers protesting proposed shipment of these and other veterans of European fighting to act as occupation troops in the Far East.

New Veteran's Administration

General Omar Bradley took over the post of Veteran's Administrator today, replacing General Hines recently appointed American Ambassador to Panay.

What's Happening at Home

America raced into its peacetime future Saturday with the government swinging the axe on all sides to get out of the woods. Four days after the surrender ending the war with Japan, one of the highest government officials said,

"We don't pretend to have any master blueprint charting every action for the future. That's impossible. Our job is to get out of the woods and the first thing to do is to tackle the trees right in front of us. Here is the big picture of what has been done in this historic week and what is expected. War contracts are being cancelled right and left. Congress will come back in September to consider a bill intended to create full employment. President Truman said it's a must measure. Millions of men will come pouring back into civilian life out of the armed forces in the next twelve months. They'll have first crack at jobs. The draft is finished for men 26 or over. Food will become more plentiful but not all at once. Clothing will become more plentiful too, but gradually, picking up by Christmas. There may be no coal shortage this winter, the Army says, but Solid Fuels Administrator is not sure. Gasoline is not rationed any more. Rent control will continue and OPA Boss Bowles says price controls will continue on food while he tries to reduce prices on clothing. Taxes will come down but almost certainly not before January first, and the government is letting bosses raise wages so long as the increases don't mean a boost in prices."

Reconversion Policy

President Truman Saturday outlined a reconversion policy designed to lift as many controls as possible while holding prices and living costs against inflation. Mr. Truman outlined the policy in an Executive Order which, to a large extent, made effective plans already announced by various government agencies in some respects, however, it strengthened the policies already proclaimed by the agencies. It directed that the Price Administrator and the Secretary of Agriculture, subject to directives of the Stabilization Director, "Take all necessary steps to assure the cost of living and the general level of prices shall not rise." The Chief Executive said guiding policies will cover all federal departments and agencies with problems arising out of the transition from war to peace.

Some Japs Surrender in Manchuria

Japanese troops laid down their arms in growing numbers in Manchuria Saturday, while spearheads swept within 70 miles of Hansing, puppet capital of Tokyo's Empire, and plowed out gains of 19 to 70 miles toward Harbin. War bulletins, although ambiguous, indicated that more than 25,000 enemy troops gave up the fight during the day, for a two-day surrender total of 45,000. But thousands of other Jap troops had not obeyed the "cease fire" order. The Russian Army newspaper, Red Star, estimated that there were more than one million crack Jap soldiers in Manchuria, Korea, India and southern Sakhalin Island. Meanwhile, at the headquarters of the Soviet Far Eastern Commander, Marshal Vashilevsky, at Khabarovsk, conferences were believed in progress with a Jap surrender emissary, who was picked up by a Soviet plane Saturday at Harbin.

Really?

Hard-headed Foreign Minister Namuro Shigemitsu Saturday flatly informed the Japs that they must face the facts. "Unfortunately," a Domei Broadcast quoted him as saying at a press conference, "we have to face the fact that we have been defeated."

Burma Japs Refuse to Quit

Jap forces facing the British Imperial Twelfth Army on the Burma front were reported Saturday by an authoritative source as showing no disposition to surrender. It was believed that forceful demands would be stayed until the Japs signed MacArthur's document.

O.K. with Texas

Governor Stenson said Saturday that he will inform three inquiring Marines from Texas that this state will go along with the Commander In Chief in accepting Japan's surrender offer. He said he would give that answer to the three who asked by telegram from Quantico, Virginia, "U.S. accepts Japanese unconditional surrender terms. Please advise status of Texas. May we quit too?"

Mass Production Heroes

The largest mass award yet of the Congressional Medals of Honor will be made by President Truman Sunday morning to 27 Army officers and enlisted men. The White House said the ceremony will be held at ten A.M. on the south lawn of the White House with relatives and a group of officials present.

Bulgarians Warned

The United States Saturday warned the Bulgarian government to cooperate after the Russian Army moved in to free its forthcoming election from fear and intimidation so that they may be truly democratic. Otherwise, Secretary of State Byrnes made clear this country will not consider signing a peace treaty with them, a former Axis satellite nation. Britain backed up the American position. A foreign office commentator in London said the two nations were presenting a common front in the attitude that the present regime does not represent all the democratic elements of Bulgaria.

"Cease Fire"

A three year old boy in Seattle, Washington, out playing with the rest of the kids, had his own reconversion problem and he rushed into his dad for help.

"They're still shooting me down for a Jap," he wailed, "and the war is over. You go tell them."

Sub Nets Lifted

Anti-submarine nets which guarded the approaches to Los Angeles Harbor will be lifted next week. The Navy announced that the operation of raising the huge steel mesh will require several weeks. Similar nets have already been lifted from the entrance to San Francisco Bay.

Line Company Marines prefer STB Day to V-J Day. In Marine parlance, "Secure the Butts" Day is the day to look forward to.*

The Marine Corps DPR issued guidelines for dispatches reporting war activities. The U.S. Navy, needing to borrow any extra correspondents available, hand delivered guidelines for end of the war reporting.

Communication from the Navy

FROM: CINCPAC ADV HQS
TO: ALPAC 159
RESTRICTED 270847/159 PRIORITY

1. ALPAC 142 which outline steps necessary to report to American public the story of Navy's part in winning war in Pacific is amplified as follows: when practical in formulating ships histories and home town stories it is desired to emphasize the following basic missions of the fleet and how well they have been accomplished.
   A. Elimination of the Japanese Navy.
   B. Maintenance of the complete underseas surface and air blockade which cut off vital supplies.
   C. Support and participation in seizure of stepping bases to Japan.
   D. Maintenance of the continuous supply line to the fleet, to ground troops and to shore based air forces.
   E. Surrender of Japan because submarine, surface ship, and air attacks had destroyed its Navy and exposed the homeland to naval blockade and its cities and interior communications to destruction by bombardment and bombing even though its Armies were largely intact and a very large Air Force remained.

* The newsletter is part of the Claude R. "Red" Canup Collection.

2. Recent surveys made for Navy Department by sampling agencies similar to gallop poll have forcefully demonstrated the following facts:
   A. The newspapers use Navy stories of all types when Navy's operations are in the news.
   B. A very efficient way of telling Navy story is through home town story about individual.
3. The press surveys indicate the necessity for accenting the following facts in preparing home town stories.
   A. Part individual plays in Japanese occupation as reflected in job aboard ship or ashore.
   B. Eye witness accounts from individual and his past war experiences.
   C. Geographic location of man and his ship.
   D. Reports of promotions and awards or citations.
   E. Fullest details on civilian background and family.
   F. Any accounts of heroism or special commendation.
   G. Anecdotes of human interest.
4. With return of peace, the number of Navy home town stories which will be acceptable to the press in the United States will rapidly diminish. A story received in the fleet home town news center in Chicago by 1 October may be twice as effective as one on 1 November. Enlisted naval correspondents are limited in number and spread too thinly through out fleet to meet present urgent need for home town news stories. Commanding officers shall insure that collateral duty public information officers utilize all practicable talent and facilities in getting a large volume of home town news stories in hands of fleet home town news center before press interest in Navy's accomplishments fades.

BY HAND 270847/159 31 AUGUST
ADJ/ INTELL/ PUBLIC RELATIONS/ ALPAC FILE/*

* The guidelines are part of the Claude R. "Red" Canup Collection.

PART 4

Japan

13. OCCUPATION DUTY CALLS

September 7–16, 1945

Marine Aircraft Group 31, one of four MAGS in 2ndMAW, was the only aircraft group selected for Japan's initial occupation. Some leathernecks were concerned the move would delay their discharge but soon realized everybody wanted to go to Japan. The MAG arrived at Yokosuka naval base, Japan, on September 7, 1945, only days after the Japanese left the facility.

It Pays to Go

"Colonel John Munn," Red recalled, "was my favorite commanding officer. Any number of instances could be recounted as to why I valued my association with him. I remember most vividly his assigning troops for either sea or air transportation for occupation of Japan. Naturally, all the officers wanted their men transported by air, but few planes were available. The various unit commanders were summoned by Colonel Munn to a meeting in his Quonset hut for transportation assignment.

"I didn't know that, of course, until my Captain—not very close to the Colonel—told me to go to the meeting and request air transportation for our six member combat correspondent unit and a jeep. I protested slightly, but orders are orders.

"About twenty-five to thirty officers blocked the door and most of the view inside—where a bunched up line waited for assignment. The Colonel was calling officers up to his desk. One spotted me and questioned my being there. 'Orders,' I answered. He raised his eyebrows.

"I heard the Colonel say, 'Gentlemen, excuse me.' The screech of his chair on bare floor parted the khakis. Through the door he strolled with me in step right behind him. Some thirty yards from the hut, the Colonel headed for a big tree. His objective—relieving his kidneys. My objective—his attention as we shared the tree. I told him my purpose for being there. The Colonel peed and cussed the officer for not having enough damn guts to come himself. After polishing the brass, we headed back to the hut, the Colonel telling me to follow him.

"The officers separated for the Colonel to get back through but closed ranks almost immediately, positioning me again at the door. I heard the Colonel's chair slide, and all the sudden he yelled out, 'Sergeant Canup, where are you?' I said, 'I'm back here, sir.'

"'Come here,' he ordered. Those officers turned and gave me a glare like you would not believe, but they moved over so I could get to the Colonel's desk.

"When I got there, he said, 'Now, sergeant, what did you want?' I explained, 'Colonel, the Captain asked me to request space on one of your planes going to Japan for six men and a jeep.'

"The Colonel made a few appropriate comments about the Captain, and then said, 'I'll let you have six spaces for six men.' He scribbled something on a piece of paper and handed it to me. Barely sliding enough for me to get out, those officers could have put me under with their fierce looks, not liking what had happened at all.

"The moral to this story is when you must go, you must go—even when you don't want to go, it pays to go."

HIGHLIGHTS OF THE ACCOMPLISHMENTS OF MAG 31 FROM INVASION OF OKINAWA TO OCCUPATION OF JAPAN

YOKOSUKA, JAPAN Today, September 7, 1945, battle scarred Hellcats and Corsairs of Marine Aircraft Group 31 arrived at this prized Japanese naval base, "the Pensacola of Japan." Here MAG 31 continues its successions of firsts—the first American pilots to land at Yokosuka and on Japanese mainland soil. Almost one year to the day since some members of MAG 31 left California, September 9, 1944, Marine pilots left Chimu Airfield, a fighter strip cut from Okinawa's rugged hills by Seabees, and landed at Yokosuka naval base, Tokyo Bay, Japan.

MAG 31 was based on the closest American airfield to Japan during the last 131 days of the war, on the "road to Tokyo."

On April 3, 1945, 2ndMAW squadrons were the first arrivals on Yontan Airfield, Okinawa, two days after Marines of the First Division went ashore.

On April 7, 1945, pilots from this MAG made the first kill by Okinawa-based planes. Seven Kamikaze planes bagged attacking shipping in the harbor while MAG 31's equipment was being unloaded.

On August 8, 1945, Second Lieutenant William E. Jennings scored the last kill by the 2ndMAW, the last kill before the Japanese surrendered. MAG 31 squadrons shot down 192 enemy aircraft, 22 different types, many on one-way trips to Okinawa waters.

This group's Corsairs and Hellcats rode herd over bombers and ships from Okinawa to the China Sea and over Kyushu, but most of their victories were scored just north of Okinawa intercepting the enemy flying down from mainland bases. Hell's Belles, one of the Corsair squadrons equipped with 20mm cannons, shot down 71 planes without a loss to the enemy, topping other squadrons.

Significant MAG 31 Statistics from April 7 to August 15, 1945

1. Fighters flew 13,102 sorties.
2. One Hellcat and three Corsair squadrons flew 40,714 hours during 131 days.
3. Hell's Belles, a Corsair squadron with 20mm cannons, fired 215,230 rounds on strikes and interceptions. Other MAG 31 squadrons, armed with 50 caliber guns, fired 457,196 rounds.
4. Corsairs and Hellcats, converted into fighter-bombers for special missions, dropped 564,000 pounds of 500 pounders, 514 napalm bombs and fired 6,637 rockets.
5. Targets—bridges, caves, warehouses, fuel dumps, vehicles, troops, A-A and mortar positions, planes, and shipping—from Okinawa to Kyushu.
6. Suri Castle, Naha and Sugar Loaf Hill—supported Marines and soldiers, southern Okinawa, May and early June—rocketing, strafing, and napalm bombing.
7. Commended by Admiral of the First Fleet and the Secretary of the Navy for setting up Yontan Airfield on April 3 in the face of enemy artillery, mortar, and sniper fire. The Japs dug in less than 15 miles to the south, infiltrated, and attempted amphibious landings on nearby beaches.
8. June 21—island secured. Bombing, strafing, and suicide actions continued both on land and sea.
9. Under went 185 red alerts in 131 days.
10. In the Okinawa campaign—24 killed, 54 wounded, and two missing. The two missing and 20 of the dead were pilots.
11. 2ndMAW, consisting of four aircraft groups which included MAG 31, was awarded the Presidential Unit Citation for extraordinary heroism. (7Sept45)

Yokosuka

"I didn't want to leave Okinawa," Red noted, "since I thought my discharge might be forthcoming—but in the Marines you do what they say do—and I occupied one of those six seats on the plane taking the combat correspondents to Yokosuka, Japan.

"The correspondents made camp in the Japanese barracks right on Tokyo Bay after we arrived, among the first at Yokosuka. What impressed us most was the size and number of rats in the barracks and, matter of fact, all over the damn place.

"Our combat correspondent office was on the second floor of one of the buildings. We would stand there looking out the window at all the rats running around on the ground. Bottles of cola were available, and after we drank the contents we would lean on the window and try to drop the bottles on the rats which were down below trying to scrounge something to eat.

"It didn't seem to bother the ones under our windows or any of them that we were around. As we walked around the base, there would be two or three rats on the sidewalk trying to eat something. They wouldn't get out of your way. You'd have to give them a wide berth. They weren't afraid of anything."

YOKOSUKA, JAPAN
SEPTEMBER 8, 1945

Here I am in Japan! I had expected to come here for some time, but the plans went into operation suddenly Thursday. I flew up here Friday, and here it is Saturday morning

Yokosuka is on the Pacific side of the island about 20 miles or so from Tokyo. It is only 12 miles from Yokohama, which is pretty well leveled. This base was left in fair-condition. It was not a special target. Our planes picketed the ships in the bay and concentrated on the industrial city of Yokohama and Tokyo itself. Not much sign of war here. One big Jap battlewagon is in the harbor.

I am walking on pavement for the first time in a year. Yesterday I spent the afternoon scouting around, and my dogs ached from the hard asphalt . . . quite different from sloshing through mud.

I am thankful for the move. The chow is better because we are eating with the Seabees until our outfit gets set up. We are living in Jap barracks and have an office also. Lots of chairs and desks here, also lots of rats and mosquitoes. Place is not very clean for a naval base.

The weather here is much cooler than Okinawa. We are about 800 miles further north. This is more like Los Angeles and Santa Barbara. The days seem to be warm enough, but the nights are quite cool. Some people use two blankets, but last night I slept through with only a sheet—my one sheet.

When we left Chimu Airfield Friday morning of course it was raining. Once we got our altitude and settled off on the course, we had fair weather. Even with fair weather the trip was not too warm. The plane I came in was a PBJ. That is what the Marines call them, but it is the B-25, Billy Mitchell medium bomber, same type planes that Doolittle and the boys flew in the first Tokyo raid.

YOKOSUKA, JAPAN
SEPTEMBER 8, 1945

This is still Saturday. I have just returned from my first visit to the city of Yokosuka.

A friend and I managed to get out of the naval base gates before an order came out stopping all liberty in town. We walked casually to the main highway, which is the main street of a small number of little towns that stretch eight miles or more. We went about a mile and caught a ride with an interpreter. We had such an interesting conversation we forgot about distance and wound up eight miles from our main gate.

It was still early so we went through the business section and stopped in a jewelry store where some officers were making purchases. The MPs came along and ordered all Americans out of town. We were allowed to stay—power of the press.

We walked too much of the way back but caught a couple of rides—one with one of Doug's looeys in a big black Jap car similar to our Packard. We were tempted to stay with him—he was on his way back to Tokyo—but didn't have the nerve to go AWOL!

At the gates we talked with the guards while we rested the tired dogs. Along came another big empty black car driven by a Jap chauffeur for a Marine battalion commanding officer. We asked for a ride and were driven in style to battalion headquarters. The Jap jumped out, saluted, and opened the door for us. After the ride, we acted like a couple of big shots . . . sauntered to the main building, entered through the front door, and exited out a side door without stopping. The Jap must have thought us generals or something. Some fun! I'm not kidding myself into believing the majority like us any more than we would have liked them if our side had lost, but they are being treated a hell of a lot better than we would have been.

Jap planes are all over the airfield. Ammunition, engines, copper, machinery, whole planes—you name it—have been found stored in more underground caves than you can imagine. Caves are everywhere. Much of the industry moved into caves—huge caves fixed up like outdoor buildings with floors and lots of lights. This place would have been difficult to take. The terrain is like Okinawa —lots of hills and caves.

Some of the Japs in the army and navy have been retained to work, but lots of men are in the city where they were discharged. Some seem happy, others anything but. The men wear a mixture of clothing. Almost all—even the kids—wear something used by the army or navy, such as caps, pants, etc. Although this is a big industrial center on Tokyo Bay, the people seem to be poor and they apparently have had it tough for many months.

When you see Linda and Buzz tell them Daddy is in Japan and seeing lots of little Jap boys and girls. I have found that kids are alike everywhere I have been in the Pacific—just kids!

IRONY OF WOOD

"The Marines will have lots of fun using that wood," remarked Major General Louis E. Woods as he observed large stacks of salvaged lumber at this Japanese naval air base now occupied by a group of his 2ndMAW.

The General and the leathernecks were thinking of the lumber shortage Marines had faced in all of their campaigns up to the war's end. On every island it had been the same story: beg, borrow, and appropriate by moonlight issue boards needed to build decks for tents, writing tables, and chairs.

Here there was enough wood for everybody, according to Staff Sergeant Claude R. Canup, Marine Corps combat correspondent. Even so, skeptical Marines figured there was a catch. And they were right.

The catch: Marines are quartered in barracks recently occupied by Japs—barracks complete with modern conveniences. Yes, even to chairs, desks, benches, and floors. (9Sept45)

DIFFERENT CARGO

Billy Mitchells, medium bombers which the Marines fly under the name PBJs have been converted into cargo and transport planes in the occupation of Japan.

They are familiar sights to Japanese of the Tokyo area—the same which Doolittle's raiding party used in the initial attack on that city.

The Mitchells designated for the occupation job, according to Staff Sergeant Claude R. Canup, a Marine Corps combat correspondent, are now based at Chimu Airfield, Okinawa, and operated as a unit of MAG 31 in the closing

MAG 31 ordnance men cleaning a Hellcat's guns, Okinawa, 1945. From the left: P.F.C. Elroy J. C. Karl, P.F.C. Joe. L. Levy, Sgt. Herbert W. Curtis, and Cpl. Leland L. Wheeler. Photograph by T. Sgt. Charles V. Corkran, DPR with MAG 31. Claude R. "Red" Canup Collection.

days of the war. Now they are helping move the MAG and its personnel to this naval base.

The Marine operated Mitchells, flying from Iwo Jima before transferring to Okinawa, flew night patrols over this and the Tokyo area, searching for coastal shipping. (9Sept45)

LEARNING TO FLY AGAIN

Fighter pilots, veterans of the Okinawa campaign, almost had to learn to fly again after occupying Yokosuka naval base airfield.

The reason, explains Captain Robert Baird is their Corsairs and Hellcats are stripped of about two and a half tons of combat weight not needed for reconnaissance patrol. The fighters now carry less ammunition, no bombs, and no auxiliary gas tanks.

Captain Baird says the planes fly easier and faster, and that "It is just like changing from a Model T to a V-8." He has been awarded the Distinguished

Flying Cross, the Air Medal and a gold star in lieu of a second Air Medal. (10Sept45)

YOKOSUKA, JAPAN
SEPTEMBER 11, 1945

We moved to a new office today in the administration building replacing the room we were assigned in the barracks, also moving to new living quarters. Even with all the shifting, time is dragging here except in the rare case of something happening. This morning I checked myself in the mile long chow line. It took an hour and twenty minutes to get into the mess hall, eat a couple of flapjacks and get out again. We are doubling with the Seabees now until the Marine galley sets up.

I still haven't been to Tokyo. I'm giving them time to clean up the mess. If the places I have seen are any indication, I have a pretty good idea what it is like there.

The base is pretty well crowded now with many people coming ashore and flying here. Everybody wants to come to Japan and not many of them have business. Things should settle down to business-like routine in two or three months. Then it will be just like being at a base in the States.

UNEXPECTED

A Marine, telling friends about the movie he had seen downtown, explained that "It was like our own, but I couldn't make heads or tails of it because the talking was all in Japanese."

"I wonder why they didn't have English explanations," inquired a listener.

"I don't guess they figured on us being here when they made the picture," volunteered a leatherneck. (11Sept45)

ANSWERED FROM ABOVE

A Marine looked at the changed expression on the faces of Japanese in this city today and found the answer to a military question.

"I was walking along a crowded street," he explained, "and the natives stared at me like I had stolen their last bowl of rice. Those standing in front of shops and dark doorways made me feel better about having taken along my .45 automatic. Some of those who passed me on the street didn't even bother to look at me, but I had a pretty good idea of what they were thinking. Almost everyone glued their eyes on my pistol.

"Then some of our Corsairs came over pretty low. There must have been a dozen of them flying over the city, their white stars shining like new silver dollars. Boy, was I proud of them! And you should have seen those Japs. Every one of them stopped and looked up. Their expressions changed, and after the planes went by I felt better about everything, because the Japs looked less defiant or resentful and nodded or smiled at me."

Just before this leatherneck's Corsair squadron left Okinawa to come here, he wanted to know "Why are they using fighter planes in the occupation? I don't see how they can be any help just flying around." (11Sept45)

THIS IS YOKOSUKA, JAPAN

Two teen-age boys walked up the street to the theater, purchased a couple of tickets, handed them to the aged, almost toothless, dirty doorman and went inside for a movie already underway. The boys chose seats near the rear of the theater, joining half-dozen others sitting on slightly padded wooden benches. Some viewers fanned themselves—no air conditioning.

A few doors away three barbers relaxed in their comfortable chairs. Across the street, two blocks down, another barber shop was full, two chairs occupied, and three men waiting. One barber a woman.

Along the streets, crowded with pedestrians forever dodging carts, bicycles and motor vehicles, moved the people of this city shaking war shackles and emerging from caves and other hideouts.

These street scenes in this city along Tokyo Bay are little more than five hours by air from Okinawa, last major battlefield of the war. From the air, silenced guns draped with white flags of surrender, American flags and Red Cross flags are visible.

The Yokosuka naval base, used until the last Jap planes were downed, yielded training devices for suicide bombers. The barracks and offices, found dirty and stripped, are clean now and house officers and men of MAG 31.

Several civilian cars and buses, in the service of the Jap navy, are parked on the base. Some will run if pushed far enough. Motors are damaged by cheap fuel and wiring is faulty. Steering wheels are on the right side and gears shifted with left hand. Tires stand out, nothing wrong with them. They look good, and unusual, on civilian vehicles.

Marines, suddenly plucked from Okinawa and killing Japs, find themselves brushing past Japanese trained to kill them. For many U.S. military men, this is the first Oriental city they have visited and the conquered Japanese are the first Orientals they have seen. Japanese civilians are surprised by the troops making purchases in shops instead of looting. The Japanese, distant and suspicious at first, use their English skills to admit they did not expect such kindness and are warming up to the Americans.

There was no trouble here and none was expected. Guards and military police are on the alert day and night. The scene is quiet, the atmosphere is friendly. Our men on liberty in the city no longer wear side arms. Quickest, friendliest smiles and courteous bows come from the children and old men. Military age eye us suspiciously.

The streets stay crowded, and the people seem to be going somewhere; yet, if they vanish down the road, there is another taking the place of everyone leaving. Pedestrian traffic is heavy. Many carts and bicycles force our military vehicles to slow down to the plodding pace of congested areas. Not all streets have sidewalks. Civilians defiantly walk in front of trucks and jeeps.

Manners seem forgotten here, the ones concerning staring, by Americans and Japanese. Marines size up civilians while they are being stared at by civilians.

In the States, particularly now, there are more women than men. Here it seems just the opposite. The definite scarcity of young women becomes more obvious as the number of liberty parties increase. Women here wear bloomer type pants instead of skirts. When a Japanese girl takes an American to her home, the family will serve tea, which is plentiful, but food is scarce. Our troops are getting used to the Oriental custom of taking their shoes off before entering a house. Shoes must be removed, also, before entering some shops.

Cigarettes are more popular than either Japanese or American currency. The power of a package of cigarettes is amazing. Some prices are figured in the number of cigarettes a service or article is worth, and some big-hearted Joe that starts tipping can tip the scales. For instance, a civilian movie charged two cigarettes for admission yesterday. A big-hearted Joe tipped one or two smokes. Today the price for admission may be four or five cigarettes—and we can't even understand the movie. (13Sept45)

"I'm Monahan!"

"Even though our jeep was left on Okinawa, like good marines and resourceful correspondents we were able to secure transportation," Red reminisced. "A combat photographer named Odie Monahan was the ring leader of the correspondent group, at least on this occasion, when he managed to 'borrow' an English Ford. He designated himself the driver and drove us all over the place.

"Our first trip was into the foothills of Mt. Fujiyama, location of beautiful little towns that escaped the bombs. More memorable was a trip into Tokyo to the emperor's palace. Monahan drove beside one of the guarded moat gates.

All guards were from MacArthur's military police and they were all over the place.

"There were four or five of us in the Ford, and Monahan leaned over the front seat passenger and yelled, 'I'm Monahan!' The guards snapped to attention and saluted. 'Yes, sir,' the soldiers said as the gate opened. We drove over the moat in the direction of the Imperial Palace grinning widely like school boys pulling a prank. Cruising the streets, we slowed down to read names on the mail boxes. We did find a few princes and other important cats. Mostly we just drove around, laughing and trying to guess who the guards might have thought we were. This is one time not having chevrons on our sleeves was a good thing.

"Monahan had a way of getting things done and getting us into places, some maybe we should not have gone."

TOKYO

The most amazing site in Tokyo is the downtown devastation. The buildings in the business and financial section are either leveled or gutted. Safes are the only configurations recognizable in the rubble, damaged only on the outside. The destruction is so widespread the safes saved little. Residential areas on the outskirts of the capital fared better. Remains of the homes are being cleaned for the beginning of a tremendous rebuilding program.

In densely populated residential sections, the survivors are living in shacks made of burned tin salvaged from the ruins of stores and factories. Smokestacks are all that remain of the war plants that turned out the instruments of death and damage.

Along the eight mile highway from Yokohama, an industrial city targeted for bombing, to Tokyo only the results of war can be seen—abandoned trolleys, buses, cars, trucks and other vehicles—left where our bombers caught them. In limited numbers buses, trolleys and electric trains, express lines into Tokyo, still run. All are crowded. It is a common sight to see American troops hitching rides on the rear of overloaded trolleys.

Business is good in Tokyo. Service men on liberty, used to quick flights to Australia and New Zealand, are enjoying the department stores and other shops. The few towns and villages captured on small islands were destroyed and looted before even our land troops arrived. Today a line of mostly service men, most of those sailors, stretched a half block long waiting for a leading department store to open. Sailors could not take a chance on another visit to the city. Even on Okinawa, shore leave for the sea-going didn't offer much of a chance for souvenirs except on the battlefields, and there the infantry got the cream.

For the most part, however, souvenirs bought this early in the occupation are articles bringing a good price here but that sold in American stores for much less not many years ago. Nevertheless, they are real souvenirs from Japan. Everybody, it seems, must take home a souvenir. (16Sept45)

Lunch in Tokyo

Describing lunch in Tokyo, Red recalled, "Our combat correspondent gang visited the capital. Walking aimlessly around the city, the four of us spotted a nice looking hotel and decided to have lunch. All the hotels were occupied by MacArthur's Tenth Army who had taken over the town. The restaurants, we weren't sure about.

"We walked into a beautiful lobby. Amazed it had managed to survive all the bombing, we gawked for a few minutes before noticing the lowest ranking person in the lobby was a full colonel. At that time early in the occupation, we had our side arms and looked maybe important. We walked into the restaurant, were seated, and ordered from the menu.

"We were served some sort of raw fish about the size of our sardines. We ate a little and pretended we knew what we were doing. We piddled around with our fish, acted like we enjoyed it, and then got the hell out of there.

"Being stared at by all those colonels and generals and maybe a few admirals takes your appetite when you're the only enlisted people in the room and have weapons. That experience maybe could have landed us in jail as armed marines in the wrong place. By the army, I mean. The Japs didn't give a darn."

14. PRISONERS OF WAR

September 16, 1945

Always in search of material for dispatches, Red interviewed recently released POWs on the U.S. Navy hospital ship Benevolence, *docked in Tokyo Bay.*

S. R. LUFKIN—POW

A prisoner of the Japs since December 10, 1941, Marine Corporal Sewell Robert Lufkin, 27, Fortuna, Calif., was captured on Guam. He wrote in his diary on August 14, one day before the war ended, "Heat terrific. Around 110 degrees. Work hard, with guard over you constantly, making you work. Several men pass out nearly every day. Saw a Japanese fighter plane shot down about a quarter of a mile away by four of our Grumman fighter planes. Felt so good that I squared my shoulders and gave all the Nips in general a 'go to hell' appearance." The Marine made the notation in a dirty notebook he kept hidden from the Japs.

Corporal Lufkin has not seen his parents since July 1941. During the 40-odd months he had been a prisoner, Lufkin received 20 letters from home. He wrote at regular intervals but does not believe the Japs sent his messages home. He explained, "For the past year and a half my mother wrote as if she were terribly worried and not certain I was alive." He added the Japs were known to read outgoing mail then destroy it.

Treated for malaria and looking little the worse off for the mistreatment administered by the Japanese military and civilian guards, Lufkin was unusually cheerful as he related his experience in prison camps. After his capture, he was taken to Zentsuji on an island lying between Kyushu and Honshu where he remained until June 9, 1942, when he was taken to Osaka. He was at that seaport on the west coast of Honshu until released.

"When we were first thrown into prison camp," Lufkin recalled, "we were fed soup and rice, not enough all day for a good breakfast. At Osaka, we were the first prisoners and sort of a novelty. They were kind to us, even gave us cigarettes. They were winning the war then; but, later on when the tide turned, they began getting rough. That was the winter of 1942–43. They cut down our rations and we had to steal food.

"Twenty of us were farmed out to a stevedore company handling bauxite. We worked aboard a ship, down in the hole, and the Jap guards carried baseball bats used to club prisoners thought were not working hard enough.

"I saw one guard hit a little fellow with a club so hard that it knocked him six feet. We couldn't help a wounded prisoner. It made us see red. We were helpless. It was so cold during the winter for the men from the Philippines that they died like flies from flu, pneumonia, malaria, and malnutrition. A man had to be almost dead to get into what the Japs called a hospital, and it was just a case of him going there to die."

But death held no fear for the prisoners, according to the Marine who enlisted in 1937. He said they knew they were likely to die any day and did not seek shelter when our bombers hit the area.

A form of punishment the Japs used was to have a prisoner hold a pail of water in front of him until his arms became weak, and he splashed the water. Then he was beaten with clubs. Sticklers for military courtesy from prisoners, Lufkin said the Japs lined up 30 men at attention and beat them across the face with three-foot limber sticks if they failed to snap to attention fast enough to satisfy a guard. "I was struck five or six times across the face," he recalled.

He said they had "some sort of church service" once at the camp, but the Japs held annual services for dead prisoners. "It was mockery," he explained, "and men, forced to stand at attention during the services, fainted from exposure."

He said the worst punishment he received was working when he was sick. "If you were able to stand, they figured you were able to work," he explained, "and if you didn't produce enough work to suit the guards, they would beat you."

Like some other prisoners interviewed aboard the ship, Lufkin said, "You can get better stories from the other fellows. I wasn't treated as cruelly as some of them."

Corporal Lufkin plans to remain in the service. (16Sept45)

EMMETT SHAUL—POW

"It was a cold day—one of the coldest of the winter—five-foot tubs of water, filled to the brim and buried in the ground, were frozen over. A prisoner of war, an American held by the Japanese, was thrown into the water container, breaking the thin coat of ice as he landed with a breath-taking splash. He was left in the water at least a half-hour. When the Japs pulled the freezing prisoner out of the tub, they beat him senseless with clubs, leaving him lying on the ground for two hours. I have seen quite a few prisoners of war given that treatment," Marine Corporal Emmett W. Shaul, 24, said today as he rested aboard the navy hospital ship BENEVOLENCE in Tokyo Bay.

Shaul, of Bakersfield, Calif., was captured on Guam December 14, 1941. Taken to Zentsuji off Honshu in January 1942, he remained there until June when he was transferred to the POW camp at Osaka on the west coast of Japan's home island. He was at Osaka until October 19, same year, when he was moved to Hirohata. He stayed in that area until September 9, 1945, when occupation forces emptied the camp.

Another pet punishment administered by the Japs, according to Shaul was to beat prisoners with clubs shaped like swords. "They would prance around a prisoner, making feints at him with the stick," Shaul explained, "and then hit him with the broad side of the club, knocking him down. They would kick the prisoner in the stomach and groin until he got up. If he was knocked senseless, they would bring him to by throwing water in his face and beat him some more." Shaul said he had received some of that treatment.

There were other forms of punishment. Putting a water hose into a helpless and weak prisoner's mouth—then turning the water on—would almost drown a man. Men were also beaten with heavy clubs and ropes, cutting the skin and drawing blood. "I have seen the Japs take off their belts and hit a man across the face with the heavy buckles," Shaul said.

"When tired, weak prisoners would return to the camp from a day of hard labor," Shaul recalled, "they were lined up for inspection. Sometimes a hat would not be straight, or a button not buttoned, or maybe the prisoner would not be clean," he recalled. "Punishment for these minor infractions of rules established by the Japs would be to run the prisoner for an hour or more, the Japs riding along side them on bicycles and beating any man who fell behind."

Shaul, who last saw his parents in April 1941, said while he was a prisoner he received three letters and a card. Aboard COLORADO after his rescue, Shaul met his step-brother Gunners Mate Second Class Carl Winslow. "That made me feel good," he beamed.

He wanted to thank everybody for every favor since his release. "I don't know how to say it. Such things as clean clothes, a bed and sheets, and good chow—it seems so unreal," he said as he looked about the hospital ward, finding it hard to believe that all of this was not just a dream.

Corporal Shaul enlisted July 6, 1939. (16Sept45)

HOWARD C. JORDAN—POW

Marine Sergeant Howard C. Jordan was captured May 6, 1942, at Corregidor. A member of the Fourth Marines, he had been in the Philippines only six days, traveling there from Shanghai.

Sergeant Jordan, who has not seen any of his relatives since 1927, explained he was older than most of the prisoners and knew more about the Japs. "I wasn't treated as badly as some of them. I knew enough to keep my nose clean," said the 38 year old, a Marine since December 1928.

The worst punishment Japs meted out to prisoners of war in the camps where Sergeant Jordan was held were beatings with what the American dubbed "reform bats." He described the special sticks as the size and shape of baseball bats adding they were used freely for the slightest reason.

Jordan recalled the day the guards gave him a going over with the clubs. While out of camp on a job, he obtained two matches and forgot to get rid of them before returning. He remained conscious while he was being clubbed but said some others were beaten senseless by enraged guards who would work themselves into a frenzy while beating prisoners.

Under the worst of conditions, sick men were forced to work if they could stand, and the St. Louis leatherneck received his worse punishment in this form. Pneumonia was contracted in the winter of 1942 and he was off the job only three weeks. The arthritis in his hip and lower spine is attributed to working in the rain. He also explained that when the B-29s came over making large bombing raids in the area, all the prisoners had to run a mile and a half for shelter.

The leatherneck was first taken to a prison camp at Manila, but on May 27, 1942, was shipped to Cababuan on Luzon where he was held a year and a half. He was sent to Mojii on the southern tip of Honshu. On October 5, 1943, he was in a detail of 400 dropped off at Hirohata, a steel mill town south of Kobe. The last day the prisoners worked was August 15—the day the prisoners were told the war was over. The only official announcement was a report of the death of President Roosevelt. Even then the Japs did not break the news but told one of the prisoners, an acting first sergeant, who relayed the message to the others.

Sergeant Jordan, who plans to stay in the Marines, said when the prisoners were told even by their own men, "We didn't believe it." (16Sept45)

ALVIN L. CASE—POW

Marine Platoon Sergeant Alvin L. Case, whose father is 86-years-old, today thought about the three years and three months of Japanese prison camp life and commented, "I was pretty lucky. I got only two bad whippings."

Sergeant Case, 34, was with the Fourth Marines on Corregidor when he was captured May 6, 1942. After two transfers he wound up at Hirohata, south of Kobe, October 19, 1943, and worked in that steel mill town until the occupation forces freed him September 9, this year. He and other Americans were farmed out to civilians and worked aboard a ship.

The first time Case was beaten he was accused of not coming straight from a toilet. "I was beaten with vitamin sticks, tripped, and kicked in the stomach and groin." He said two Jap guards beat him five minutes with the wooden sticks cut to resemble a sword. "We called them vitamin sticks," he explained, "because the Japs didn't feed us enough and used these sticks to get more work out of prisoners."

The sergeant doesn't know why he was beaten the second time. "They did a good job with the plastic ruler type stick which was limber, an inch wide, and a foot and a half long. I was struck across the face and hands. That beating closed one eye and crippled my left hand for a week."

Sick for three months and unable to stand because of malnutrition, the Japs tried to cure this and other POW illnesses with something they called "punk" —seaweed in small bags. Depending on the disease, the punk was placed on various parts of the body and burned. If the patient felt no pain he was sick. If the patient showed pain from the punk burning on his skin, he was declared well and forced to work. This treatment was used by the Japs on themselves.

He showed scars on his feet where the Japs had burned punk on them to cure beriberi. The pain was likened to a burning cigarette held to his skin, and he felt no pain for several months. Punk was applied to the back to cure dysentery. "You'll find lots of prisoners with punk scars," Case stated.

"Bug gravy" was fed to the prisoners—burned rice and dried cocoons. While not tasty, the combination did provide nourishment.

Sergeant Case, who enlisted July 16, 1930, married an Oklahoma girl in February 1940. "I haven't heard from her since November 1941," the Marine recalled. He is looking forward to a long furlough and plans to remain in the Marine Corps. (16Sept45)

FRANK E. PICK—POW

Although he was beaten 117 times by the Japanese, whippings and clubbing were not the worst experiences in prison camp for Marine First Sergeant

Frank E. Pick, 33, who was captured on Corregidor May 19, 1942, and released September 1945.

"The worst thing that happened to me," recalled the leatherneck from Freemont, Neb., "was the day I had to stand in ice water up to my arm pits for seven hours. That was in February of this year, and it was freezing weather."

Sergeant Pick was a honcho, squad leader, and did not have to work. Second in command, he always looked out for his men. His punishment, he explained at the evacuation hospital here, was for stealing and contempt. "We had to steal food or starve," is the way he put it. He was forced to stand in the huge tub of ice water for slapping a guard who threw the prisoners' food away. The prisoners had not moved fast enough to suit the guard during an air raid. "The men were hungry and had been working hard. When I saw their chow dumped, I jumped the guard, cursed him, and slapped him in the face," Pick said bitterly.

The sergeant, from Athens, Ind., is now suffering with sinus problems brought on by the "water treatment." Placing a water hose over his nose and mouth, the Japs used the water's high pressure to inflict more pain.

Sergeant Pick, who was wounded in the left leg by machine gun slugs on May 6, at Corregidor, was captured when the Japs seized the hospital at Malinta Tunnel. "Kicked out" of the hospital, he was taken by boat to Manila where he marched in the "Humiliation Parade" to Bilbide prison five miles away. Next day he was in a detail sent by train to Cabanatuan. From there, he walked 20 miles to another camp.

In August 1943, he left the Philippines and returned to Manila. From there, he sailed to Mejii on Honshu. There only five days, a steel mill in Hirohata was his final destination before being freed on September 8.

On August 30, 1945, Pick and the other POWs in his camp made an American flag from the silk lining of blackout curtains, struck the Rising Sun, and ran their improvised Stars and Stripes on the Jap flagpole on September 2. A few Japs were still in camp but had quit giving orders following the end of the war. "They were even good to us," the sergeant explained.

Sergeant Pick looks forward to seeing his daughter for the first time. He left for the Pacific in March 1939 and she was born a month later. Several pictures of her reached him in prison camp, and he reports she is "mighty pretty."

The liberated Marines and soldiers assisted the Eighth Army with the search and release of other captives until the latter part of the month. Only after completion of their last mission did the men agree on processing necessary to be speeded home. The sergeant, who became a Marine in August 1931, plans to stay in the service. (24Sept45)

CHARLES E. MAURER—POW

It wasn't the beatings with fists and sticks—or any of the other physical forms of punishment administered by the Japs—that cut deepest into Marine Sergeant Charles E. Maurer, 26, prisoner of war.

"The worst part of it all," explained Maurer from Coleman, Alberta, Canada, "was the humiliation we had to tolerate—and we tolerated it because we knew that some day we would be free."

Sergeant Maurer, attached to the Fourth Marines, was captured May 6, 1942, on Corregidor. Practically all his confinement was at Cabanatuan and Osaka. The freedom for which he suffered such humiliation came on September 2, this year. Like so many other leathernecks and soldiers released from captivity, Sergeant Maurer joined the Eighth Army in the liberation of other prisoners on Honshu rather than returning home immediately.

Sergeant Maurer stated he had no grudge against the smaller prison officers. "I blame the camp commanders and the Swiss delegation for conditions which prevailed in the concentration camps. The commanders ordered the rough treatment, and the Swiss delegation painted rosy pictures of camp conditions to our government. I blame them. They are the ones who should pay," the sergeant recounted.

The leatherneck, a former Chicago resident, received "over a dozen" beatings with fists and sticks, and he also suffered from lack of food and clothing. August 15 was the last day the prisoners were forced to work. The Japs did not tell them the war was over—they explained there would be no work for a few days. "We knew something was up," he stated, "and believed the war was over because the Japs began treating us better." The three weeks of improved treatment gave him a healthy appearance at this processing station—his last stop in this country before returning home.

The Red Cross, recounted the Marine, furnished one issue of American shoes for men in the camps. They later began making their own shoes. "We got so good at making shoes and other leather goods," described the sergeant, "that pretty soon the Japs had us making things for themselves and their families."

The mail service was poor. Sergeant Maurer revealed men received four year old letters.

A member of the Marine Corps since July 31, 1940, Maurer plans to stay in the service after a lengthy furlough. He last saw him mother in 1939. (24 Sept45)

CHESTER C. ALDERMAN—POW

Corporal Chester C. Alderman, 25, processed here the latter part of September after many months in a Jap prison camp. When he and others of his camp were freed, they joined with the Eighth Army assisting in the liberation of prisoners from other camps. The Marine from Flora, Ill., was captured on Corregidor May 6, 1942, and gained his freedom September 2, 1945. The leatherneck looked well and showed only in his eyes the horrors of Jap prison camps.

After being released from hospital ship BENEVOLENCE, he wants to remain in Japan to assist occupational forces. "I can speak a little Jap," he revealed, "and I know these people. I could make them understand all right."

Corporal Alderman, happy over the prospect of a reunion with relatives, was processed here with eight other Marines and a large number of other POWs. They were greeted at the railroad station by top ranking American officers of the Tokyo Bay area and, described by one general, a score or more of "the best looking nurses we could find in the hospitals and on the ships here." They were the first American women many of the POWs had seen in five years.

Following his capture, Alderman was forced to march in what the Japs called their Manila "Victory Parade." He recounted it was a humiliation parade for the Americans.

The leatherneck spent five months at the Cabanatuan No. 3 camp. Transferred from there to Umeda at Osaka, he remained until May 20, 1945. Tsuruga was his last camp. The Japs released all prisoners in that camp September 2.

Corporal Alderman went through less punishment than most prisoners; however, his never-to-be-forgotten experience was standing at attention and being beaten across the face with a doubled army belt. "During an air raid," he explained, "I went to the toilet. It was on the outside of the barracks. Instead of going down the hallway, I took a side door and walked on the outside. A guard saw me. For that offense, or at least what they termed offensive, I was stood at attention and given 30 blows across the face and about the head with a double army belt."

The corporal enlisted in the corps at Dallas on August 15, 1938, and plans to remain in the service. (24Sept45)

FRANK E. COPELAND—POW

"You'll have to excuse me. It's that music. I can't keep still."

While a band of American and British musicians played one of the latest jitter-bug tunes in a huge warehouse on the docks here, Marine Corporal Frank E. Copeland posed for a picture and told of his experiences during three years and seven months as a prisoner of war in Japan.

The 23-year-old from Denver, Colo., admitted he didn't know the latest steps in rug-cutting but planned to waste no time learning when he reached the States. His last stop in Japan was this evacuation center.

Young Copeland, who looked none the worse for his POW experiences, remained in Japan a few weeks more than was necessary to help the Eighth Army free other prisoners. He went along with the liberation forces as an interpreter. Learning to speak Japanese through associations with the enemy and also studying, he wants to stay in Japan and serve with the army of occupation. A Marine since February 1, 1940, he plans to remain in the service.

Captured on Guam December 10, 1941, the corporal had been in camps at Zentsuji, Tanagawa, Umeda, and Tsuruga, released from the latter September 2, this year. He came through this processing station with 200 other prisoners —Marines, merchant marines, sailors, and soldiers.

Corporal Copeland had little to relate concerning prison camp treatment simply stating, "I was once forced to stay in a kneeling position four hours."

But all of that was no more than a bad dream now. The music was playing and he wanted to get back into the warehouse where the high notes were almost deafening. Too, he couldn't keep still. (24Sept45)

15. -30-

October–November 14, 1945

After the war ended, Red continued filing dispatches—reports of awards, human interest stories, and descriptions of the defeated country. All the CCs waited for their discharge papers from DPR in Washington, their discharge date determined by a system of points accumulated. Many of Red's colleagues with earlier enlistment dates left for home soon after the occupation. Red, the noncommissioned officer in charge of the remaining correspondents, prepared the first Public Relations Group Summary Activities Report for the first month of occupation.

PUBLIC INFORMATION SECTION
MARINE AIRCRAFT GROUP 31

8 October 1945

MEMORANDUM TO: Commanding Officer, Marine Aircraft Group 31.

1. The following is a report of press and radio material submitted by this section to the Director, Division of Public Information, Headquarters, U.S. Marine Corps during the first month of occupation duty with MAG 31 at the Yokosuka Naval Air Base:
   (A) Forty seven (47) total news and feature stories: (4) Lt. Vance JOHNSON, (19) S/Sgt. Claude CANUP, and (24) Sgt. Don BRAMAN.
   (B) Seventeen (17) radio interviews with officers and men for broadcasts over their local stations by T/Sgt. Herman MARKOWITZ and Pfc. Jim NUTTER.
   (C) Thirteen (13) watercolor and black and white paintings by S/Sgt. Paul ARLT.

(D) Forty-five (45) news photos with negatives by S/Sgt. Odie MONAHAN and Sgt. Charles MCDADE. In addition to MAG 31 pictures, these photographers made news photos for Lt. Harold MARTIN, transient Public Relations Officer, and the Public Relations Section of the Fourth Marine Regiment.

2. In accordance with directives from Headquarters, personnel of this section have assisted civilian newspaper and radio correspondents, both at this base and at Press Headquarters, Tokyo, in obtaining news relating to MAG 31.
3. At the request of the Commanding Officer, this section has prepared reports of atrocities against Marine Prisoners of War, interviewed in Yokohama, to be posted for the information of MAG 31 personnel.
4. The strength of this section has been reduced to Correspondents CANUP and BRAMAN, Photographer MCDADE and Artist ARLT. Others mentioned above have been recalled to Headquarters Squadron, Second Wing. ARLT and CANUP, near the end of their tours of duty, are awaiting orders to the Wing this month.
5. This report is submitted for the information of the Commanding Officer. In accordance with a request by the Executive Officer, extra copies of stories by MAG 31 Correspondents will hereafter be presented to the Commanding Officer, along with monthly reports.

S/Sgt. C. R. CANUP
NCO in charge*

JAP MECHANICS

Japanese airplane mechanics handled the first American plane to land on their field as if it were one of their own, according to Major James A. Bulman, Jr., Seattle, Wash., executive officer of a Marine fighter squadron here.

Major Bulman landed on Yatobe, 30 miles north of Tokyo, recently when he observed Jap planes still apparently operative. He learned that the few with propellers were without carburetors and the Japanese were standing by waiting for American troops to occupy the field.

"I was treated royally by the base commander," Major Bulman told Marine combat correspondent S/Sgt. Claude R. Canup, "but what amazed me was how the Jap mechanics brought me in. After buzzing the field a couple of times, I came in for a landing. They immediately directed me to a revetment and then gave me 'cut and switch' just like my own men." When the major returned to this Marine air base to make his report, a squadron of Corsairs already had begun a search for him. He was hours overdue.

* The 8 October 1945 memorandum is part of the Claude R. "Red" Canup Collection.

Even though he flew to this base with his wheels down, he reported all was well. The Japs had presented him with a Zenith radio and inside the wheel well was the only place it could be stored on a fighter plane.

"Frankly," Major Bulman said, "I would have trusted those mechanics to work on my plane. I was the first American they had seen since the war ended, and they impressed me with their courtesy and sincerity." (3Oct45)

JAPS SING MARINE HYMN

Leathernecks always lend an attentive ear or join in the singing when they hear the Marine Hymn. They did both in Yokosuka the other day.

A half-dozen mechanics, looking over merchandise in a souvenir store, were amazed when the Japanese male clerk began singing: "From the halls of Montezuma to the shores of Tripoli . . ."

When the boy, recently discharged from the Japanese army, reached the line: "We will fight our country's battles . . ." several women clerks joined in, and pretty soon the Marines, no longer amazed but amused, added their voices.

"Again," smiled the male clerk twice as he led the Americans and the Japanese women through the song.

It was a double surprise, according to Marine correspondent S/Sgt. Claude R. Canup, because the Japs not only could carry the tune perfectly but knew every word. Yet, they did not know enough English to make conversation.

"That beats any sales talk I ever heard," remarked one of the Marines. (9Oct45)

ONCE IN A LIFETIME

You can expect just about anything in Japan as Marine correspondent S/Sgt. Claude R. Canup has learned.

The correspondent, on duty at this Japanese naval base, went souvenir shopping in Yokosuka. He priced ladies handbags.

"Five yen," said the clerk as she took the purse for inspection. She then went to another counter to assist another customer.

The correspondent ran his hand inside the bag, felt a piece of paper and pulled it out. The paper was a five-yen note.

"I'll take this one," he said to the clerk when she came back to the counter. He handed her the five yen found inside the handbag and said, "I would like to look at another one, please." (9Oct45)

POINTS AND APPOINTED

For the first time to the knowledge of men in MAG 31, a Seabee has failed to come through for leathernecks.

Seabees and Marines have fought and worked side-by-side all the way from the Solomons to Japan and many stories can be told of the favors—big and small—leathernecks received from men of construction units.

There always has to be a first time for everything, and this is it according to Marine correspondent S/Sgt. Claude R. Canup of Anderson, S.C., who quickly explains that the case in hand did occur after the shooting was over.

This being let down by a Seabee happened when MAG 31's flight echelon came to occupy this base which was already accommodating a CB unit. There was no room in the Marine planes for a barber. Naturally, the Marines looked up the CB barber—a very busy man. Appointments had to be made two days ahead—on Friday for Sunday.

Sunday came and Marines went to the barbershop only to discover the Seabee had changed the appointment to Monday according to the date book hanging on the wall. The leathernecks returned to the shop on Monday morning—no barber. Not even the date book was there.

Explained a passer-by, "The barber? Oh, he had points and went aboard ship this morning for home."

"First time I was ever stood up by a Seabee," mumbled a leatherneck . . . whose hair was curling up on the back of his neck. (10Oct45)

WINDOW PEEPING

Several hundred Japanese can vouch for this story according to Marine correspondent S/Sgt. Claude R. Canup of Anderson, S.C.

A fighter pilot on occupational patrol from Yokosuka naval air base reported to intelligence, "A loaded troop train moving north . . ." He gave the time and place.

"How do you know Japanese soldiers are aboard?" asked the intelligence officer.

"I flew down to 10 feet and looked in the windows," grinned the Marine Corsair pilot who a few weeks before had been flying combat patrol from Okinawa. (11Oct45)

*This letter was tucked away for safekeeping and found among Red's treasures in the cardboard box.**

* The letter to Linda Canup is part of the Claude R. "Red" Canup Collection.

YOKOSUKA, JAPAN
12 OCTOBER 1945

Hello, Sugar Baby,

This is the first bright day we have had in sometime. The rain stopped last night, the wind shifted, and the skies cleared. This morning the sun streaked across Tokyo Bay, and the air is crisp. You are probably having the same weather at our house, but not as much rain as they get here in Japan. Sometimes it rains here all day and all night flooding roads, filling cellars, and making everyone miserable because most of the roofs leak. When there is a strong wind with the rain, the water blows right through the thin walls of some of the houses.

You would enjoy a visit to Japan. It is very different. For instance, the babies are not carried in carriages or strollers here, and the people do not have automobiles. When they go out they walk and strap the baby on the back of a child or man or woman—sort of like the Indians do—but, here they do not put the baby in a basket or pouch. The baby is put into a little harness and strapped around the shoulders of someone. I have seen babies out in cold, damp weather hanging on the backs of girls and boys not as big as you are. Only a few people carry babies in their arms because these people have to work with their hands.

Children here don't grow large like they do at home. A girl your size might be several years older than you. The children are short, stocky, and brown. They all have black hair.

Most of the people wear wooden clogs which have straps to hold them on their feet. They can't afford shoes. Even as cold as it is now lots of people don't have socks and some go barefooted.

I went to see a family in Tokyo yesterday. When I entered their Japanese home, I stopped at the door and took off my shoes because they don't wear shoes inside. In the living room we sat on thick straw mats because there are no chairs. They have no beds and sleep on the mats.

Most of the girls your size and on up to grown women wear pajamas all the time. The smaller girls and boys wear kimonos. Some of the children are clean, but too many are dirty and ragged. They wave at passing cars and yell "Hello." When our soldiers walk along the street, the children say "Hello" and "Choc-lit." Those are the only English words they have learned. When they say "Choc-lit" they want candy. They have not had candy here in a long time. The war has left them without most of the things you have, but the children seem fairly happy.

I don't notice much playing by the children in Japan. They seem quiet and are often in the streets.

I am looking forward to coming home. When I do come back it will be to stay, and we will play every day. Maybe I will be home for Christmas. Until then I send my love to all three of you.

Daddy

JAPS REVIVE BASEBALL

Baseball, abandoned during the war because it is American, is being revived throughout Japan—because it is American.

The Japanese, gifted contortionist among many lines, are performing the difficult trick of leaning over backwards and bowing at the same time to satisfy the Allies with social and economic reforms. One way to play ball with the Americans, obviously, is to play baseball.

Tokyo's English language Nippon Times seldom lets a day pass but what it carries a story in which baseball is mentioned. It gave liberal space to the World Series.

The press headlines the revival of sports in general, baseball in particular; and recreation stories stress the importance of baseball, editorially holding our national pastime as a "must" in government-sponsored sports programs.

Recreation is under the welfare ministry, and no matter how often there may be a cabinet shakeup, the Japanese will find official blessing for sports, of which baseball is admittedly the newest and most popular.

An editorial recently pointed out that in the few years baseball has been played in Japan it proved its popularity, even surpassing ancient and traditional Oriental sports spectator appeal.

Former Welfare Minister Kenzo Matsumura, who turned in his uniform in the October cabinet turnover, keynoted the government's aim toward a sports revival when he said: "For the last eight years the people suffered much, not only materially, but physically and spiritually. Therefore, the revival of sports is urgent for the sake of the people.

"Physical education, however, must be conducted at the people's initiative, with the government in the position of giving encouragement and eliminating obstacles.

"I hope that all sorts of sport groups which were abolished during the war will be revived and resume activities."

Revealing the government's change of policy with the ending of the war, the one-time minister promised no interference, stating "as sports are chosen in consideration of individual interest, circumstances and age, no regulations will be enforced in connection with the choice of sports."

In the next breath he plugged the great American pastime, adding: "I hope baseball matches, tennis tournaments and Sumo (Japanese wrestling) will be conducted from this fall on."

That was the cue for the Japs to throw off their wraps and pull baseball equipment out of hiding.

Receiving prominent publicity in the press is the revival of the war-killed baseball series between Waseda and Keio universities. The Times' writer remembers that "the last match was held in October 1943, as a send-off function for the students who were to leave their respective universities to serve either in the army or the navy."

Now many of the players have returned, ready to play again.

Further evidence of Nippon's all-out baseball efforts is shown in the creation of a Sportsman Club at Saitama prefecture. Times story of the organization points out that "for the first time in many years in Japan since the outbreak of the war, a baseball game was scheduled . . ."

There is a difference of opinion among writers here as to how long baseball has been in Japan, but the Japan Baseball Federation is bringing back the country's professional league "after exactly 12 months since it was suspended in November of last year" with a game in Koishikawa. The Times is quoted on the date.

The professional circuit has five positive starters in the Tokyo Giants, Nagoya Dolphins, Hanshin, Hankyu and Ashi. The Giants are owned by the federation.

Further evidence of Americanism is brought to light by Saburo Yokozawa, former umpire of the Seitesu club. He is forming a new team, nicknamed "Senators."

A seventh team is expected to be ready for the opening league series next spring.

But the fans will not have to wait. Just as Kenzo Matsumura wished while serving in the cabinet, games are planned this winter with demobilized soldiers and remaining club members.

The Times reveals full government sanctioning of baseball with the apparently shocking announcement that "the old baseball phrases of 'balls' and 'strikes' will be used," and editorialized hopefully for games with the army of occupation.

Meanwhile, at this MAG 31 base in Yokosuka and throughout the Tokyo Bay area, American forces apparently are not giving much thought to baseball. It is football season back home.

Anyway, all they talk about is how many points they have—points toward going home. (15Oct45)

YOKOSUKA, JAPAN
OCTOBER 15, 1945

Your mention of the trip to the mountains made me lonesome for the trail of the lonesome pines, or the chestnut trees or whatever it is that grows up there "in them thar hills." I have seen about as much of Japan as I care to. The people are nice as hell, but who wouldn't be in their position.

When will I be home? That's a good question. My term is from 14 to 18 months. I think I have a fair chance of splitting the middle and making Christmas in Anderson. In my setup I don't have to wait for a unit to be relieved. I am treated as an individual. I feel like millions of other guys who want to get back home and get in some real living.

We old codgers are not getting any younger. I read somewhere that a woman had written her congressman asking that her husband be discharged so that she could have a baby before it is too late. She is 38.

TOKYO BAY MASONIC CLUB

The Tokyo Bay Masonic Club, believed to be the first of its kind in Japan, was organized September 18 at Yokosuka naval base. Occupation officers, enlisted men and civilians who are Masons or are members of affiliated organizations are invited to join.

The next meeting of the TBMC will be held in the MAG 31 chapel at the Yokosuka naval air base Tuesday night at 7:30 according to Marine First Lieutenant Stewart L. Baughman.

Marines and Seabees now make up the membership, and a special invitation is extended by Baughman to army and navy men in Tokyo and adjoining stations. (15Oct45)

On October 16, 1945, Red was promoted to technical sergeant. On October 20, the first and only weekly report was submitted, with Red sending copies to the public information officer of the 2ndMAW.

PUBLIC INFORMATION SECTION
MARINE AIRCRAFT GROUP 31

20 October 1945

FROM: NCO in Charge.
TO: Commanding Officer.
VIA: Intelligence Officer.
SUBJECT: Weekly report of activities

1. The Section moved into new quarters at the beginning of the week, leaving the office in the Administration Building 15 October and setting up in a room adjoining Group Intelligence. Packing, moving, squaring away and making necessary repairs at the new office were completed Tuesday.

2. The Section was placed under the command of the Group Intelligence Officer 15 October and was directed to submit a weekly report of activities to the Commanding Officer.

3. Staff Sergeant Claude R. CANUP prepared six news stories.

4. Staff Sergeant Paul T. ARLT executed one water color painting of the Yokosuka harbor from drawings made on the base.

5. Sergeant Donald W. BRAMAN prepared three news stories, interviewed Mrs. Lydia Schapiro in Tokyo for information concerning feature story on son Isaac, released news copy prepared by this section to the Nippon Times, Stars and Stripes and Armed Forces Radio Services. (Copy for Tokyo publications was on organization of a Masonic Club at this base and an invitation to occupation forces in area to join).

6. Sergeant Charles E. McDADE was loaned to the navy to make news photos to accompany stories on personnel in Construction Battalion Maintenance Unit 602. A letter from the Navy's Overseas Correspondent to the officer in charge of CBMU 602 requesting that McDADE be commended is attached to this report. In addition, McDADE carried out routine duties with this section.

7. Lieutenant R. J. BATTERSBY, Public Information Officer of the Second Marine Air Wing, paid a brief visit to the section 16 October and expressed complete satisfaction in the way the men in his charge are performing their assigned duties.

CLAUDE R. CANUP*

S.C. MARINES POLLED

South Carolina Marines who were in the invasion of Okinawa and were among the first leathernecks to occupy Japan are practically unanimous in the opinion that the United States should have compulsory peace-time military training. The South Carolinians represent almost every section of the state. All are in MAG 31.

Other things on the minds of the scores of South Carolina Marines:

Eight plan to return to pre-war jobs, four will seek new employment; eight of 20 are married, and five will pop the question upon return to civilian life.

* The 20 October 1945 weekly report is part of the Claude R. "Red" Canup Collection.

On the purchasing side of the picture, eight want to buy a new automobile, nine would like to own a home, two plan to buy farms, two others want to see the state from a jeep, and one intends to see the country from a bird's-eye view in his own plane.

Only one of the men is interested in remaining in the service but remains undecided.

Less than a third of those questioned expect to borrow money or attend college under privileges contained in the G.I. Bill of Rights. (23Oct45)

N.C. MARINES POLLED

What are North Carolina MAG 31 leathernecks with occupation forces in Japan thinking about?

They are thinking about returning home as quickly as possible, resuming their old job, buying a car, marrying and seeing to it that the United States has a trained reserve army that will find the country prepared for quick action in the event of another war.

Of 23 North Carolina officers and men polled in MAG 31, which came here in September after participating in the entire battle of Okinawa, 43 per cent plan to return to their former jobs, 47 per cent want to buy a home, and 57 per cent are in favor of compulsory peace-time military training.

Getting down to straight figures, five of those interviewed here at Yokosuka and on Okinawa are married and three others hope to be soon.

Six of the 23 will buy a car, and three others prefer a jeep. One, a fighter pilot, plans to own a plane.

On the real estate side of the ledger, only one is interested in purchasing a farm. He worked for an industrial plant before entering the service. Only three plan to change from old to new jobs.

To the question of staying in the Marines, 20 gave a flat "no" while one was undecided. Two pilots plan to remain in service. (23Oct45)

GEORGIA MARINES POLLED

Half of the single Georgia Marines who were in the battle of Okinawa and later came to Yokosuka with MAG 31 are planning to marry when they return home. Some are now on their way to the States.

In a recent survey of leathernecks, 16 Georgians revealed their opinions on military training and disclosed major post-war plans. Those polled were from 19 to 27 years of age and represented every section of the state from Habersham Gap to the coast. They were employed in such pre-war jobs as textile worker, insurance salesman, letter carrier, bank teller, lineman and multi-graph operator.

Both the married and the single agree almost unanimously on two military questions. More than three-fourths favor compulsory peace-time military training. With the exception of one, there will be no re-enlistment.

The value of learning a trade in service is borne out by five of the Georgians planning to continue in civilian life the same type work they are now doing in the Marine Corps.

Twenty-five per cent plan to purchase a house as soon as possible. Half that percentage is interested in farms.

Nine plan to buy automobiles, but only two have been sold on the jeep. A fighter pilot wants to buy an airplane. (24Oct45)

SERGEANT SAUDER DECORATED

Sergeant Paul D. Sauder, 22, Crabill, Ind., left Yokosuka this week for home. Sauder, who enlisted May 16, 1943, served on Okinawa and in the initial occupation of this naval air base.

As an aerologist, he made many flights from Okinawa over Japan, Korea, China and other enemy territory. For 15 of these combat flights he received the Air Medal and two stars.

Sauder was wounded July 4 this year when the Privateer in which he was riding was hit during an attack against enemy shipping off southern Korea. The Purple Heart was awarded for this action. (25Oct45)

ATTORNEY ZENOFF DECORATED

Marine First Lieutenant David Zenoff has been awarded the Bronze Star medal for activities during the capture of Okinawa. Lieutenant Zenoff, a former Milwaukee attorney, who recently left for the West Coast and a discharge, plans to return to that city and resume the practice of law.

The decoration was accompanied by a citation which read in part:

"First Lieutenant Zenoff assumed the full administrative burden of the squadron when the tactical operations occupied the attention of the commanding officer and executive officer both day and night. Displaying sound judgment, a high standard of loyalty, and exceptional qualities of leadership, he looked after the general welfare and discipline of the troops and kept up the morale of the organization under the most difficult circumstances. He formed a plan and trained the troops to combat airborne attacks, and when such an attack took place on May 24, his tactics succeeded so well that not a man in the squadron was wounded despite heavy fire being directed into the squadron area." (26Oct45)

MARINE ACE BAIRD DECORATED

Captain Robert Baird, holder of the Corps' record of night fighter victories with six, has been awarded the Distinguished Flying Cross, the Air Medal and a gold star in lieu of a second Air Medal.

The medals were accompanied by citations signed by Major General Louis Woods, commanding general 2ndMAW. The night-fighter pilot was cited for "extraordinary achievement while participating in aerial flights in connection with military operations against the enemy in the Ryukyu Islands . . ."

Captain Baird, South Gate, Calif., recently completed his tour of duty and will be discharged in the States. Post-war plans for the young captain are to fly for an airline company in America. (26Oct45)

PHARMACIST BURKS IS HERO

First Lieutenant William N. Burks, 26, a pharmacist from Jefferson City, Mo., who joined the Marine Corps and won the Bronze Star medal during the assault and capture of Okinawa, is returning to his civilian job. Lieutenant Burns left Yokosuka recently for the West Coast after participating in the initial occupation of Japan.

Burks, intelligence officer of a night fighter squadron, was awarded the medal by Major General Louis E. Woods who cited the officer "for tireless energy and unusual professional ability. He collected, evaluated, and disseminated intelligence which was necessary for the success of his squadron. He toiled indefatigably to establish his section rapidly on Okinawa, and he worked to the limit of his endurance to prepare reports, brief pilots, and supervise the work of his section." (26Oct45)

CAMPBELL DECORATED

First Lieutenant Clark C. Campbell, 25-year-old from Elizabeth, Pa., has been awarded the Bronze Star medal for outstanding work as ordnance officer of a night fighter squadron and for heroism during an enemy raid on Yontan Airfield, Okinawa.

The medal was accompanied by a citation for maintaining "an outstanding ordnance section, which was a valuable asset to the squadron throughout its operations against the enemy. While on Okinawa, his squadron was assigned to night intruder missions. It was necessary for him to quickly prepare the aircraft to carry rockets, bombs, and napalm."

When enemy suicide troops landed on Yontan Airfield, Okinawa, Campbell learned that several men were trapped on the standby line without weapons or cover. He armed himself and accompanied by another man went to the line through enemy fire and returned the men to safety.

The former school teacher, who participated in the initial occupation of the naval air base in Yokosuka, recently sailed for the United States and a discharge. (27Oct45)

"Good morning, Colonel"

"Phil Storch," Red recounted, "another combat correspondent, and I were walking along in front of the barracks in Yokosuka one morning. We had been in Japan on occupation duty about two weeks. We met Colonel John C. Munn and, as we had always done on Okinawa during the war, we simply said, 'Good morning, Colonel,' . . . and walked on.

"All the sudden we heard him say, 'Sergeants!'

"We turned around and said, 'Yes, Sir!'

"The Colonel remarked, 'I just wondered what had become of the old marine custom of saluting?'

"We snapped him a salute . . . which told us quite plainly that the war was over and we were now serving in peacetime."

The last monthly report of correspondent activities was sent on October 29 to the 2ndMAW's public information officer and to the Public Information Officer Section, U.S. Marine Corps. Red's last dispatch, #398, was included in the transmittal.

PUBLIC INFORMATION SECTION
MARINE AIRCRAFT GROUP 31

29 October 1945.

FROM: NCO in Charge.
TO: Public Information Officer, Second Marine Air Wing.
SUBJECT: Monthly report.

1. The Section this month filed the following material:
   (A) Stories numbered 385 through 398 by Technical Sergeant Claude R. CANUP.
   (B) Stories numbered 315 through 325 by Staff Sergeant Donald W. BRAMAN.
   (C) Water colors numbered 155, 156 and 157 by Technical Sergeant Paul T. ARLT.
   (D) Fifty-one (51) negatives by Sergeant Charles E. MCDADE and two Photo Lab photographers.

2. Attached to this report is letter commending the Section's Sergeant McDade for assisting Navy Correspondents.
3. Enclosed are two copies each of stories prepared by this Section this month.
4. Sergeant Braman left the Section 26 October to return Stateside with the MAG's 60-point men for discharge.
5. Technical Sergeants Canup and Arlt, with 14 months overseas service and 58 and 62 points, respectively, are standing by for orders to report to Headquarters, 2ndMAW, as the first step toward returning Stateside.
6. The Section this month was visited twice by Public Information Officer R. J. Battersby, 2ndMAW, and by Captain A. G. Campbell, representing Public Information Section, Air FMFPAC.
7. The Section's Ford, a Japanese vehicle appropriated shortly after the MAG moved to the Yokosuka naval air base 7 September, was this month placed in the Transportation Pool.

C. R. Canup*

PUBLIC INFORMATION SECTION
HEADQUARTERS, MARINE AIRCRAFT GROUP 31
C/O FLEET POST OFFICE, SAN FRANCISCO, CALIFORNIA

29 October 1945.

FROM: NCO in Charge.
TO: Public Information Officer Section U.S. Marine Corps, Crocker Building, San Francisco, California.
VIA: CINCPAC Pearl, Marine Corps Station (Public Information Section).
SUBJECT: Public Information material, transmittal of.
ENCLOSURES: (A) Four (4) stories by Technical Sergeant Claude R. Canup, numbered 395, 396, 397, and 398, with negatives. (B) Six (6) negatives, complete with captions, numbered MAG 31 "55" through MAG 31 "60".

1. Submitted for review and disposition.

C. R. Canup†

* The 29 October 1945 monthly report is part of the Claude R. "Red" Canup Collection.
† The 29 October 1945 transmittal memo is part of the Claude R. "Red" Canup Collection.

16. THE "RUPTURED DUCK" FLIES HOME

November 15–December 25, 1945

Members of the U.S. Army, Navy, Marine Corps, and Coast Guard were given lapel pins when honorably discharged. The pin, featuring an eagle with outstretched wings perched in a circle, was nicknamed the "ruptured duck."

Back to Pearl Harbor

"On November 15, 1945, about a month before my discharge date," Red narrated, "I received orders at Yokosuka that I should proceed to San Francisco with T. Sgt. Philip H. Storch, combat correspondent; S. Sgt. Paul T. Arlt, combat artist; and S. Sgt. Edward B. Talty. That meant as NCO in charge I was to find transportation.

"I immediately made a beeline for the airstrip to find a plane with room for four headed in the direction of the West Coast. A mail plane returning to Okinawa was our ticket off the Japanese mainland. On November 16, 1945, we hitched a ride on that plane to Okinawa. After getting squared away in the transient camp on Okinawa, I began looking for transportation to Honolulu. I knew if I could get us there I could get us the rest of the way to San Francisco.

"I checked around and found that a marine captain was flying to Pearl Harbor on his last flight before heading home. I looked up that officer. As well as I remember, he had an R4D that carried about twelve or fourteen passengers. Six Seabee officers were the only passengers booked on the plane, and the pilot agreed to take on four more. We met him the next morning, boarded, and headed for Iwo Jima.

"On Iwo Jima, I met a marine sergeant who offered to take us by jeep to the top of Mt. Suribachi. Of course, we accepted. The jeep ride to the top and walking near where that famous flag was raised was quite an experience.

"The next day we flew to Guam. Unfortunately the navigator became ill the day we landed. Spending three extra days there with nothing to do and nobody to report to was a blast. Meeting three guys I knew, we went all over that damn island.

"When the navigator recovered, we flew on down to Majuro to spend the night. That was the most beautiful little island I had seen in the Pacific. The officers from our plane were greeted by another officer. Since we didn't have any stripes or anything to identify our rank, we didn't object to being recognized as officers and treated as such. We got our liquor—just like the officers—and a good meal—just like the officers. Majuro was very enjoyable.

"From there we landed on a little island named Johnston. I had never heard of it. We spent the night and in a few hours arrived in Pearl Harbor."

PEARL HARBOR
NOVEMBER 26, 1945

If everything goes well I should be seeing you in a little more than three weeks because I understand my dream boat will leave here Monday, or at least I am to board her then. I don't know what she is or how long she may hang around these waters after she accepts me; but, no matter her name, I'm sure she is a lady. At least, I'll give the old gal every benefit of the doubt if she'll deposit me in Frisco inside of six days after I get aboard. I have been here since last Saturday, a week tomorrow.

Four of us are traveling on the same orders, and we were transferred into a transient squadron this morning getting our names on the list of men awaiting passage back to the States. According to information I could gather in Japan and later on Okinawa, I am about a week or more ahead of schedule now. I am really impatient being held up here this long. As the goal draws nearer, my patience becomes shorter.

I've figured this thing pretty close in a way, but practical enough, I think. I'm allowing a week before we should be steaming under the Golden Gate Bridge, or drawing close to some part of the California coast—our orders read San Francisco. I figure a week to clear things up there, and a week to get across country. That's counting on a discharge on the coast.

I don't have any idea as to which way I will come home, since I don't know if I'll come under orders or a free man. I am toying with the idea of trying to hitch a plane ride once I get to the States but am afraid I might get bumped

Red, Marie, Linda, and Buzz celebrating Christmas Day 1945, in Anderson, S.C. Claude R. "Red" Canup Collection.

anywhere, even at some remote field. Anyhow, I won't mind a comfortable train ride for a few days. At least the seats will be soft which is something entirely new in my book now.

Should I be able to breeze in the newspaper office a bit ahead of schedule, I might give them a hand a few days before Christmas. I catch myself being in a hurry to get back in the harness and high gear with deadlines.

I will come back home in fair physical shape but not like I was when I returned from boot camp. I have done little physical work out here and am pretty soft.

I have little taste for liquor now and have turned down many drinks. Haven't talked with women in so long that I will have to watch my language. I've learned to eat with elbows on the table, even feet—it's comfortable. I haven't felt a wintry blast in so long I'll probably catch pneumonia when I get back just looking out the window at a frost-bitten plant.

Tell the band to start practicing . . . I'm coming home!

Home for Christmas

"The destroyer trip," Red remembered," took about five days to get to San Diego. We spent the night there at the transient base. It was early December by then. The next day we traveled to San Francisco and reported for duty and paperwork at headquarters—discharge date, December 15, 1945.

"Like tens of thousands of other World War II servicemen recently returned to the West Coast from duty in the Pacific, I was trying to get home for Christmas. When the weary ticket agent in San Francisco looked up from three large volumes of train schedules and asked me, 'What large city is South Carolina near?,' I knew I had a problem.

"As a marine combat correspondent I was able to get around the Pacific several times as events prompted. After thumbing rides all the way from Japan to San Francisco, I was really a bit amused that the confused ticket agent did not know South Carolina was near Atlanta. She did finally sell me a ticket to Seneca, South Carolina, and I caught a ride with relatives the thirty miles or so down to Anderson.

"I was able to keep my Santa Clause date with Marie and our young children, Linda and Buzz. That was quite an occasion!"

This column, appearing with his familiar picture, in the Anderson Independent *on December 25, 1945, is the first writing Red did as a civilian. Reprinted with permission granted from the* Independent-Mail.

HERE WE GO AGAIN!

This is the Christmas Bing Crosby has been singing about the last few years—the one a lot of guys have been dreaming of. Even so, it isn't a hundred per cent as peace-time Christmases go. Santa Claus will make his scheduled rounds—and, it is a white one.

However, some of the guys are still waiting to get back from "Somewhere in the Pacific," and they are still dreaming. But, as the beginning, hopefully, of an unbroken string of "peace on earth" seasons in a world finally at peace, it is off to a swell start. And it is going to be a pleasure to look forward to the others.

The Best Gift—a Duck

To tens of thousands of men who long ago learned about Santa, the top present of the season was the little gold lapel button which is commonly referred to as the "ruptured duck."

That present—a gift from the Army, Navy, Marine Corps, and Coast Guard—is being more warmly received than anything the bewhiskered old boy could cram into his over-sized seabag. It is the one article for which there is no substitute because it is what has brought fathers, husbands, and sons home—to stay.

Some say the image on our discharge button looks more like a duck than an eagle—and all of us lucky enough to receive the gift probably did take off for home like a "ruptured duck," not that any of us ever saw a duck that was ruptured.

Tens of thousands home this Christmas no longer have to dream of this day. Events of the past few years won't be forgotten overnight; but, instead of being lived, they will be carried as memories. Those memories of the horror of war may very well be the best guarantee against another world-wide mistake.

The New Year ends another dream. No more will people sit and plan for the post-war. This will be the opportunity to put the planning into action. What happens from here on out will not depend so much on war dreams, or post-war plans, but on the will and the energy of every man who is ready to release his pent-up ambitions.

Most of us have had to contend with so much bickering and jealousies and just plain cussedness so long that we want the country back to its normal self as soon as possible. Just as we have quit dreaming of other things, so would we like to stop dreaming of the kind of America we once knew and live again in an America of greater freedom, an America unhampered by out-dated laws and politicians, and an America in which Americans pull together.

Many of us can remember when people retired at night without locking the front door. Neighbors trusted each other—even strangers. Maybe we'll never throw away the front door key, but we at least could have more faith and fewer feuds and strikes.

In Anderson and all over the country the New Year holds promises of regaining much of what was paid for with such a high price to retain.

The Independent as well as other businesses is getting back the men who for the past few years took on a more important job. With their return post-war plans will take shape. The sports section of *The Independent,* more or less propped up to take care of a curtailed sports program in a country that had its mind on other things, soon will come back bigger than ever. This section will again cover the field—local and national. And the emphasis will be on our own counties and neighbors across the river.

It is too early to forecast what sudden growth sports will take in this neck of the woods, but people seem to be more recreation conscious than before; and, whatever the growth, *The Independent* sports section will keep pace and then some. That's not a dream.

So, it is with pardonable pride that I grab off this much space in the Christmas edition to sort of work my way back into the old job. But, I just wanted to let you know that if you've been missing sports news and comments—Here We Go Again!—and happy to be in South Carolina ringing in the New Year.

Red Canup, Anderson Independent *sports editor, checking his daily column, circa 1950. Claude R. "Red" Canup Collection.*

My Christmas Wish for You

May this be the Christmas you've been dreaming about and may the dreams dreamed in damp foxholes, on lonely flights, on dark decks, and in leaking tents come true . . .

And God bless the "ruptured duck."

GLOSSARY

-30-. Symbol used by journalists to denote the end of an article.

ADJ. Adjutant; staff officer who helps a commanding officer with administrative affairs.

Air Medal. Military decoration; presented for a single act of merit or heroism or for meritorious service while participating in aerial flight(s).

Allies. Nations united against Axis in World War II; primarily the United States, Great Britain, and the Soviet Union.

ALPAC. All Pacific.

Armistice Day. November 11, commemorates the anniversary of the armistice ending World War I in 1918. Since 1954 called Veterans Day.

Axis. Nations that opposed the Allies in World War II; primarily Japan, Italy, and Germany.

Baka (Baca). Japanese for "fool or idiot;" a rocket propelled, human-guided suicide missile carried underneath a "Betty" Japanese aircraft; after release from the Betty's belly, a pilot glided toward a ship, fired three solid-fuel rockets then finished mission by aiming the missile at the target ship.

Betty. Allied nickname for a Japanese twin-engine bomber that carried the Baka bomb.

bogey. Enemy plane; unidentified aircraft.

Bronze Star. Military decoration; medal presented for individual acts of heroism or meritorious service in close personal contact with the enemy.

carrier. Warship designed to deploy and recover aircraft, thus serving as a seagoing airbase.

Chimu Airfield. Allied airfield constructed by Seabees on Okinawa, twenty miles north of Yontan Airfield and closer to Japan; completed before July 1945.

CINCPAC. Commander in Chief Pacific.

CO. Commanding officer.

combat correspondents. Civilian media specialists recruited by the USMC in World War II to gather, relate, and prepare information documenting the marine war story for the American public and USMC history. Assigned to Pacific combat zones, they included journalists, illustrators, photographers, cinematographers, artists, public relations specialists, and radio broadcasters. Today combat correspondents are classified under the military occupation specialty Public Affairs. The Defense Information School, Fort Meade, Maryland, is responsible for their training.

Corsair. F4U; carrier-capable U.S. fighter aircraft of World War II; built by Chance Vought.

cruise. Time spent away from home base, usually overseas.

D-day. Day of invasion.

Denig's Demons. Nickname of first combat correspondents; after Brigadier General Robert L. Denig, who was charged with the recruitment and assignment of the first group.

Devil Dog. Nickname for marines; a translation of the German term "Teufel Hunden"; reputed to have originated during World War I after the Battle of Belleau Wood, when Germans thought the victorious marines were so ferocious they called them "Teufel Hunden."

Dinah. Allied nickname for a twin-engine Japanese reconnaissance aircraft.

dispatch. World War II marine term for combat correspondent news release; written in the field, censored at Pearl Harbor, and sent to headquarters for distribution; also called a story, a report, or an article. Venues for dispatches were marine's hometown newspapers, national and fraternal magazines, the Corps newspaper *Chevron,* and the Marine Corps' *Battle News Clipsheet.*

Distinguished Flying Cross. Military decoration; awarded for heroism or extraordinary achievement while participating in aerial flight or for voluntary action above and beyond the call of duty.

dogface. Nickname for enlisted army personnel.

Domei. Japanese news agency.

Essex. Classification for large aircraft carrier ships that were the backbone of the U.S. Navy's combat strength during World War II.

flimsy. Paper used in World War II for typing dispatches; also onionskin.

FMFPAC. Fleet Marine Force Pacific.

Frances. Allied nickname for a Japanese twin-engine land based bomber.

Frank. Allied nickname for a single-seat fighter aircraft, considered to be best Japanese fighter in large scale operations in World War II.

Galloway, Joe (1941–). Nationally syndicated military columnist and author; reported from combat zones during Vietnam War; received Bronze Star for carrying men to safety.

G.I. Bill. Servicemen's Readjustment Act of 1944; furnishes low interest home loans and educational benefits for returning veterans.

giretsu. An attack by an elite Japanese suicide force; a rough translation is "act of heroism."

Grable, Betty. A famous Hollywood star and a favorite World War II pinup girl; her image decorated the walls of barracks, bomber jackets, and aircraft.

Greatest Generation. Americans experiencing both the 1929 Great Depression and World War II; term popularized by *The Greatest Generation,* a book written by newscaster Tom Brokaw.

grunts. Enlisted marines.

Hamp. Allied nickname for a Japanese fighter plane.

Hellcat. U.S. fighter plane, the Grumman F6F, which was built to counter Japanese Zero aircraft; it was the U.S. Navy's first choice to deploy with *Essex*-class carriers.

Higgins boat. Landing craft used to transport troops and materials from ship to shore during amphibious invasions, with the contents being released through a boat ramp, also known as an LCVP; named for Andrew Higgins, its builder.

HORNET. A large Essex-class aircraft carrier.

Il Duce. Benito Mussolini; Italian Fascist premier, executed April 25, 1945.

Intell. Intelligence.

Iwo Jima. Pacific Island secured at great cost of American lives in World War II; location of Mt. Suribachi, site of civilian photographer Joe Rosenthal's Pulitzer Prize–winning photograph of marines raising the U.S. flag and marine combat correspondent Sergeant Lowery's military photograph of the same.

Jake. Allied nickname for a Japanese naval reconnaissance float plane.

"Joe Blow." An average or ordinary man.

kamikaze. Japanese air attack force assigned to crash into a target; the explosives-laden plane used in such an attack; a rough translation is "divine wind."

Kate. Allied reporting name for a Japanese carrier-based standard torpedo bomber with a crew of three; also a land-based bomber.

leatherneck. A marine; the name originated from the leather that once lined inside of collars of marine uniforms.

liberty. Off-duty time for military personnel.

liberty ship. A cargo ship, especially one built cheaply and quickly during World War II by welding rather than riveting the hull.

LST. Landing ship, tank; a naval vessel that support amphibious operations by carrying large quantities of vehicles, cargo, and landing troops directly on shore.

MAG. Marine Aircraft Group.

MAW. Marine Aircraft Wing.

MOS. Military occupation specialty.

Nansei Shoto. Ryukyu Islands, Japan.

Navy Cross. Military decoration; the second highest individual honor for exceptional heroism in action, second only to the Medal of Honor.

NCO. Noncommissioned officer.

night fighter. Combat pilot guided, or vectored, to targeted enemy aircraft by radar controller.

Nipponese. Japanese.

Nips. Allied nickname for Japanese military personnel.

Okinawa. Site of last great battle of World War II; largest island of the Ryukyu Islands, southwest of the Japanese mainland.

Pearl Harbor. U.S. Pacific naval base on the Hawaiian island Oahu, bombed by the Japanese on December 7, 1941, leading the United States to declare war on Japan on December 8, 1941.

pillbox. Low-roofed concrete mounting for machine and antitank guns.

pin-ups. Photographs of young women (usually in bathing suits) often displayed in military living and working quarters.

Presidential Unit Citation. U.S. military decoration awarded in the name of the president; the highest and only group award for exceptional heroism in action.

PT. Patrol torpedo; small boats equipped with radar for night attacks of smaller vessels.

Purple Heart. U.S. military decoration; awarded in the name of the president to individuals wounded or killed while serving with the military.

Pyle, Ernie (1900–1945). Nationally syndicated military columnist killed by Japanese machine gun fire while reporting on fighting in the Pacific Theater; 1944 Pulitzer Prize–winner.

R4D. Twin-engine marine or navy transport aircraft.

Ryukyu Islands. Island group closest to Japan.

Sally. Allied nickname for a Japanese heavy bomber.

Seabee. Member of the U.S. Navy battalions that build naval aviation bases and facilities; also CB.

Siegfried Line. Defensive line of pillboxes and strong points ordered built along German western frontier by Adolf Hitler.

Silver Star. U.S. military decoration; awarded for gallantry in action against an enemy of the U.S.

Skivvies. A trademarked name for men's underwear.

SMF. Supplemental monetary funds; the form used to request advance funds, before credit cards became commonplace.

staging. Assembling, holding, and organizing personnel, equipment, and sustaining material in preparation for a move onward.

Tactical Air Force Ryukyus. Large joint U.S. military operation during World War II, headquartered at Yontan Airfield, Okinawa.

theater (theatre). Large geographical areas for military operations.

Tojo. Tojo Hideki, Japanese prime minister during World War II; also the Allied nickname for a Japanese single-engine fighter aircraft.

Tony. Allied reporting name for a Japanese fighter plane.

USMCCCA. United States Marine Corps Combat Correspondents Association.

USO. United Service Organization; the U.S. military's "home away from home"; civilian volunteers supporting morale and providing entertainment for servicemen.

Val. Allied reporting name for the Japanese dive bomber, primarily carrier borne, that participated in most actions, including Pearl Harbor. Vals sank more Allied military ships than any other Japanese aircraft.

vector. To line up enemy aircraft in a straight line in U.S. fighter aircraft gun sights; at night planes *vectored* to enemy aircraft with the assistance a radar controller at the airfield.

V-J day. Victory over Japan Day, August 15, 1945.

VMF. Marine aviation fighter squadron.

VMF(N). Marine aviation night fighter squadron.

Wilhelm. Wilhelm II, German emperor during World War I.

WWI. World War I.

WWII. World War II.

Zeke. The official Allied reporting name of a long-range Japanese fighter aircraft used in kamikaze operations during final years of World War II; usually referred to as a Zero.

SOURCES

Badders, Hurley E. *Anderson County: A Pictorial History.* Norfolk, Va.: Donning Company, 1983.

Barker, A. J. *Okinawa.* London: Bison Books Limited, 1981.

Brokaw, Tom. *The Greatest Generation.* New York: Random House, 1998.

Claude R. "Red" Canup Collection, 1944–1998. Private collection.

542nd Marine Night Fighter Squadron. Baton Rouge, La.: Army and Navy Publishing Company, 1946.

Hawthorne, Hugh. "Marine Aircraft Group 31 Historian." *Jet Stream* (MCAS Beaufort), January 13, 1984, 1–2.

Holcomb, Thomas. Letters of Instruction No. 506, 2195-30, AO-278-nsh. 1943. General Alfred M. Gray Research Center and Archives, Library of the Marine Corps, Quantico, Virginia.

Keaton-Lima, Linda M. Canup. "Combat Detour: Marine Night Fighter Squadron 542." *Leatherneck,* May 2010, 36–40.

———. "Giretsu Attack." *Naval History,* June 2010, 46–48.

"90 Days of Operation Tactical Air Force Ryukyus, April 7–July 6, 1945," July 6, 1945. USMC "restricted" handout. Claude R. Canup Collection.

Shaw, Henry I., and Benis M. Frank, Jr. *Victory and Occupation.* Vol. 5 of *History of U.S. Marine Corps Operations in World War II.* [Washington, D.C.:] Historical Branch, G-3 Division. Headquarters U.S. Marine Corps, 1968.

Sherrod, Robert. *History of Marine Corps Aviation in World War II.* Baltimore: Nautical and Aviation Publishing Company of America, 1987.

Stavisky, Samuel E. *Marine Combat Correspondent: World War II in the Pacific.* New York: Ballantine Publishing Group, 1999.

The War in the Pacific, Okinawa: The Last Battle. Task Force 56, Chart III Organization of Expeditionary Troops for the Ryukyus Campaign, U. S. Army in World War II. Center of Military History, January 1945.

Ward, Geoffrey C. *The War: An Intimate History, 1941–1945.* Directed and produced by Ken Burns and Lynn Novick. New York: Alfred A. Knopf, 2007.

Weinberg, Gerhard L., and Mark R. Peattie, consultants. *World War II Chronicle.* Lincolnwood, Ill.: Publications International, 2007.

INDEX

ABOUT THE EDITOR

A native of Anderson, South Carolina, LINDA M. CANUP KEATON-LIMA is a graduate of Lander College. She earned her master's and doctoral degrees at Clemson University. Keaton-Lima spent more than thirty years in public schools and community colleges in South Carolina and North Carolina.